THE ATLANTIC SALMON TRUST

THE INSTITUTE OF FISHERIES MANAGEMENT

LINNEAN SOCIETY OF LONDON

STRATEGIES FOR THE REHABILITATION OF SALMON RIVERS

Proceedings of a Joint Conference held at the Linnean Society
on Thursday 29 to Friday 30 November, 1990

Edited by
DEREK MILLS

With a Foreword by His Royal Highness, The Prince of Wales

THE INSTITUTE OF FISHERIES
MANAGEMENT

THE ATLANTIC SALMON
TRUST

LINNEAN SOCIETY OF LONDON

STRATEGIES FOR THE REHABILITATION
OF SALMON RIVERS

Proceedings of a Joint Conference held at the Linnean Society,
on Thursday 29 to Friday 30 November, 1990

Edited by
DON A MILLS

With a foreword by HRH The Royal Highness The Prince of Wales

It is most encouraging to learn that so many rivers are being rehabilitated for the Atlantic salmon, throughout its whole geographic range. This has been made possible by strenuous efforts to reduce pollution in rivers and estuaries, to soften the impact of land drainage work, to improve access and counter the effect of dams and barrage works, to reconstruct lost habitats and to impose stricter controls on the use of water for domestic, agricultural and industrial purposes. It is certainly gratifying to read of the successful salmon restoration schemes in the United Kingdom, particularly in the Taff and the Thames. In this regard the National Rivers Authority, with their predecessors, are to be congratulated on their achievements.

The rehabilitation strategies that are being adopted are ingenious, and I hope that more work can go into the genetic studies which seem to be the crux of the matter when decisions are taken on the source of fish for restocking. The successful reconditioning and holding of kelts in fresh water to provide a source of eggs in subsequent years shows an intriguing advance from the disdain with which the humble kelt was once treated. The development of a whole range of tags has provided fishery scientists and managers with valuable techniques for identifying and tracking individual fish on their return from the sea.

The continuing management of our rivers is obviously essential to provide a healthy and secure environment for an optimum number of adults and young, and it is very interesting to read of the restoration of gravel to denuded river beds, of the provision of fish passes at the sites of numerous dams and weirs and of the transport of adult fish to safer upstream areas.

It is, I think, sensible to see the salmon not simply as a quarry for anglers and netsmen. For many people who love to see this splendid fish, just to know that it is <u>there</u> is reassuring. Its very presence is a sign that our rivers are healthy; when we see it return once more to rivers that we have worked to restore many will know that something positive is being done to protect the environment and our heritage.

BIOGRAPHICAL NOTE

Derek Mills graduated from Queen Mary College at the University of London in 1953 and took up a temporary appointment at the Marine Laboratory, Aberdeen before joining the staff of the Oceanographic Laboratory, Edinburgh in 1954. He left this post in 1956 and spent a short time with the Fisheries Research Board of Canada at St.Andrews, New Brunswick, before returning to the Marine Laboratory in Aberdeen in 1957. He was seconded to take charge of a newly established Salmon Research Laboratory at Contin, Strathpeffer, and supervise the running of a salmon research scheme funded by the Scottish Home Department and the North of Scotland Hydro-electric Board. Much of his time over the next eight years was spent studying the effects of hydro-electric installations on the movements of salmon, the survival of hatchery-reared salmon fry and goosander and cormorant predation. He was awarded a Ph.D. for this work in 1964 and a year later joined Edinburgh University's Department of Forestry and Natural Resources where, with the help of his postgraduate students, he has continued his work on salmon, particularly on the Tweed.

He was invited to join the Trust's Honorary Scientific Advisory Panel in 1972, and is now its chairman, and the Council and Committee of Management in 1981. He represented the Trust on official visits to Greenland (1980) and the Faroes (1982) and also at the EEC in Brussels and the Council of Europe in Strasbourg. He has been the Trust's observer at ICES each year since 1984. He was chairman of the Organizing Committee of the successful Third International Atlantic Salmon Symposium held in Biarritz in 1986.

Derek was responsible for setting up the Scottish Branch of the Institute of Fisheries Management in 1973 and was its first chairman. He has been editor of its journal, *Fisheries Management* (now the *Journal of Aquaculture and Fisheries Management*) since 1975 and is a member of the Training Committee. He was elected a Fellow of the Institute in 1982.

CONTENTS

1

LIST OF CONTRIBUTORS

S.N. Axford, NRA: Yorkshire Region, 48 Skeldergate, York YO1 1HL.

J. Banks, NRA: Thames Region, King's Meadow House, King's Meadow Road, Reading RG1 8DQ.

A. T. Bielak, R.W. Gray, T.G. Lutzac, M.J. Hambrook and
P. Cameron,
Department of Fisheries and Oceans, Gulf Region, Fish Habitat and Enhancement Division,
Science Branch, P.O.5030, Moncton, N.B., Canada E1C 9B6.

A.S. Champion, NRA: Northumbria Region, Eldon House,
Regent Cresent, Gosforth,
Newcastle-upon-Tyne NE3 3UD.

P. Dulude and G. Pustelnik*,
Department of Recreation, Fish and Game, Direction régionale de Québec, 9530 rue de la Faune, C.P. 7200, Charlesbourg, QC, Canada G1Q 5H9.

*Musée Aquarium, 3 rue du Cdt Maratuel, 24200 Sarlat, France.

R. Gardiner and I. McLaren,
The Scottish Office Agriculture and Fisheries Department,
Freshwater Fisheries Laboratory, Faskally, Pitlochry, Perthshire

S. J. de Groot, Netherlands Institute for Fisheries Research, P.O.Box 68, 1970 IJmuiden AB,
The Netherlands.

L. P. Hansen,
Norwegian Institute of Nature Research, Tungasletta 2,
N-7004 Trondheim, Norway.

G.J.A. Kennedy and W.W. Crozier,
Department of Agriculture for Northern Ireland, Aquatic Science Research Division, Fisheries Research Laboratory,
38, Castleroe Road, Coleraine, Co.Londonderry.

B. Lamy, Association Internationale de Défense du Saumon Atlantique, 195 rue Saint-Jacques,
75005 Paris, France.

G.W. Mawle, NRA: Welsh Region, Rivers House, St.Mellons Business Park, St.Mellons, Cardiff CF3 0LT.

D. H. Mills, Institute of Ecology and Resource Management,
University of Edinburgh,
Darwin Building, Mayfield Road, Edinburgh EH9 3JU.

M. F. O'Grady, J.J. King and
J. Curtin*, Central Fisheries Board, Mobhi Boreen, Glasnevin, Dublin 9, Republic of Ireland.

*Office of Public Works, Newtown, Trim, Co.Meath, Republic of Ireland

D.J. Solomon, Foundry Farm,
Kiln Lane, Redlynch, Salisbury, Wiltshire SP5 2HT.

K. Whelan, Salmon Research Agency of Ireland,
Farran Laboratory, Furnace, Newport, Co.Mayo,
Republic of Ireland.

M.Windsor and P. Hutchinson,
North Atlantic Salmon Conservation Organization, 11 Rutland Square, Edinburgh EH1 2AS.

INTRODUCTION

The Atlantic salmon originally occurred in every country whose rivers flowed into the North Atlantic Ocean and Baltic Sea. In some instances the country has no coastline bordering either of these waters, for example Czechoslovakia, Luxembourg and Switzerland, and the salmon had to undergo long upstream migrations up such rivers as the Vltava (Czechoslovakia) and the Rhine (Luxembourg and Switzerland). Salmon have now disappeared from the rivers of these countries due to the erection of navigation locks, the construction of dams and pollution.

Although these countries were the first to lose their stocks of salmon, other countries through which these and other large rivers, such as the Seine, Meuse, Douro and Thames, ran were soon to experience a similar loss as a result of water abstraction, impoundment and pollution. The same situation was experienced in North America for similar reasons, and salmon in the rivers of New York, New England and Maine, such as the Housatonic, Connecticut, Merrimack and Penobscot, quickly dwindled as these waterways were harnessed for power and factory production of numerous commodities. There are copious records of rivers "teeming" with Atlantic salmon right up until the middle of the last century, with some of the more fortunate rivers holding an abundance of salmon up until more recent times.

Whichever country one cares to choose, with the possible exception of Iceland, the same story of dwindling salmon stocks unfolds. In the United Kingdom, the late nineteenth century brought with it increased river pollution, particularly of the lower reaches, and the Clyde, Tyne, Tees, Taff, Trent, Ribble and Ouse, to name but a few, fell victim to the thoughtless actions of polluters. Spain saw the demise of salmon in many of its rivers like the Mino and Naton through dam construction and excessive water abstraction for irrigation, while stocks dwindled almost to the point of extinction on the Dordogne, Garonne, Bresle, Gironde and Loire from pollution and the construction of dams for mills and hydro-electric power. The salmon streams of Canada's province of Nova Scotia experienced the destruction of salmon stocks from logging activities, resulting in rapid run-off and excessively high water temperatures while most of the north shore rivers of Quebec from the Saguenay west to Lake Ontario, including the Jacques Cartier, became polluted and lost their salmon runs. Even Norway, a country renowned for the number and size of its salmon, did not escape the effects of industrialisation, and pollution resulted in the loss of salmon from rivers such as the Akerselv and Drammenselv, while hydro-electric power has been a cause for concern for salmon stocks on rivers like the Laerdal. However, worse was to come.

By the end of the last century acidification as a result of sulphur dioxide emissions was starting to affect southern Norwegian rivers like the Tovdal and is now responsible for the total loss of salmon from many of the rivers in southern Norway and the west coast of Sweden and is also affecting rivers in south-west Scotland, mid-Wales and parts of eastern Canada. Since the Second World War major power developments in Norway, Scotland, Sweden and eastern Canada have resulted in further reductions in both salmon numbers and the salmon's environment. In Sweden, as a result of some whole river systems being harnessed, the stocks of salmon previously supported by the rivers Indal, Angerman, Ume and Lule, and others, have had to be maintained artificially by smolts reared in local hatcheries and released into the lower reaches of these rivers below the lowermost dam. In Scotland and Canada, too, some salmon spawning areas have been lost due to flooding by reservoirs and stocks have had to be maintained by hatchery production. Although threat from river pollution is starting to abate as a result of better pollution legislation, acid rain, water abstraction, afforestation, land and arterial drainage schemes continue to be a threat to the salmon's survival, as does over-exploitation by illegal and interceptory fisheries.

A detailed chronicle of these past disasters in the history of the salmon's distribution and welfare has been written with some feeling by Tony Netboy in his books "*The Atlantic Salmon - A Vanishing Species?*" and "*Salmon - The World's Most Harassed Fish*".

However, the story is not all one of "doom and gloom". Stock enhancement of course has been practised as long as one cares to remember and with varying success, but probably not as much as one might imagine from the millions of eggs, fry, parr and smolts planted out in rivers of many countries where salmon stocks have shown signs of dwindling. Poor survivals of introduced stock have been due in the past to lack of knowledge of the implications, some genetic, of such practices. Now the story is changing. We have more knowledge of fish genetics. There is also a greater environmental awareness generally and, as water quality improves, there is increasing pressure to protect the aquatic environment from various forms of land and water use and to reinstate degraded rivers. Such actions are to be welcomed and will be noted by the Greenland and Faroese salmon fishermen, who were quick to point out to us the polluted state of some of our rivers when we in the Trust, along with representatives of the Atlantic Salmon Federation, visited Greenland and the Faroes in 1980 and 1982 respectively.

In the United States, salmon rehabilitation was under way in the early 1960's on the Dennys, Aroostook, Sheepscot and Narraguagus rivers in Maine and by the mid-60's plans to restore the Penobscot in Maine had been completed. In the early 1970's arrangements were well advanced for the restoration of the Connecticut and Merrimack in New England and New Hampshire. Elsewhere at this time similar work had started. In France, the Bresle was the first stream to have salmon restored to its waters, although it would not be long before many more French rivers were successfully rehabilitated. At this time, also, restoration and improvement work was under way on a number of Newfoundland rivers including the Upper Terra Nova, Great Rattling Brook and Noel Paul's Brook. The late 1970's saw restoration work start on the Dordogne in France, the Drammenselv in Norway and the Morell, Nepisiguit, Jacques Cartier and Exploits River in Canada. By the following decade salmon rehabilitation was snowballing. Projects were starting in the early 80's on the Tyne and Thames in England, on the Akerselv, flowing through Norway's capital city, Oslo, and on Point Wolfe River in Newfoundland. By the mid to late 80's the Taff, Torridge, Loire-Allier, Boyne and Meuse had joined the list and salmon were recorded straying into rivers such as the Clyde and Trent, whose water quality was beginning to improve.

A conference on the Restoration of Salmon Rivers (*La Restauration des Rivières a Saumons* eds. M. Thibault and R. Billard), held in France in 1987, and entirely devoted to this subject, indicated the need for those involved in rehabilitation work to get together to discuss mutual problems. However, it attracted little attention from those concerned with salmon rehabilitation in the United Kingdom and the Republic of Ireland. So, in recent discussions between representatives of the Atlantic Salmon Trust (Gordon Bielby, Jeremy Read and the late Gerry Hadoke) and the Institute of Fisheries Management (Kevin O'Grady) it was decided that strategies for the rehabilitation of salmon rivers would be an appropriate and timely subject for a joint conference. It was hoped that overseas experience would be forthcoming as well as that from work at home, particularly from the National Rivers Authority regions who are heavily involved in salmon rehabilitation. London was chosen as the location and the venue was provided by the Linnean Society of London through the offices of its Executive Secretary, Dr. John Marsden. The organisers are to be congratulated on obtaining generous sponsorship from Fish Eagle Co. (fish tag designers and manufacturers), J & B Rare Scotch Whisky Ltd. and National Power. The three organizations were most honoured by the presence of His Royal Highness, The Prince of Wales, Patron of the Atlantic Salmon Trust and Honorary Member of the Linnean Society of London.

The whole conference, which was attended by over 100 people, was a great success, as you will appreciate from the following proceedings - so please read on.

Derek Mills

AN OVERVIEW OF TECHNIQUES USED IN ATLANTIC SALMON RESTORATION AND REHABILITATION PROGRAMMES

KENNETH F. WHELAN

Salmon Research Agency of Ireland

1. INTRODUCTION

Rehabilitation and restoration schemes to enhance or re-introduce Atlantic salmon stocks are not recent inventions. For almost as long as man has destroyed the delicate habitat of the salmon, he has sought vainly to replace or improve upon that which he has destroyed or inexorably altered. de Groot (1989) and Netboy (1968) provide numerous examples of primitive restoration programmes. In recent years better planned and better publicised programmes have taken place, particularly on major river systems such as the Thames, Trent and Clyde in the U.K. (Mills, 1989) and the Connecticut, Merrimack and Jacques Cartier Rivers in the USA and Canada (Anon, 1989).

Such projects are, of necessity, immensely expensive undertakings and generally involve both a private and public resource base. In order to promote and sustain interest in, and commitment to, the project it is important to initially define the aims of the restoration or enhancement programme.

These have been neatly summarized, as follows, for the restoration of the Jacques Cartier (Frenette, Dulude and Beaurivage, 1988) and serve as a useful model for similar programmes:

1. The restoration and conservation of the river and its environment.

2. The increase in value of the salmon resource.

3. The valuation of the banks.

4. The provision of structures permitting the return of salmon and the use of the river for recreational tourists.

5. The use of the river for teaching and research.

6. The development of the culture and heritage of the river.

7. The confirmation and strengthening of the development of the socio-economic aims.

8. The control, the management and the taking into custody by the local people (of the river).

As mentioned previously, the enhancement and restoration of salmon rivers has been on-going for at least the last two hundred years and as a consequence a whole gambit of biological, chemical and physical techniques have been used; some of which were specifically geared towards individual restoration programmes (Bielak, 1989).

It has proved a difficult task to identify the 'key methods' used since invariably some techniques of vital importance to specific programmes will be excluded. Equally, it would be a rather pointless exercise to describe in detail fundamental methods such as electrical fishing, standard chemical analyses or classic fish pass designs.

I have, therefore, decided to give an overview of the most commonly used strategies quoted in the literature and to make specific reference to novel techniques, particularly those emanating from North America (Bielak, 1990).

2. WATER QUALITY

Basic to the success of any restoration programme is the assumption that at least a tolerable water quality regime exists, not alone within the juvenile habitat area but throughout the whole migration route of both the adult and juvenile fish. Indeed, in the case of many such programmes it is a major improvement in the water quality of the system which stimulates interest in the total rehabilitation of the catchment and its restoration as a salmon bearing river (Gough, 1982; '83 and '87). Suggested water quality criteria for Atlantic salmon are given by Solbé (1988) and de Groot (1989).

In larger systems it may prove extremely difficult to achieve consistently high levels of purity, particularly in the estuarine waters where tidal flow, wind and the general topography of the estuary may combine to concentrate pollutants. Lethal levels of heavy metal or other toxins may result; or more commonly an oxygen deficient wedge or interface may exist between the fresh and salt water. Such unsavoury conditions, even where they prove to be short lived, may lead to high smolt mortalities or prevent adults from entering the main river channel.

Recent research has also shown that the synergistic effect of a mix of pollutants may have serious implications for fish stocks, and managers should be aware that in a heavily industrialised catchment the long-term lethal joint effect on fish, of toxicants in mixtures, may be markedly more additive (Anon, 1987).

An even more insidious problem is the eutrophication or over-enrichment of river channels. Recent work in Ireland has shown that even in areas devoid of heavy industry or high population density this may become a serious problem (Anon,1986) and can lead to a dramatic reduction in the ability of such channels to harbour high densities of juvenile salmonids. Heavy growths of filamentous algae (*Cladophora* spp) and an increase in macrophytic growth can result, at times, in severely reduced oxygen levels and fish kills. Caffrey (1986) has developed an index using the abundance, presence or absence of key macrophyte communities to define the level of eutrophication in such enriched waters.

Acid rain is a major environmental problem which has afflicted many waters in both North America and Europe. It is now recognised that the only satisfactory permanent solution to the problem of acidification of Atlantic salmon rivers is the elimination of the source of acidity. Feasible short-term mitigation measures are liming, stocking and the preservation of genetically diverse stocks. The complete liming of an affected salmon river is complex and expensive. However, partial liming is proving successful in certain catchments. The insertion of cofferdams, containing crushed limestone, is one novel method of dealing with the problem (O'Neil, 1990).

3. PHYSICAL ACCESS

Another prerequisite for the survival of any fish species is free access to spawning and nursery areas. In the case of salmon, both Pacific and Atlantic species, there is a long history of weirs, impoundments and hydroelectric schemes blocking or impeding such free passage (Netboy, 1968; Benson, 1970; de Groot, 1989). Several detailed reviews of the effectiveness of various fish pass designs have been produced, both in terms of upstream and downstream migrating adults and kelts and downstream migrating smolts (Anon, 1975; Benson, 1970; O'Neil, 1990). In general it has been concluded that successful fish passage is only achieved where the skills of both the engineer and the fish biologist are closely integrated. Basic salmon behaviour patterns have often confounded even the most complex and sophisticated fish pass designs (Netboy, 1968; Mills, 1989) and site specific design is generally fundamental to success.

In addition to the classic fish pass many related designs such as fish ladders, fish lifts, light arrays and bubble screens are also in general use. In North America, where a long series of impassable or difficult barriers lie in the way of the salmon, both juveniles and adults may be trucked to the desired locations, either upstream or downstream. Ensuring fish passage is expensive; for example over $100m dollars has been spent, to date, on the Connecticut River in New England (Mills 1989; Anon, 1989).

In situations where the protection of the ascending adults is proving difficult or where an accurate census of returning adults is required the erection of a fish fence or salmon protection barrier is frequently used.

Salmon protection barriers basically utilize a large salmon-holding pool usually located at the downstream end of a salmon sanctuary area, both upstream and downstream fish barriers are used, with the downstream one containing an upstream-migration trap. The barriers are installed at the start of the salmon run; they are given 24 hour per day protection by on-site crews, and are assisted by flood lights, dogs and other warning devices. The fish are counted into the pool as they arrive and are held there until just before the onset of active spawning when they are allowed to move upstream - the protection crew moves up with them.

On the 30-mile long Northwest Upsalquitch (New Brunswick, Canada) a closed water sanctuary had long been protected by conventional means, i.e. federal and provincial patrols and provincial wardens located at several major holding pools. Despite these efforts very few fish were surviving to spawn. This fact was documented by fish counts made in 1975 and 1978. The clear, usually low water at the end of August or first week of September allowed accurate fish counts to be made by staff monitoring the river. A second count was made in mid to late October, just before the onset of spawning. Results of these dual counts revealed an average of 40% survival, but it is estimated that actual losses were closer to 90% when fish arrivals/removals before the counting period are considered. Since the introduction of the barrier protection scheme, the survival is about 90% (range 85-95%) with virtually all of the losses attributable to furunculosis, now endemic in the Restigouche drainage (Redmond, 1990).

4. HABITAT ASSESSMENT

Assuming that one of the principal aims of the restoration programme is the creation of a discrete self-sustaining population, it is important to assess the availability of suitable nursery and spawning habitats and to calculate, as accurately as possible, the potential holding capacity of the system. Various methodologies have been developed in this regard (Mills, 1989) but more recently computer modelling is being used to predict, in a more quantitative manner, the carrying capacity of short stretches of river for fry and parr. One such programme is HABSCORE which is currently being developed by the NRA: Welsh Region for use with both juvenile salmon and trout. (Milner, 1982).

In mountainous catchments it is often wise to survey all potential nursery areas, including those above seemingly impassable barriers. In the North Esk in Scotland and more recently in the River Erriff in Ireland the stocking of such areas has resulted in an appreciable increase in the overall productivity of the system. The resultant adults cannot, of course, reach these highland areas but production from these zones does make a very real contribution to the various commercial and recreational fisheries

When assessing the potential of a catchment to produce or nurture juveniles it is important that full cognisance be taken of the potential of main channel spawning, particularly in situations where projects are geared towards a near-restoration of historic levels of adult salmon in a given catchment. Whelan, Roche and O'Maoileidigh (in preparation) have shown that, in the case of the River Feale, in Ireland the main channel spawning produced some 60% of total parr, despite the presence of many fine spawning tributaries within the catchment. The extent of the main channel nursery and spawning areas was so great as to minimise even the most productive of the tributaries.

Redds, or more correctly redding areas, are not evenly spread throughout a catchment but are concentrated into discrete zones. In the larger Irish salmon fisheries there are generally five or six major redding zones present and these may be located in the main channel or along major tributaries (Whelan *et al.* in preparation). The protection of these areas from either mechanical or biological damage is vital to the well being of the system. In situations where a restoration programme is planned historical information on the location of such spawning areas could prove a vital link in the success of the rehabilitation programme, particularly if the physical composition of the river bed has remained largely unchanged.

Adult habitat in terms of resting pools or salmon lies should also be assessed, particularly in situations where the returning adults must navigate long distances through a channel which has been altered by man's activities. In long canal-like sections of river the provision of suitably designed lies, at key locations, would doubtlessly assist in the survival of healthy, un-stressed adults.

In situations where spawning habitat is limiting greater use could be made of spawning channels which are designed to reduce competition and to optimise juvenile production (Bielak, 1989; Mills, 1989). This is particularly true in the case of European restoration initiatives.

Commercial gravel removal is also a major problem in many areas (Cuinat, 1988; Whelan and Roche (in preparation (b)). The latter study was carried out on the River Inny, a small salmon and sea trout fishery in the south west of Ireland. Removal of gravels had resulted in serious bank erosion problems and an overall drop in productivity. Free passage of adult migratory salmonids was also affected.

5. SURVEYS AND SURVEY TECHNIQUES

As indicated previously the whole planning phase of a rehabilitation or restoration programme should be based on detailed physical, chemical and biological surveys of the catchment. Unfortunately, much of the survey work is carried out at this initial phase and the level of performance monitoring is often appreciably less. This is unfortunate since an accurate evaluation of the success of each phase of the programme will be beneficial, not alone to the project on hand, but also to future projects. Both Harris (1978) and Kennedy (1988) have shown that this is particularly true in the case of monitoring the relative success of stocking programmes.

Monitoring the descent of juvenile salmon and the ascent of resultant adults has taxed the ingenuity of fisheries scientists and engineers for many years. Various direct trapping mechanisms have been used, particularly mobile and permanent Wolf trap type designs. The use of these forms of traps has given cause for concern, particularly in relation to the handling of fully silvered smolts and fresh adults. Stress and mechanical damage can lead to direct mortality or disease outbreaks. Existing developments are currently taking place in the use of both acoustic and video detector methods (Carlton, pers.com.). The use of internal pit-tags, although expensive, seems also to hold great potential. Detectors for the location of internal magnetised micro-tags are also currently being developed.

The use of semi-quantitative methods of assessing juvenile salmon populations were described by Kennedy (1981) and Kennedy and Strange (1982). The technique involves a single fishing, using standard electrical fishing equipment and standard fishing crews. All salmonids are retained and the appropriate statistics are recorded. The technique permits a large number of sites to be sampled in a comparatively short timespan. Strange *et al.* (1989) have evaluated this technique against a commonly used quantitative method and recommend its use in extensive juvenile monitoring programmes. Whelan *et al.* (in preparation) have used a similar technique to carry out preliminary surveys of large salmonid catchments in Ireland but recommend the use of standard quantitative techniques to calculate salmonid standing crops within the zones or eco-types described by the basic 'blitzing' or semi-quantitative technique.

6. BIOLOGICAL CONSIDERATIONS

It is still not certain what constitutes a unit stock. However, it is certain that each major catchment will contain one or perhaps more unit stocks. Over time, nature has genetically sculptured individual races or stocks to suit their particular freshwater environment. Some would claim that even the phenotype of such races has been manicured to suit its surroundings; lakes or slow flowing rivers are often characterised by races of deep bodied, broad shouldered salmon and grilse, while sleek, sea-trout-like salmon are often associated with the faster flowing spate systems

(Whelan, 1990). Recent genetic work has also shown that discernible differences do exist between various races or stocks of wild salmon (Cross and Ward 1980; Cross and Healy, 1983; Cross and King, 1983; Wilkins, 1972 and 1986).

The task facing those seeking to restore a salmon run is to produce a race of salmon, which may quickly become adapted to that particular system. It is important to realise that it is not a direct analogy with the original race of salmon that is required but rather a race which will adapt well to present day features of the catchment. It is, however, vital that the stock type should be matched as closely as possible, both physically and biologically, to the 'new' river (Thorpe, 1988). In the past, lack of success in the restoration of salmon rivers has been due to the restricted range of donor stocks available (Stolte, 1980).

Having chosen an apparently suitable donor stock a decision must be made whether to stock: ova, parr, smolts or even adults.

Kennedy (1988) has provided a detailed review of stock enhancement techniques. The most favoured methods are the use of eyed ova in various forms of hatching boxes (Shearer, 1961) or in artificially constructed redds (Kennedy and Strange, 1981); and the stocking of either feeding or unfed fry (Egglishaw et al., 1984; Harris, 1978). The use of both parr and smolts has also been recommended by various authors (Elson, 1957; Isaksson, Rasch and Poe, 1978).The use of semi-natural rearing channels is gaining in popularity and a great deal of work on this method is on-going in Canada (Bielak, 1989). Enhancement of basic stocks by stream remedial work is also popular. This would include: the stocking of areas inaccessible to adults but where free downstream passage of smolts is possible, the creation of resting pools and spawning channels and the construction of fish passes into the upper reaches of the catchment.

The use of lakes within a catchment as a semi-natural rearing area has been extensively reviewed by Harris (1973). More recent investigations in Newfoundland and Ireland have indicated that some juvenile salmon utilise lake habitat naturally (Chadwick, 1985 and Anon 1986-89). In Canada, small lakes or ponds are being increasingly used as semi-natural rearing areas (Bielak, 1989).

Transfer of adult salmon from below impassable barriers or from overstocked areas to spawning channels, or other underutilized parts of the same system, has been used with some success in Canada (Davis and Scott, 1983). Similar experiments were also attempted on the River Taff in Wales. Despite a relatively high mortality of released fish it was generally concluded that with adequate handling facilities such a strategy had potential. One of the major advantages of this technique is that the progeny of transferred adults will be of "wild quality" compared with juveniles produced in hatcheries and released in streams (Kennedy, 1988).

The possibility of using aquaculture reared adult spawners is also being investigated in Canada (Legault, 1990). The progeny of the basic wild stock are grown to maturity in the cosseted environment of an aquaculture installation. The resulting ripe adults are subsequently re-introduced into the wild. The principal advantage envisaged is the avoidance of the interceptory fisheries. Additionally during the restoration period, protection efforts are reduced to five or six weeks annually compared to five months for wild adults. Aquaculture reared adults do not exhibit homing behaviour which would cause them to migrate to the ocean in search of their natal river.

During the initial years of a restoration programme each adult return is of immense importance and every effort must be made to breed from these individuals. The use of kelt reconditioning is a technique which has obvious potential in terms of recycling Atlantic salmon and the provision of several generations of eggs or milt from known adult returns. Total survival after the first year of reconditioning is in the region of 60% (50% for males and 70% for females); while sexual maturity increases over time in the female salmon (from 34% in first year to 88% in the fourth year). All males mature annually (Turgeon, 1990).

It has also been shown that the presence of juvenile salmon in a system may encourage the straying of adult salmon from other systems. It is hypothesised that pheromones or metabolic products of the newly stocked population may attract non-native adults into the system. Solomon (1973) describes experiences from the River Parrett in Somerset, which is an estuarine tributary of the Severn and whose confluence is on the opposite side to those of the Usk and Wye. Following stocking of the River Tone, a tributary of the River Parrett, increased numbers of tagged Usk, Wye and Severn salmon were recorded in the estuary of the Parrett.

Predation is a key element in both the juvenile and adult life stages of the Atlantic salmon. Mills (1989) has reviewed the available data and has shown that heavy predation by fish (Mills, 1964; Wheeler and Gardner, 1974); birds (Elson, 1962; Kennedy and Greer, 1988) and mammals (Rae and Shearer, 1965) may seriously affect the overall survival of a salmon stock. Elson (1962), for example, showed a seven-fold increase in the survival of stocked under-yearlings through the control of mergansers and belted kingfishers. Kennedy and Greer (1988) estimated that total daily predation rates of cormorants, feeding on the River Bush in Norther Ireland, were 1083-2023 wild smolts, 176-382 hatchery smolts and 691-1285 brown trout.

Mills (1989) lists a whole range of sea fish species which prey on adult and juvenile salmon and quotes the work of Rae and Shearer (1965) in relation to predation from both common and grey seals.

From work carried out to date on the Burrishoole system in Ireland it is obvious that specific individuals or 'rogues', are often responsible for the bulk of predation and the removal of these individuals can greatly increase survival. Otters are a particular problem at present in this catchment and live trapping commenced in 1990. It has been estimated that as many as 50 adult salmon were taken by otters in 1989. One otter has been trapped and transported out of the catchment during 1990.

7. ECONOMIC STRATEGIES

Finally, I should like to consider the economic strategies or fund raising activities which underpin these expensive restoration initiatives. As we have seen previously, Frenette *et al.* (1988) have produced a series of objectives for the restoration of the Jacques Cartier. Laudable as these objectives may seem I would suggest that funding may also result from objectives which have more to do with self interest than aesthetics.

There are doubtlessly individuals, or groups, who will contribute towards an enhancement or restoration programme with their sights firmly set on a productive recreational or even commercial fishery. There are others, particularly those involved in local government, whose only motivation in funding the programme is to bolster their own political image, particularly where stringent pollution control mechanisms have been put in place on the system.

I would suggest that the results from the restoration programme must, if it is to be sustained, pander, at least in part, to all of these diverse motivations. Long-term funding from public and private sources is basic to the success of these initiatives.

What then, do our contributors require for their money? Is it assurances that at least 10 adults have made it back to the headwaters to spawn; a series of pretty colour prints and a shapely brochure? Is it isolated salmon, trapped in fish passes, to be viewed by visitors and school groups? Is it salmon acting as canaries in a mine, ensuring that clean water prevails throughout a system?

It is my view that after a decade or more of a costly restoration programme the general public expect fish and a substantial number of fish.

Again, I would revert to objectives and draw a clear distinction between the two extremes of any system which is being restored. The upper reaches quite obviously need to be enhanced, with the clear objective of maximising production and generating a self sustaining stock. Even when fully developed this may be far lower than historic values for the system. For example, it has been estimated that the Connecticut will accommodate some 6,000 adult salmon when fully restored (Jones, 1988).

Let us contrast this with current stock levels in Ireland. It has been calculated that the River Corrib has an annual river stock of some 20,000 - 30,000 grilse (Browne, 1988); while based on similar estimates of exploitation and survival it is estimated that the River Moy produces a river stock of 50,000 - 60,000 grilse per annum, with a minimum rod catch in 1989 of 11,500 grilse! These catchments are physically far smaller than the Connecticut River basin.

It is clear from the above examples that enhancing the stock will, at best, produce only a very modest recreational fishery. However, there is another strategy which I feel has not been given adequate attention in the context of restoration programmes; that is ocean ranching.

Ranching is a commercial operation designed to provide a commercial harvest. The fish are released as near to the estuary as possible with a view to obtaining optimum survival. The fish are harvested low down on the system and provide either fish for consumption, broodstock, a rod fishery or adults for enhancement. The objective of such a programme, in a restoration context, would be to achieve maximum survival and the largest possible return of adult salmon.

There is at present a large restoration programme taking place on the River Guddena, in Denmark and here they are adopting such a strategy. The pre-smolts are placed in imprinting ponds adjacent to the main river. They are then transferred into a large floating pen and driven very slowly some 100km to the estuary. They are released into the outer estuary beyond any pollution problems and well beyond many of the inshore predators. On their return the fish are trapped adjacent to the imprinting pond and held as broodstock.

By twining the strategies of enhancing and ranching, particularly if innovative techniques such as those on the River Guddena are used, all of the major objectives of a restoration programme may be met. Relatively large numbers of returning adults are to be seen in the system and their progeny may be used to enhance the all important spawning stocks or to provide a valuable recreational fishery.

Finally, I should like to mention briefly a major enhancement scheme which took place in Ireland during the last century and which was most successful. It was on the Ballisodare River, Co. Sligo and historically this system was barred to salmon by an impassable rock barrier. When a fish pass was constructed in the 1850's the fish gained access to the system and thrived. Only the most primitive of juvenile and adult stockings took place (Went, 1969). It is now one of the most productive fisheries of its size in Ireland and produces some 800 grilse a year to the rod!

The moral is quite clear. Where man struggles to replace lost habitat his task is a daunting one; but where he strives to utilize nature and a pristine habitat, success is all but guaranteed.

REFERENCES

Anon. (1975) Symposium on the methodology for the survey, monitoring and appraisal of fishery resources in lakes and large rivers - panel reviews and relevant papers. EIFAC Technical Paper No. 23 Supplement 1 - Vol II. 747pp.

Anon. (1986) Water Quality in Ireland: General Assessment Part Two: River Quality Data. Environmental Research Unit, Dublin.

Anon. (1986-1989) In: Salmon Research Trust of Ireland, Inc. Annual Reports for year(s) ending 31st December 1986, 1987, 1988 and 1989.

Anon. (1987) Water quality criteria for European freshwater fish. EIFAC Technical Paper No. 37 Rev. 1, 75pp.

Anon. (1989) US Atlantic salmon stocks - a ten year review. NASCO Paper NAC (89) 12.

Benson, N.G. (ed.) (1970) A century of fisheries in North America. Special Publication No. 7. American Fisheries Society, Washington, D.C. 329pp.

Bielak, A.T. (ed.) (1989) Innovative Fisheries Management Initiatives. Annual Meeting of the Canadian Wildlife Federation. Canadian Wildlife Federation, Ottawa, Ontario, Canada. 29pp.

Bielak, A.T. (ed.) (1990) Proceedings of the 1988 Northeast Salmon Workshop. Special Publication Series No. 16, Atlantic Salmon Federation, St.Andrews. N.B., Canada. 156pp.

Browne, J. 1988 The use of Leslie Matrices to assess the salmon population of the River Corrib. In: Atlantic Salmon: Planning for the Future. (Eds. D. Mills and D.J. Piggins). Croom Helm, London and Sydney, 275-300.

Caffrey, J.M. (1986) Macrophytes as biological indicators of organic pollution in Irish rivers. Proceedings of the Royal Irish Academy. Symposium on Biological Indicators of Pollution. Pages 77 - 87.

Chadwick, E.M.P. (1985) Fundamental research problems in the management of Atlantic salmon, *Salmo salar* L., in Atlantic Canada. Journal of Fish Biology, 27 (Supplement A): 9-25.

Cross, T.F. and Ward, R.D. (1980) Protein variation and duplicate loci in Atlantic salmon, *Salmo salar* L. Genetics Research, 36: 147-165

Cross, T.F. and King, J. (1983) Genetic effects of hatchery rearing in Atlantic Salmon. In: Genetics in Aquaculture. (Eds. N.P. Wilkins and E.M. Gosling). Elsevier Science Publishers B.V. Amsterdam. Oxford and New York. 33-40.

Cross, T.F. and Healy, J.A. (1983) The use of biochemical genetics to distinguish populations of Atlantic salmon, *Salmo salar*. Irish Fisheries Investigations. Series A., No.23.

Cuinat, R. (1988) Atlantic salmon in an extensive French river system; the Loire -Allier. In: Atlantic Salmon: Planning for the Future. (Eds. D. Mills and D.J. Piggins). Croom Helm, London and Sydney, 389-399.

Davis, J.P. and Scott, D.C. (1983) Exploits River Atlantic salmon development programme 1978, 1979 and 1980. Freshwater and Anadromous Fisheries Management Programme, Dept. of Fisheries and Oceans.

Egglishaw, H.J., Gardiner, W.R., Shackley, P.E. and Struthers, G. (1984) Principles and practices of stocking streams with salmon eggs and fry. Department of Agriculture and Fisheries for Scotland. Scottish Fisheries Information Pamphlet, No.10, 22pp.

Elson, P.F. (1957) Using hatchery-reared Atlantic salmon to best advantage. Canadian Fish Culturist, 21: 1-17.

Elson, P.F. (1962) Predator - prey relationship between fish - eating birds and Atlantic salmon. Bulletin of the Fisheries Research Board of Canada, 24: 731-67.

Frenette, M., Dulude, P., Beaurivage, M. (1988) The restoration of the Jacques Cartier: A major challenge and a collective pride. In: Atlantic Salmon: Planning for the Future (Eds. D. Mills and D.J. Piggins). Croom Helm, London and Sydney, 400-414.

Gough, P.J. (1982) Salmon rehabilitation scheme report. Thames Water, Directorate of Scientific Services.

Gough, P.J. (1983) Salmon rehabilitation scheme report. Juvenile salmon production in the Thames Catchment, 1981-1982. Proceedings of the Annual Study Course of the Institute of Fisheries Management, City University, London.

Gough, P.J. (1987) Thames salmon rehabilitation - the next steps. Atlantic Salmon Trust Progress Report, December 1987, 23-24.

de Groot, D.J. (1989) Literature survey into the possibility of restocking the River Rhine and its tributaries with Atlantic Salmon (*Salmo salar* L.). RIVOMO 88-205/89.2. Netherlands Institute for Fisheries Investigation IJmuiden, Netherlands.

Harris, G.S. (1973) Rearing smolts in mountain lakes to supplement salmon stocks. International Atlantic Salmon Foundation, Special Publication Series, 4(1), 237-52.

Harris, G.S. (1978) Salmon propagation in England and Wales. A report by the Association of River Authorities/ National Water Council Working Party. National Water Council, London, 62pp.

Isaksson, A., Rasch, T.J. and Poe, P.H. (1978) An evaluation of smolt releases into salmon and non-salmon producing streams using two release methods. Journal of Agricultural Research in Iceland, 10(2): 100-13.

Jones, R.A. (1988) Atlantic salmon restoration in the Connecticut River. In: Atlantic Salmon: Planning for the Future (Eds. D. Mills and D.J. Piggins). Croom Helm, London and Sydney, 415-426.

Kennedy, G.J.A. (1981) The reliability of quantitative juvenile salmon estimates using electro-fishing techniques. Atlantic Salmon Trust Workshop on Data Acquisition. Atlantic Salmon Trust, Farnham.

Kennedy, G.J.A. (1988) Stock enhancement of Atlantic salmon. In: Atlantic Salmon:- Planning for the Future (Eds. D. Mills and D.J. Piggins). Croom Helm, London and Sydney. 345-372.

Kennedy, G.J.A. and Strange, C.D. (1981) Comparative survival from salmon (*Salmo salar* L.) stocking with eyed and green ova in an upland stream. Fisheries Management. 12(2): 43-8.

Kennedy, G.J.A. and Strange, C.D. (1982) The distribution of salmonids in upland streams in relation to depth and gradient. Journal of Fish Biology, 20: 579-591

Kennedy, G.J.A. and Greer, J.E. (1988) Predation by cormorants (*Phalacrocorax carbo* L.) on the salmonid populations of the River Bush. Aquaculture and Fisheries Management. 19(2): 159-70.

Legault, M. (1990) Atlantic salmon enhancement project using aquaculture reared adult spawners - Port Daniel River. In: A.T. Bielak (ed). Proceedings of the 1988 Northeast Atlantic Salmon Workshop: 40 Special Publication Series No. 16, Atlantic Salmon Federation, St. Andrews, N.B. Canada.

Mills, D.H. (1964) The ecology of the young stages of the Atlantic salmon in the River Bran, Ross-shire. Freshwater and Salmon Fisheries Research, Scotland, 32, 58pp.

Mills, D.H. (1989) Ecology and Management of Atlantic Salmon. Chapman and Hall, London and New York. 351pp.

Milner, N.J. (1982) Habitat evaluation in salmonid streams. Proceedings of the Institute of Fisheries Management, 13th Annual Study Course, University College of Wales, Aberystwyth 47-52.

O'Neil, S. (1990) High-technology salmon enhancement techniques. In: A.T. Bielak (ed). Proceedings of the 1988 Northeast Atlantic Salmon Workshop: 45-53. Special Publications Series No.16. Atlantic Salmon Federation, St.Andrews, N.B.Canada.

Netboy, A. (1968) The Atlantic salmon - a vanishing species. Faber and Faber, London. 457pp.

Rae, B.B. and Shearer, W.M. (1965) Seal damage to salmon fisheries. Marine Research Series, Scotland, 2, 39pp.

Redmond, M.A. (1990) Provincial/state research summary. Province of New Brunswick. In: A.T. Bielak (ed). Proceedings of the 1988 Northeast Atlantic Salmon Workshop: 93-95. Special Publications Series No. 16. Atlantic Salmon Federation. St. Andrews, N.B. Canada.

Shearer, W.M. (1961) Survival rate of young salmonids in streams stocked with 'green' ova. International Council for the Exploration of the Sea, Salmon and Trout Committee 1961, No.98, 3pp.

Solomon, D.J. (1973) Evidence for pheromone - influenced homing by migrating Atlantic salmon, *Salmo salar* L. Nature Vol. 244: 231-232.

Solbé, J. (1988) Water quality for salmon and trout. Atlantic Salmon Trust. Pitlochry 72pp.

Stolte, W. (1980) Planning as related to the restoration of Atlantic salmon in New England. In Atlantic salmon: its future. Proceedings of the Second International Atlantic Salmon Symposium, Edinburgh. Fishing News Books, Farnham, Surrey, 135-45.

Strange, C.D., Aprahamian, M.W. and Winstone, A.J. (1989) Assessment of a semi-quantitative electric fishing sampling technique for juvenile Atlantic salmon. Aquaculture and Fisheries Management. 20(4): 485-492.

Thorpe, J.E. (1988) Salmon enhancement: stock discreteness and choice of material for stocking. In: Atlantic Salmon: Planning for the Future (Eds. D. Mills and D.J. Piggins). Croom Helm, London and Sydney, 373-388.

Turgeon, Y. (1990) Reconditioning of Atlantic salmon. In: A.T. Bielak (ed). Proceedings of the 1988 Northeast Atlantic Salmon Workshop: 34-36. Special Publications Series No.16. Atlantic Salmon Federation. St. Andrews. N.B., Canada.

Wheeler, A. and Gardner, D. (1974) Survey of the literature of marine fish predators on salmon in the northeast Atlantic. Journal of the Institute of Fisheries Management, 5(3): 63-66.

Went, A.E.J. (1969) Historical notes on the fisheries of the two County Sligo rivers. Journal of the Royal Society of Antiquaries of Ireland. 99(1): 55-61.

Whelan, K.F. (1990) Priorities for Irish salmon research. In: Proceedings of the 20th Annual Study Course. 12-14th Sept. 1989. Galway, Ireland. Institute of Fisheries Management.

Whelan, K.F., Roche, W. and O'Maoileidigh, N.P. (in preparation) A pre-impoundment study of the River Feale catchment, Co. Kerry, Ireland.

Whelan, K.F. and Roche, W. (in preparation) The effects of extensive in gravel removal on the physical and biological characteristics of the River Inny, Co. Kerry, Ireland.

Wilkins, W.P. (1972) Biochemical genetics of the Atlantic salmon. *Salmo salar* L. II. The significance of recent studies and their application in population identification. Journal of Fish Biology. 4: 505-517.

Wilkins, W.P. (1986) Salmon stocks: A genetic perspective. Atlantic Salmon Trust, Pitlochry, 30pp.

ASSESSMENT OF PRACTICABILITY

JOHN BANKS

NRA: Thames Region

This conference is about rehabilitation, so in considering the assessment of practicability we already know that the rivers being considered were suitable places for salmon to complete their life cycle. The previous paper considered rehabilitation techniques, and some main strands that already point to the areas in which assessments of its practicability must operate. The task for this paper is to structure the steps which should be gone through, or might be gone through, in reaching a decision on whether or not to attempt rehabilitation.

Let us not delude ourselves for one moment with the idea that assessment is a coldly calculated amalgam of science and economics, clearly it is not. Since the eventual economic gains from a rehabilitation project are likely to be conjectural, and at least partly intangible, sentiment, politics, public relations and a sheer determination to see things 'put right' are likely to play a considerable part in determining whether resources will be available. Without such motivation rehabilitations may never get started, so they are not to be underrated, but they do need to be kept separate as far as possible from the scientific appraisal of a proposal. In practice these strong forces are quite likely to determine that rehabilitation will be attempted in advance of the scientific assessment.

If we imagine a pristine salmon river we will know that there was once an adequate flow, the water was sufficiently clean and there was a sufficiently unobstructed passage to the spawning grounds to permit the completion of the life cycle and presumably to provide enough surplus to be regarded as a worthwhile resource for angling and perhaps netting. This population has been reduced or extinguished, and the suggestion is made that the population should be restored. The assessment of this task can conveniently be considered under seven headings.

1. RESPONSIBILITY: RESOURCES

Immediately these two questions arise. Who would carry out the work of assessment and then perhaps implementation? Will resources be available? Even where, as in England and Wales, there is a clear statutory responsibility to maintain, improve and develop fisheries placed on the National Rivers Authority and its predecessor Water Authorities the requirement for internal resources for a rehabilitation project must compete with other claims within fisheries and outside it. Without such a clear statutory power and backing would-be rehabilitators are thrust back onto whatever funds they can gather from voluntary sources. On the Clyde, for example, the Clyde Fisheries Management Trust were attempting to co-ordinate action for the reconstruction of fish passes. Under Scottish salmon administration a Clyde Salmon Fishery Board could be established and could raise funds if everyone agreed, but such agreement cannot be assumed. This point is discussed later under 'Requirement'.

In the Rhine rehabilitation project several nations are involved without any formal overall authority or direction. This is bound to make an efficient use of resources much harder to achieve.

Answers to these apparently straightforward issues may thus be quite complex. However, the importance of a clear understanding from the outset cannot be understated.

Following these basic issues there come three questions which relate to the technicalities of restoration:

    i   What parts of the life cycle are now blocked or restricted, and at what points is rehabilitation possible?

    ii   Is the population relict or extinct?

    iii How far is it intended to restore the population in terms of numbers and inhabited area?

2. RESTRICTIONS

Although the salmon has been described as an "opportunistic generalist" this relates more to its ability to be flexible in timing its breeding cycle than in its more basic environmental requirements. The limits to flexibility are therefore quite closely defined in many instances.

The life cycle	Sources of difficulties
Adult return	Quality of water in estuary
	Quality of water upstream
	Obstructions
	Quantities of flow
	Interrelations of these three with time to produce the right combinations at the right seasons
Spawning	Does potentially suitable gravel still exist
	What quantities are present
	What is its condition
	Will there be adequate flows over it in the spawning season
Nursery areas	Area available
	Quality
	Reliability in terms of flow and water quality
Smolt migration	Presence of potential diversions eg. fish farms or potable water abstraction
	Is water quality downstream, eg in the estuary, adequate at the time of migration

If the difficulties with quality or flow are sufficiently severe it may indicate that further improvements in these areas are needed before rehabilitation can be attempted. For example, when fish began to repopulate the tideway the return of salmon in the Thames was mooted in the early 1970's, but it was quickly recognised through modelling that the sewage treatment investment programme for London would have to run its course for another 8 or 9 years before restoration could be seriously considered. Although the answers to these questions on the life cycle may be apparently clear I suggest that the full checklist should be worked through. Calculations should estimate the potential production of eggs, fry, parr and smolts and their survival potential to know how many adults will be needed to sustain the population (assuming that this is the objective). A margin of safety is required in order to assure survival through the bad years as well as the good. It should also not be forgotten that a newly re-establishing population may be less efficient at survival of the marine phase and successfully locating the river from which it has migrated.

Even in large and prestigious projects, like the programme for the Connecticut River where millions of dollars have been spent in providing fishways at the formidable dams, Ben Rizzo was quoted in the latest edition of the *Atlantic Salmon Journal* as saying that the problems of ensuring efficient smolt migration at these dams had been seriously underestimated. The whole programme was negated without attention to this problem which looks as if it will require rather more money to solve than that for the original fishways for the adults. Following re-evaluation this aspect of the problem is being tackled vigorously.

3. RELICT OR EXTINCT

Where a salmon population is struggling, but surviving, data gathered on the relicts will be of great assistance in answering some of the restriction questions just posed.

A relict population can be encouraged and expanded once its strongholds are known. Most importantly there will be a stock of fish with a proven genome to provide the basis for expansion once the conditions are right. There is a great difference in the scale of the problem of assessing practicability for the restoration of an extinct population. There are no observations to be made from nature, and no population base. Everything has to be developed from first principles unless, as in the Taff for example, the river was first repopulated by straying fish once the water quality was improved sufficiently, and now of course rehabilitation is being undertaken more actively.

The most difficult circumstances are provided by rivers like the Thames where the population has been extinct for over 150 years, or the Rhine where the gap is more like 50 years. Inevitably the rivers and their uses have been developed without reference to a salmon population. In the Thames, where salmon were extinguished by a combination of lethal water quality in the estuary and pound locks in freshwater, there was more than one attempt during the mid to late 19th Century to restore the population. These attempts were doomed because the hopeful restorers of the period simply lacked the knowledge to make a realistic assessment of their chances. The stimulus to think about rehabilitation again was the spectacular recolonisation of the estuary as the sewage treatment investment of the 1960's began to produce results. At

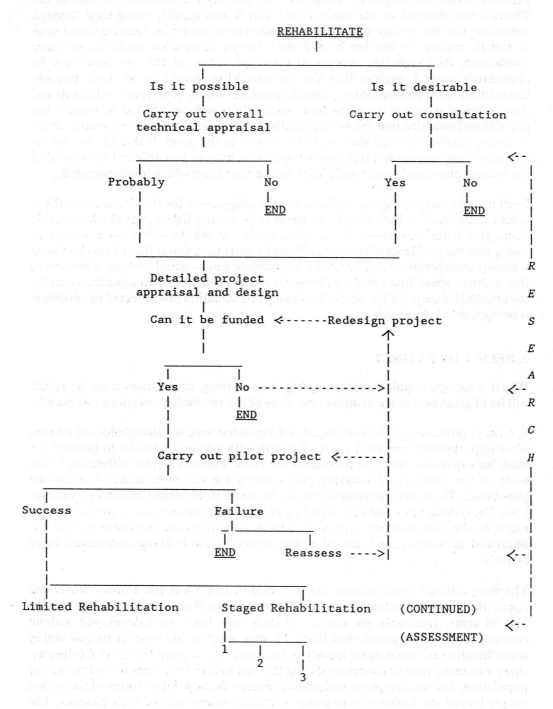

Figure 1. Summary of practicability assessment.

the beginning little thought was given to managing the rest of the life cycle. Compared with the millions spent on cleaning up the estuary the remaining problems for a salmon population must have seemed trivial. In fact they are quite formidable, because of the construction of obstacles, the dredging of spawning or nursery areas and water quality problems in freshwater. All of this will mean that the new population is unlikely to need to be a reproduction of the old one, even if that were possible. A choice of parent stocks is required for the new population. The issues involved are discussed by Wilkins (1985) and Cross (1989).

4. RESTORATION EXTENT

The answer to the question of how far to attempt restoration is likely to depend on the problems with restrictions and the issue of resources. The project appraisal must consider how much can be restored, and whether it is sensible to attempt it in a phased manner, perhaps related to obstructions. If, for example, the balance between spawning and nursery areas is not right consideration could be given to addressing it through habitat-improvement.

5. REQUIREMENT

Whilst consideration of the technical problems is proceeding this is another vital part of the overall assessment which must be faced.

Is the project desirable, and desired by those who may be affected by it? Using the Thames example, this question was addressed in the late 1970's through a process of consultation, not just with the statutory committees of the Water Authority but with the public at large. Comment and objection were invited by means of advertisement. The results of this exercise were considered by a working party containing outsiders like representatives from the Association of County Councils, The Country Landowners Association, the Greater London Council and the London Boroughs Association as well as representatives of fishery interests. The consultation dealt very much with two concerns of existing fishery users, would they run the risk of being priced off the water by salmon anglers, would the cost of the scheme be borne through licence charges from the pockets of anglers with little interest in salmon fishing? There is no need to say more here than that these fears were sufficiently allayed by examples of peaceful coexistence like the Severn to convince most that the scheme was sufficiently in the general interest to go ahead. However, these fears do exist and are frequently raised when NRA officers meet anglers' groups and the subject of salmon is raised.

In the Clyde it also became clear that many trout anglers in the upper parts of the river were not in favour of the return of salmon. Whilst the Thames is clearly well suited to coarse fishing the Clyde would adapt very readily to salmon fishing. The likely overlap of fishing seasons for salmon and trout on the Clyde are a further factor in suggesting that the requirement for rehabilitation could be a very real issue in such a river.

For many rehabilitation projects it is unlikely that the question of desirability will need to be raised so seriously, but wherever the hoped for benefits are intangible as much as they are in hard cash for a particular interest group, like fishery proprietors, the questions of who pays, who benefits, and who may suffer disadvantage are very real. These questions need to be in the public domain.

If it is finally agreed that restoration is desirable the last stage is the production of a detailed and costed implementation plan. Depending on circumstances it may well be sensible to divide this into a pilot project and staged implementation as more of the river is reopened. On the other hand the whole project could depend on the removal of a single block. Whichever is being dealt with I suggest that it is essential to have the means, and to have secured continuing resources from the outset which will make it possible to identify success or failure. This may be done by counting adults, perhaps through parr surveys. Whatever is to be done needs to be a part of the overall plan. Without this capacity for ongoing assessment the project will be limited. In a major project the justification for continued funding will be jeopardised. However, the dangers of linking funding to over-optimistic assessments should be borne in mind. All parties need to recognise from the beginning that successful rehabilitation is likely to take time.

6. RESEARCH

At any stage from the initial technical appraisal right through to implementation a problem may be foreseen, or arise unexpectedly, where the solution does not seem to be available from existing experience. The assessment of practicability may require research effort at some basic issue, and the answers will need to be fed back into the assessment process.

The process of assessing practicability is summarised in Figure 1.

REFERENCES

Wilkins, N.P. (1985) Salmon Stocks: A Genetic Perspective. Atlantic Salmon Trust, Pitlochry, 30p.

Cross, T.F. (1989) Genetics and the management of the Atlantic Salmon. Atlantic Salmon Trust. Pitlochry, 74p.

FINANCING AND LEGISLATION

BERNARD LAMY (Chairman) and FREDERIC MAZEAUD (General Secretary), Association Internationale de Défense du Saumon Atlantique

In twenty years from 1954 to 1974, the level of salmon captures in France had dwindled from 180 metric tons to 20 tons. At the time of the first oil crisis, there was a need for an urgent solution to this situation.

In a common move, the majority of associations in charge of environment, species conservation or fisheries issued a request underlining that with proper management, our rather outstanding hydrographic network should be able to appeal to the well-off sport fishermen, traditionally attracted by foreign fishing grounds. It should also attract other customers interested in Atlantic salmon fishing as well as in a touristic, cultural and gastronomic journey in France.

Moreover, the brand new (three year old) *Ministère de l'Environnement* had not committed itself to any project which, used as a spearhead, could clearly show that impossible missions could be achieved despite modest budgets.

These pressures prompted our governmental minds to adopt the idea of a *"plan quinquennal saumon"* under the responsibility of the *Ministère de l'Environnement* for the 1976-1980 period. This was followed by a *"programme poissons migrateurs"* for 1981-1985. Since then, numerous spot actions were conducted as a follow up to these actions, the latest being a *"plan grands migrateurs"* under the same authority and for the 1990-1995 period.

There are two major aims to these planned actions.

    A   To find a solution to problems occurring in the 16 rivers where *Salmo salar* were still present in significant numbers in 1974:

in Basse Normandie:

SIENNE
SEE
SELUNE

in Brittany:

LEGUER
ELORN
AULNE
JET
ODET
AVEN
SCORFF
BLAVET

ALLIER in Centre Auvergne
GAVES d'OLORON and MAULEON in Béam
NIVE in Pays Basque

B   To restore and restock other rivers which formerly were renowned for their *Salmo salar* abundance:

RHINE in Alsace
SEMOY, a MEUSE tributary in Lorraine
BRESLE in Normandy
GARTEMPE, a LOIRE tertiary tributary in Limousin
GARONNE and DORDOGNE in Aquitaine
GAVE de PAU in Béam
NIVELLE in Pays Basque

In addition, other minor rivers received a somewhat beneficial effect from all these successive activities.

1. THE "SALMON FIVE-YEAR PLAN" 1976-1980

Overexploitation of the salmon resource and habitat degradation were a primary target for the first measures intended to put an end to the decrease of Atlantic salmon stocks - from 36,000 fish in 1955 to less than 8,000 in 1975 - on the French territory. Four types of measures aimed at:

1)   stock assessment and better knowledge of population structure

2)   restocking using hatcheries or intensive-care nursery creeks

3)   providing existing dams with fish ladders

4)   habitat management, cleaning and protection.

During this period, £3.5 million were spent on equipment, fish ladders, studies and training.

The positive effects of this first plan are reflected mostly by the fish ladder construction and juvenile restocking. Indeed, despite these efforts, captures were in decline except in some parts of Brittany where regional associations had initiated their own plans earlier.

2. THE MIGRATORY FISH PROGRAMME, 1980-1985

Among the first effects following the first *"plan saumon"*, a positive result was observed on all the migratory fish, mostly on sea trout whose populations have dramatically increased in numerous rivers.

For this reason, after having made an overall assessment of this first period, the decision was taken to extend the benefit of such plans to all kinds of migratory fish like sea trout, shad, lamprey, eel and sturgeon, from an either recreational or professional standpoint but with a preference for high added value species.

In a similar way, the legal background evolved in several major directions:

- classification of rivers leading to Atlantic salmon classified rivers

- regulation and even prohibition of gravel extraction in the bed of rivers

- *Loi sur la Protection de la Nature* with compulsory "*Etudes d'Impact*" of projects and mandatory evaluation and measurement of biotopes protection

- prohibition of capture for species like sturgeon still present in the Garonne-Dordogne basin

- new *Loi-Pêche* (1984 ratified 1987) introducing quotas for salmon sport fisheries, compulsory declaration of catch by everybody and fly fishing only for the last month of the season on most rivers.

To achieve this programme, £7.2 million were spent.

3. SPOT ACTIONS BETWEEN 1986 and 9189

During these four years, almost 50 million francs helped to fund the same sort of actions as mentioned above in terms of equipment. If we consider the whole period 1976-1989, 14 years, an aggregate of £15.2 million was invested in salmon and migratory fish, which amounts to approximately £20 million in 1990. Among this sum, an estimate of 3/4 (150 MF) was devoted to salmon.

4. ORIGIN OF FUNDING

A. GOVERNMENT

- general budget

- *Ministère de l'Environnement*

B. CSP

- *Conseil Supérieur de la Pêche* and other bodies

C. TERRITORIAL BODIES

- Budget of French Regions

- State/Region contracts

This list does not encompass what has been achieved in cooperation with EDF (Electricité de France, the French national electrical power company) according to an EDF/Ministère de l'Environnement contract where more than £4 million were spent in studies and amelioration of dam equipment whenever the already existing fish ladders were not operational for migratory species.

5. NATURE OF EXPENSES

			Amount in M£
A	**Investments**	78%	15.60
B	**Operating costs**	22%	4.40
	TOTAL	100%	20.00
1	Studies	35.7%	7.14
2	Restocking, equipment, hatcheries	23.0%	4.60
3	Fish ladders, counting fences, monitoring stations	31.7%	6.34
4	Habitat restoration. Improvement of spawning grounds	4.7%	0.94
5	Promotion, information, popularisation	4.9%	0.98
	TOTAL	100%	20.00

There is no doubt that works in connection with dams, fish ladders and counters represent the majority of the overall expenses. If we added the EDF contribution to the above figures, the share of heavy equipment would jump from 31.7% to 50% of the cost of programmes.

In addition, the cost of studies is also very heavy. France had indeed a wide gap to fill in this respect.

6. ROLE OF THE CONSEIL SUPÉRIEUR DE LA PÊCHE

Acting as a link between Administration and the representatives of fishermen, and competent for all continental fisheries in open or public water, the CSP is an "*Establissement Public National*" with administrative, technical and some political power.

- administrative: managing the income of our *taxe piscicole*, due by the sport fishermen according to the *12 juillet 1941* law, to the best of our continental water interests extending from the warden fees to the above mentioned expenses. CSP is especially in charge of hiring, training and backing wardens, this being done through our "*brigades départementales de garderie*".

- technical: scientific studies, experimentation, technical advice to sub-units like *Fédérations, AAPP* and *Associations Agréées de Pêcheurs Professionnels*.

- political: as a consultative organisation to the Ministry in charge of freshwater fisheries policy (*art L234-1* of *Code Rural*).

The CSP board advises the Ministry in elaborating fisheries bye-laws or regulations. In any case, it is consulted before any kind of government decision in the field of continental fisheries management takes place at the national level. In the case of our major salmon river, the *Plans Grands Migrateurs* are studied and put forward by the board of CSP.

Similarly, every year, the CSP board sets up the legal amount of the *Taxe piscicole* which is the fee included in the yearly fishing licence to be paid by sport fishermen acting in open continental waters.

Indeed, the French *Code Rural* (*art L-230-1* to *L-239-1* including, from the *Loi du 29 juin 1984 plus décret de codification du 27 octobre 1989*) regulates all that concerns continental freshwater fisheries, from rivers, canals and streams, to water bodies which permanently or sporadically connect with them, and this until the fresh water meets the sea at the salinity limit.

CSP elaborates the practical applications of the law to be approved by the Ministry and implemented by the Préfet (regional representative of the Government) according to *Code Rural*: *arrêtés ministriels* or *arrêtés préfectoraux* for salmon classified rivers, for migratory fish protection etc.

It is worth mentioning a few dispositions of *Code Rural* outlining the management of migratory or amphihaline species.

- *Article L 236-11*

  Regarding rivers or canals flowing into the sea,"*des décrets en Conseil d'Etat*" rule certain conditions in a uniform policy for continental or marine capture of alternatively fresh water or sea water living species:

  1) calendar time when fishing is prohibited

  2) minimal size

  3) measures to be taken for reproduction, development, conservation and sale

  4) list of species whose marketing and sale is prohibited

  5) list of species whose introduction is prohibited

  6) number and size of permitted nets, traps or fishing instruments

In correlation to this text, not yet enforced for want of a *décret* approved by the authorities in charge of freshwater management as well as those in charge of the Sea, the *loi de 1984* gives authority to the CSP wardens to control conditions of capture beyond the salinity limit of the fish living alternatively in fresh water or sea water (*article L 237-1* of *Code Rural*, 6°).

Other dispositions of *Code Rural* set up some more obligations or restrictions:

29

- to restore a free circulation at the dam level (*L 232-6 Code Rural*)

- to impose a minimal discharge below the dam (*L 232-5*)

- to repress any direct or indirect discharge of substances potentially noxious to fish (pollution *L 232-2*)

- to limit or offset troubles from works in the streambed, even in the estuary (*L 232-3*, to be ratified by *Conseil d'Etat*)

All these dispositions, eligible for enforcement in the estuarine zone, bring a significant positive contribution to amphihaline migratory species management.

In addition, it should be noticed that there is legislation of a wider scope than sport fisheries and their management: the *Loi du 10 juillet 1976* on Nature Protection (*titre 1° of Livre II Code Rural*).

This legislation applies to the whole national territory, territorial waters included. It allows spot actions for the protection of some freshwater species like migratory fish. Already existing are sturgeon and salmon protection, two migratory and anadromous species.

7. MISCELLANEOUS ADMINISTRATIVE IMPLICATIONS

Although the situation outlined above might appear simple, the actual facts are not so clear. Indeed, many - too many - additional government agencies have a word to say about salmon. Among them, some have been devoted to Scientific Research like INRA or CNRS. Others like IFREMER have a scientific basis but are mostly in charge of protecting the economy of marine resources. All of them actively seek public funding to achieve research and development programmes which eventually might somewhat lack suitable coordination. Besides, it is practically impossible to stick a pound of concrete to an existing dam without getting the clearance of innumerable offices. Moreover, associations for Nature, Environment, species protection etc...are sprouting, sometimes with a strong local audience.

For all these reasons, an upstream migrating salmon has to swim across different administrative districts competing for prevalence, which indirectly influences its fate. It is compulsory for professional fishermen to tag each salmon caught with a plastic ring. This ring costs 46 francs for salmon caught in "continental water" and only 1 franc in "sea water", that is respectively above or below an abstract line crossing the estuary...

It is quite easy to understand that this situation generates serious frictions and even contradiction. For instance, on a big dam, the existence of a fish ladder which had been advocated and then constructed by sport fishermen has recently been officially questioned by a regional association for Nature Protection on the grounds that...it might threaten the salmon's future!

Again, although no party owns any rights to the salmon resource, there is a quarrel on appropriation between the freshwater sport fishermen whose officials restock the river and the marine users who harvest it as professionals in the estuary. In this case, each party refers to traditions, moral rights and finally to financial input, which results in a conflict where overbidding parallels fishing rights.

There is no clearcut frontier between wild stock management and aquaculture. Prohibition of Pacific species has resulted in the introduction of all kinds of *Salmo salar* broodstocks which have been used for restocking rivers. Today, this mixture of genetically different Atlantic salmon stocks has probably ruined part of our native broodstock with little hope to go backward: this resulting from uncoordinated efforts and conflicting technical advice issued by a congregation of scientists and wildlife managers. In the meantime, the same people have not been able to adopt an effective policy regarding ocean ranching practices, a possible way of restocking which has met so far with more contempt than attention.

Protected pollution or poaching, interests of trout anglers playing against salmon, fishing instruments devoted to other species and killing migrating salmon as a by-catch...appear like administrative dead ends in terms of regulations and salmon protection.

8. CONCLUSIONS

In terms of salmon conservation, a long series of efforts have been engaged during the past 15 years. France has now major assets to restore Atlantic salmon in several rivers and to enhance its populations.

Due to the actions successively supported by public funds, the next steps have been set up:

- a huge assortment of regulations and bye-laws allowing an exploitation and management of the resource without neglecting its protection or conservation.

- a better knowledge of migratory salmonid stocks and behaviour

- a better evaluation of the actual potentialities

- an improvement of most rivers at the level of fish ladders; de-siltation of spawning grounds

- creation of hatcheries and intensive-care nursery creeks.

However, despite these important efforts, we are still waiting for a significant improvement of the resource. Indeed, the last three years expectations have been confounded by a severe drought and although there is a slight general positive effect seen in Brittany, the other major French rivers are in poor condition.

If we refer particularly to such river systems as Loire/Allier, Garonne/Dordogne and Adour/Gaves, the recovery of the full potential is certainly dependent upon a decrease in the fishing pressure, mostly at the estuarine and coastal level. If the *Loi Pêche* were to be in effect in the maritime zone, this would certainly help.

We are still waiting for strong political views defining the priorities, chiefly according to the final resolution of the 3° International Salmon Symposium in Biarritz:

31

"In view of the greater income and employment potential of salmon angling and its appreciably smaller harvest of limited salmon populations, each national government of salmon-producing countries is urged to declare a salmon policy which will institute as a conservation measure, within its area of jurisdiction, management programmes to reduce commercial harvesting of salmon with a view to increasing salmon stocks and improving recreational salmon fisheries".

In this regard, we anticipate that the creation of a unique water management of the river, similar to the National Rivers Authority and wielding the whole decisional power would be a great step forward.

We are still waiting for a European model measuring accurately the exact impact of recreational fisheries of Atlantic salmon on local economies and societies. Such a model completing the recent evolution of our technical and legal dispositions would be expected to have very positive effects on our Atlantic salmon populations. The interest of France is at stake as well as the interest of every country blessed with salmon streams.

To the questions: what would you like to see being done instead of what has been done:

1) There is a philosophical alternative: do we need rivers well harnessed with fish ladders but without salmon, or do we need salmon even though the rivers are not suitable to welcome them?

Clearly so far, the French administration has enforced the first proposition. On our major migratory routes: Loire-Allier, Adour-Gaves, Dordogne and now Garonne, the result is: many fish ladders and less salmon or no salmon at all. When years ago, the La Bajasse dam on the Allier was not yet equipped, there were still quite a few salmon. Now, there is a good fish ladder but almost no extra salmon.

The matter now is: should we make salmon congregate at the foot of the first impassable obstacle that fish meet during their upstream migration? This goal might be achieved through a release-recapture site at the obstacle level or in a small tributary close to the estuary. It would probably cost a small fraction of a fish ladder to fund and once we get the salmon, we can demand a fish ladder! To be noted: in fact, some small rivers in Brittany have been restocked like that.

I propose: *to raise the funds equivalent to a Dordogne-style fish ladder (1 million £). To invest this money on a financial footing and get a return of 10%. With a £100000 yearly income, to purchase 50000 surplus smolts of a suitable broodstock (it won't be French!) at a cost of £25000, to keep another £25000 for expenses and to capitalize £50000 for devaluation. To release the smolts with proper technology at a site next to the sea and watch for return. In case there is no result, to give the money back. Why not this expedient?*

2) There is another philosophical alternative: shall we protect our native broodstock to the utmost point where there is no more salmon at all, or shall we introduce foreign blood for restocking and ruin our endangered native broodstock?

Clearly so far, the French administration and scientists have chosen the second proposition. However, we think that whenever the native broodstock is provided with valuable traits such as specific size and behaviour (the case of Loire-Allier or Adour-Gaves broodstock), it is worth their being protected (like the Pyrenean bear) against Scottish or Icelandic grilse contamination.

We want such a program to get started.

9. *Salmo salar*: A TENTATIVE MODEL FOR DAMAGED RIVER MANAGEMENT

A damaged salmon stream is 1) obstructed by an impassable dam 2) of acceptable water quality and discharge, although some sporadic events might be a threat 3) of restricted spawning success including smolt escapement 4) genetically polluted with non-native broodstock.

Management of such a stream does not rely on Mother Nature and should be conducted like a savings account: no balance, no salmon. We propose to take advantage of the dam and to control the whole population in an adjacent fish ladder. Those fish recognized as native will be given access to the spawning area or be kept for propagation in the "above the dam" area. Non-native fish (ie: mostly grilse in France) will be eradicated or used for restocking the river in the "below the dam" area.

9.1 Technical Outline

Above the dam, the native broodstock is given free and exclusive access to the natural spawning grounds. A hatchery might enhance its potential if natural spawning is anticipated to be short. Other problems are the same as for an unmanaged river.

Below the dam, a hatchery, either adjacent to the dam or located on a small tributary, breeds, grows and produces all kinds of smolts, no matter what broodstock it is. In a steady state hypothesis, this results in an abundant population of incoming adults.

At the dam level, all the fish entering the ladder are trapped and sorted. There are models of such operations. Every unwanted fish is killed or kept for below the dam. In the small tributary hypothesis, a total capture trap is set.

9.2 Economic Outline

The "above dam" questions are the same as in an unmanaged river.

Below the dam, the abundant population is provided for sport and commercial fishing. If needed, the native broodstock fish might be released if caught(adipose fin not clipped).

Cost

The cost of 1) purchasing the non-native smolts if needed 2) a total capture fish ladder 3) a hatchery growing juveniles up to the smolt stage 4) manpower. On most rivers, those expenses are already funded...

Legal

No doubt that in France, legal and administrative considerations would be the major obstacle to such an operation.

Objections

The above the dam situation will not be very different from now. However, if the salmon population is growing below the dam, the fishing pressure might have a negative effect on native broodstock. This negative effect should be allocated countermeasures such as a no-kill restriction for native fish.

There is not too much choice...

SALMON CATCHES

BASSINS	1975	Yearly 1980	Estimates 1985	1990
Basse Normandie + Bretagne	4,830	3,700	2,285	1,830
Loire-Allier	1,920	1,600	1,157	350
Adour-Gaves	632	1,040	1,075	1,200
TOTAL	7,382	6,340	4,517	3,380
Variations	-	-14.1%	-28.8%	-25.2%

Five Year Average Catch

	1976/1980	1981/1985	1986/1990
Basse Normandie + Bretagne	1,983	2,709	3,141
Loire-Allier	972	1,086	660
Adour-Gaves	570	745	3,834 [*]
TOTAL	3,525	4,540	7,635
Variations		+28.8%	+68.2%

[*] Exceptional year in 87 = more than 12,000 (96% by nets).

DEVELOPMENT OF STOCKS

D J SOLOMON

Fisheries Consultant

1. INTRODUCTION

The aim of this paper is to discuss the options available for obtaining and manipulating stocks of salmon for rehabilitation programmes. The intention is to deal with matters of strategy and approach rather than with detailed methodology; for important though the latter considerations are, it is felt that they are more than adequately covered in readily-available texts. The former, however, embraces areas both of developing understanding (and misunderstanding) and fascinating technological advances. Our present state of knowledge does not necessarily make decisions easier, but it at least allows the debate to be conducted in a reasonably informed manner.

2. CHOICE OF STOCK

2.1 The "genetic debate"

One of the most interesting developments in salmon biology in recent years has been the demonstration that different river stocks and sub-stocks are genetically different. The techniques involved are primarily electrophoretic separation of tissue proteins and enzymes, and analysis of mitochondrial DNA. The techniques and findings of recent research have been described in a clear and comprehensible way in two "Blue Book" publications of the AST by Wilkins (1985) and Cross (1989). However, in the manner of all good scientific discoveries they pose as many questions as they answer. What are the implications for salmon rehabilitation schemes?

While there is no doubt that there are genetic differences between stocks, and that these differences are maintained at least in part by the reproductive isolation of stocks, there is controversy about the mechanisms which are responsible for the differences. The basic question is whether the differences are adaptive, ie suit the fish to its particular riverine environment, and are thus influenced by natural selection, or whether they have occurred randomly as a result of genetic drift. While a detailed argument of the scientific evidence is not appropriate here, the answers are important in this context because, if the differences are adaptive, then

- use of a stock adapted to a different environment will be less effective in a rehabilitation programme than use of one adapted to a similar environment; and

- introduction of "foreign" and less well adapted material into a depleted stock may change the genetic constitution of the whole stock, making it less well suited to the particular environmental conditions.

There is little to glean from the studies of protein variation which indicated that the stocks are genetically distinct because the differences at this level are considered, generally, to be neutral in effect. The suggestion is that the different gene frequencies in isolated populations have arisen largely by genetic drift. Indeed, Youngson *et al* (1989) point out that if the different genotypes are found to be adaptive then the different gene frequencies between populations are in fact a poor indicator of reproductive isolation. One enzyme variation which appears to maybe have adaptive significance is at the Me-2 locus (malic enzyme) (Verspoor and Jordan, 1989; Youngson *et al*, 1989). Frequency of occurrence of the Me-2 (100) allele varies with location both within and between river systems. There is a definite clinal change in allele frequency from south to north between the Pyrenees and Scandinavia. Within one river system, the allele frequency varies between tributaries with different temperature regimes. Verspoor and Jordan suggested that the variation is due to a selective survival response to environmental temperature ie the differences are adaptive. They point out that if the different gene frequencies arise because of differential survival according to environmental temperature, they are a poor indicator of genetically distinct stocks. Youngson *et al* investigated gene frequencies in twelve Scottish strains of salmon held in captivity and the wild populations from which they were originally derived. The strains generally differed genetically from their ancestral stocks but in a pattern that suggested genetic drift or "artificial" selection. At the Me-2 locus, however, the differences in allele frequency of the reared strains were all in one direction from the source populations, suggesting an adaptive difference to the rearing conditions. However, I understand that a subsequent year of study has not confirmed this observation (A. Youngson, pers. comm.).

So what about some more obvious phenotypic attributes that might be considered adaptive - is there evidence here that they are genetically determined? Care is needed in analysing this, as an attribute that might be influenced by genetic make-up eg multi-sea-winter maturation, may be overridden or modified by environmental factors. Thus different river stocks may exhibit different attributes, without there being any difference in genotype. Saunders (1979) considering determination of grilse/older salmon and season of return habits, suggested that "genetics set the limits within which environment can exert modifications". Stock-specific variation in such traits as fecundity, egg size, growth rate, age at smolting, tendency to precociousness, age at adult return, season of return, tendency to multiple spawning and body shape could well be genetically determined, but could equally be the product of environmental influence. However, studies have shown for example that there is a genetic component in determination of differences in egg size in Norwegian stocks (Saunders, 1981), and "grilsing rate" between some Scottish and Norwegian stocks (Laird and Needham, 1984).

Riddell *et al* (1981) observed morphological differences between the salmon parr of two tributaries of the SW Miramichi in Canada, which they suggested could be adaptive. The fish from the Rocky Brook, which has a generally fast flow, had thinner bodies and larger pectoral fins than those from the slower Sabbies River. Fish from the two stocks reared under identical hatchery conditions maintained these differences, indicating that they were genetic in basis. An important point here is that these differences exist between two tributaries of the same system about 100 km apart.

36

So what conclusions can reasonably be drawn? First there are no doubt genetic differences, as indicated by allele frequencies in populations, between adjacent river and tributary stocks. The studies of protein genetics which allow us to recognize this do not however in themselves demonstrate any adaptive differences between genotypes; they merely indicate that there is reproductive isolation between stocks that could allow development and maintenance of adaptive differences. The evidence for genetically-determined adaptive differences is strong, however, and growing. Accepting this in principle, though, does not lead automatically to the conclusion that stock from other river systems will be poorly adapted to a new situation.

It is likely that a large river system contains more variation in environmental conditions, between its headwaters and its lower tributaries, than occurs between equivalent reaches of separate systems. A typical middle-sized system may have fish spawning and rearing in headwater streams at 700m or more altitude, while others spawn in the lower reaches. Some tributaries or reaches will be steep and boulder-strewn while others will be gravelly with a shallow gradient. Some sub-catchments may contain lakes where adult fish spend much of their freshwater sojourn and where many parr may live. An adjacent river system may show a similar range of habitat types, and a river system on the other side of the land mass may have headwater nursery areas within a few kilometres of the top of the river with virtually identical conditions. There is good evidence that the tributary (sub?) stocks in a system with varied topography are in themselves genetically distinct. If they are genetically adapted to local conditions, it is likely that stock from the equivalent zone of an adjacent (or even fairly distant) river system may be more appropriate for restocking than fish from another tributary of the same system with different critical environmental conditions. Some support for this idea comes from work on brown trout reported by Taggart *et al* (1981); they found that geographically close, but reproductively isolated stocks often showed very similar characteristics.

An important consideration at this point is that similarity or otherwise in the genetic make-up of stocks with respect to the neutral protein and mitochondrial DNA characteristics is likely to be a poor indicator of suitability of a stock for introduction. As the differences are believed to have arisen by genetic drift the degree of divergence is dependent upon the duration and completeness of the reproductive separation and adaptation. If the alleles studied are indeed neutral, similarities in their frequencies between stocks is no indication that the two also enjoy similar genetically determined adaptations, and differences do not necessarily indicate genetically determined adaptive differences.

2.2 Options for "extinguished" rivers

So how does the "genetic debate" help us with a choice of stocks? There is a difference whether we are dealing with a river which has totally lost its stock or one where a relict stock, however small, may remain. Considering first the former, there is little argument that importing stock will cause any "genetic harm" as there is no stock remaining. However, straying to other river systems is likely with an introduced stock, so even here it is prudent not to use stock from too distant a source, where even the most doubting scientist would agree that some adaptive differences are likely.

There are two basic philosophies. One is to choose stock from a river or, better, part of a river, with a similar environment in terms of size of stream, slope, temperature, hydrological regime, flora, fauna, distance to sea, estuary type and orientation of coastline in the hope that the fish are at least partially genetically adapted to their new home.

The alternative is to obtain stock from anywhere it is readily and cheaply available, ideally from a multitude of sources, in the hope that either genetic differences are of little adaptive significance, or that presenting the river with a wide range of genetic material will provide the basis for a new, well adapted genetic stock by natural selection. There is unfortunately little real experience to suggest which of these approaches is more likely to succeed. The main drawback of the first approach is that one might inadvertently overlook the most critical aspect of the environment and thus attempt to introduce a discrete stock which was in fact a significant genetic mismatch with the available niche. Until and unless we can identify exactly how fish are genetically adapted to particular environmental factors this approach will be uncertain.

While it is likely that the most critical conditions may often arise in the nursery tributary it may not always be the case. The distance of the nursery area from the sea may be important. For example, in an experiment reported by DAFS (1985), fish deriving from lower tributaries were stocked into streams on the Upper Tummel (Tay) catchment. It was found that their emigration from the system as smolts took place up to a month later than"natural" smolts from both the assumed streams of origin and the area stocked. This is likely to be critical as there is considered to be a fairly narrow time "window" for entry to the sea, outside which survival is much reduced. The fish appeared to be genetically attuned in a manner that was appropriate for a nursery stream lower down the large river system. Support for the suggestion that there is a genetic component here that interacts critically with environmental circumstances comes from further investigations reported by DAFS (1989). Fish from two Tay tributaries reared under identical experimental conditions showed differences in timing of onset of downstream migratory behaviour. These differences were appropriate, considering the distance to the sea and the different flow conditions of the donor sources, for the two stocks to enter the sea at a similar time. The obvious conclusion is that transferring stock between two such tributaries is likely to be of very limited success.

In some situations estuary and lower river conditions are critical. Towards the southern end of the range of Atlantic salmon distribution (eg Connecticut River) estuary waters are likely to be too warm for fish to pass during the summer months. Stocks in such situations are likely to enter mainly early or late in the season; in the case of large rivers, where the fish have a considerable journey to arrive at the spawning grounds, most would arrive early in the season. Saunders (1979) suggested that the original stock native to the upper Connecticut may have had a similar migratory pattern to those in the Serpentine River in the Upper St John catchment, which pass through the estuary in the winter a full year before spawning. Attempting to restock such areas with fish from a stock with a high tendency to return as grilse is likely to prove unsuccessful. Similar considerations apply to large rivers with a water quality problem which is most critical during the summer eg. the Thames and the Tees.

The second approach, taking stock from a wide range of sources, may in any event be forced on us by scarcity of available stock; for example, the Thames salmon rehabilitation scheme has had to take fish from throughout the UK, reared in a range of facilities, to provide adequate numbers for restocking. As long as restocking is done on a large enough scale it is likely to succeed, as natural selection will favour those fish most suited to the new situation. Survival rates overall will be low, but within a few generations one will hopefully have established a new, locally adapted stock. In theory, as long as the appropriate genetic material was available somewhere in the restocked populations, the genetic make-up of the developing stock will approach that of the original, now lost, population.

2.3 Options for depleted stocks

In the situation where stocks within the river system are severely depleted but not completely eradicated there are additional options, but the decision is even more difficult.

The conservative option is to work entirely from local material, and build up a stock by hatchery production or possibly by redistribution of adults. However, several points must be borne in mind. First, there is often strong resistance on the part of local management agencies to taking scarce broodstock from the depleted natural population for hatchery production - it can be argued that they are better left to their own devices. Second, as discussed in section 2.1, fish from a relict population in one part of the catchment may be unsuited for introduction to other parts with different critical conditions. Third, over the past hundred years or so man has changed the freshwater and estuarine environment of many salmon rivers considerably, both chemically (land use, fertilizers, acid precipitation, pollution etc) and physically (weirs, land drainage effects, water warming by effluents of power station cooling water and from sewage treatment works, and general riparian management). If stocks are closely adapted to their environment it is possible that a significant mismatch may now occur in some situations. It could even be postulated that this effect may have contributed to the decline in the stocks now requiring remedial action. In this scenario introduction of appropriate foreign stock could provide the very boost that the failing population needed. Indeed, a regular injection of a limited number of fish from a wide range of stocks could be a positive management technique for all stocks, in the hope that they could "take up" any appropriate genetic material and "discard" the rest. While this is not here proposed as a responsible course of action it does indicate the sort of paths down which the "genetic debate" can lead us!

As for rivers with extinguished stocks, the strategic choice of "foreign" material is between perceived "pre-adapted" stock from a similar habitat, and the "broad spectrum" approach. However, an interesting extra possibility is available where some local stock still exists. This is the production of hybrids between local and foreign stock, and is based upon the idea that the milt from a few males from the scarce local stock can be used to fertilize the eggs of many "foreign" females, to produce an abundant source of juveniles. Bams (1976) tried this with considerable success with pink salmon. He found that about three time as many "hybrids" homed to the river as did the pure donor stock, presumably as a result of genetic adaptation of local stocks. The definitive experiment has yet to be undertaken on Atlantic salmon but the observation that the numbers of introduced fish which successfully home to the river falls with increasing distance between the donor and recipient stream (Cross 1984) suggests that it is clearly worthy of consideration.

3. OPTIONS FOR STOCK DEVELOPMENT

3.1 General considerations

The ultimate goal of any rehabilitation programme is likely to be the establishment of a naturally spawning, self regenerating stock (or several sub stocks) throughout the river system without the need of further hatchery assistance. This is likely to take some time, and some stock development is likely to be required based on hatcheries. Further, it may be considered desirable to attempt to develop a particular trait eg spring running habit. There are a number of techniques available that can help in such stock development programmes.

3.2 Selection and line-breeding

By deriving broodstock from among fish that have returned successfully to the river having been released as fry, parr or smolts, one is utilizing a degree of natural selection which has presumably been involved in the high mortality rates. There is then the possibility of selecting from among the available stock for some attribute deemed desirable eg. large size, or multi-sea-winter habit. The rationale behind this pre-supposes that the attribute is at least partly genetically controlled. There would appear to be considerable scope for "line breeding" using such artificial broodstock selection; equally, there are apparently significant risks associated with inbreeding.

Evidence of a genetic input to the determination of sea age comes from selective breeding and release experiments (eg. Piggins, 1983). Inbreeding experiments in New Brunswick, involving the release and evaluation of smolts produced from a number of river stocks and their crosses, one stock (and its hybrids with other stocks) consistently produced the highest proportion of grilse (Bailey *et al,* 1980). The cage rearing industry also provides useful information on this. Some stocks of Norwegian origins show "grilsing rates" as low as 1% compared to 35% for Scottish stocks reared alongside (Laird and Needham, 1984). Experiments in Norway, reported by Gjerede (1984) involving breeding 2SW x 2SW, 3SW x 3SW and their "crosses", showed a high level of heritability of the trait for age at maturity. Equally, environmental factors are also known to have a major impact upon determination of age at maturity, but clearly the chances of success of developing a stock with a strong multi-sea-winter component will be increased by careful selection of donor stock, and by a selective breeding programme.

Inbreeding, caused by too few broodstock (the bottleneck effect) or by careless inadvertent selection, can greatly reduce the genetic variability of a reared stock. In future generations, the crossing of full siblings or half siblings is a real possibility. There are a number of ways in which the risk of inbreeding and loss of genetic variability can be reduced, including:

- choice of broodstock from a range of sources and a range of times during a run. This should ensure good genetic variability and reduce the risk of crossing closely-related individuals.

- using an adequate broodstock size. Opinions vary as to adequate numbers, and references have been made to 25, 40 or several hundred of the least numerous sex.

- ensuring crosses between as many broodstock as possible ie. fertilizing batches of eggs from each female with milt from many males. This will maximise the number of genetic combinations in the stock and reduce the risks of crossing full siblings in subsequent generations.

- batch marking a proportion of individual cross families to aid in cross selection in the next generation to avoid crossing full or half siblings.

- batch-crossing the reared stock with wild stock at intervals ie. constantly incorporating further genetic material.

On the other hand, the idea of developing a stock genetically suited to the new environment or with a particular life history trait (spring fish) implies selection and reduction of genetic variability. In all rehabilitation programmes it is probably prudent to consult a geneticist to develop a protocol for broodstock management which will take account of individual situation and the aims of the programme.

3.3 All-female stocks

The well-tested technique of creating broods of fish which are entirely female is of interest in rehabilitation programmes for two reasons:

- the supply of eggs is likely to be a limiting factor whereas the supply of milt is less likely to be so.

- there is a strong tendency for females to mature at a greater sea age, and return earlier in the year, than males. This makes them of greater interest from the anglers viewpoint.

The technique used is well established and fairly straightforward, the only significant drawback being the requirement to rear some broodstock to maturity in captivity. The technique was pioneered at Lowestoft Fisheries Laboratory and involves the production of paternal broodstock that are functional males but are genetically females. A stock of first-feeding fry are fed a diet that has been treated with testosterone. The females amongst them develop as males, with viable sperm, which are all X chromosome carriers rather than half x: half y, as normal males produce. This sperm is used to fertilize the eggs from a normal female, and an all female brood results. The sex-reversed fish are identifiable from normal males because the testes are ductless, the milt being obtained by dissection. For subsequent generations, testosterone treatment of a batch of fry from all-female broods will result in 100% "female-males". A good description of the approach and technique is given by Donaldson and Hunter (1982).

An important consideration here is that the all female broods produced are entirely normal fish which have not been treated with hormones in any way. The hormone-treated paternal broodstock are not released to the wild. While the

41

requirement to rear each generation of paternal broodstock entirely in captivity may limit the application of this technique, it may be a viable approach where cage-rearing facilities are available. It is also possible that some of the treated fish would mature as precocious parr, greatly reducing the rearing facilities required. It is also possible to preserve milt by freezing, thus allowing the products of a single brood or paternal broodstock to be used for several years.

3.4 Kelt rehabilitation

Kelt rehabilitation is another potential technique where broodstock are considered particularly precious and where fish holding facilities are available. High survival rates have been achieved, though a period of reacclimatisation to salt water at a salinity of 16-18 ppt has been recommended for maximum survival. However, considerable success has been achieved retaining and maturing grilse kelts entirely in fresh water. Pepper and Parsons (1987) describe a successful trial and give a useful summary of the literature covering earlier investigations. Gray *et al* (1987) describe a very thorough evaluation of the technique including measurement of the egg to adult survival of the offspring from reconditioned kelts. They concluded that rehabilitating kelts and rearing their offspring to the smolt stage for release resulted in egg deposition ten times higher and adult F1 returns over 150 times higher than if the kelts had been left in the river.

3.5 The importance of monitoring

One of the most critical aspects of any rehabilitation scheme is the monitoring of progress. Without some form of assessment one has no idea of whether the programme has been effective, or more critically, which approaches have been totally successful, partially successful or a downright failure. In a river without any stock it is a fair assumption (but by no means certain) that any returning stock have resulted from the programme, but what of rivers with depressed stocks? The history of stock enhancement is littered with stories of initiatives that may have played a part in the recovery of stocks - but no-one can be sure. To identify a technique that is successful by merely observing the apparent abundance of returning fish one would have to try no more than one approach each year, and on a scale that would boost numbers beyond the normal year-by-year variations in runs. Tagging of young fish provided an improvement on this approach, but the usual external smolt tags were suspected of causing significant mortalities among the unfortunate fish to which they were applied, effectively confounding serious analysis. The story of the development and now widespread use of the codedwire tag (or microtag) is too well known to need repeating here, but it is fair to say that it has revolutionised the approach to stock enhancement. Most major programmes in the UK use the technique extensively, including the Thames and Taff. Their use has allowed the identification of successful techniques and sources of fish by analysis of many approaches at one time. Individual "families" of fish can be batch tagged to identify promising choices of donor stocks for future broodstock, and to assist in line-breeding programmes. Different smolt release techniques can quickly be assessed. Browne (1984) used microtag returns to demonstrate a six-fold increase in survival of hatchery-reared smolts on the Corrib effected by transporting them for release at the head of tide. Bilton *et al* (1982) differentially microtagged 57 batches of hatchery coho salmon in a single year, sorting them according to size and time of release. They identified a fairly narrow "window" of size and release dates when returns exceeded 40%, with figures falling away sharply with other sizes and times. With the increasing understanding of the principles underlying stock selection, the increasing range of techniques available for stock development and a powerful approach to monitoring, we can look forward to very real advances in the science of stock development in the foreseeable future.

A most important consideration in monitoring the performance of a rehabilitation scheme is to make sure that you are in fact assessing the true aim of the exercise - generally a self-sustaining breeding population. Demonstrating a level of return of tagged fish to the estuary or to angling catch does not in itself prove that a good reproducing stock will result. For example, in the study already discussed where the performance of a hybrid local x introduced stock was compared to pure introduced stock of pink salmon, similar numbers of each group were recorded in the local inshore commercial fishery. However, about three times as many of the hybrid stock were recorded in the lower river, and about ten times as many in the tributary where the fish were released (Bams, 1976). Thus although the two stocks exhibited similar survival to return to coastal waters, the hybrid stock was clearly far superior in achieving homing to the area of release.

Two studies with released Atlantic salmon have indicated that the fish home fairly well to the area of release, but are reluctant to disperse into potential spawning ground upstream (Piggins, 1986; Ritter and Carey, 1980).Thus although returns of tagged fish to the angling fishery may indicate that the programme is successful, the scheme may in fact be much less successful if the aim is to establish or to boost the spawning stock. Not only do the fish have to disperse into suitable spawning areas, but they must reach spawning readiness at the appropriate time and find the spawning environment to their liking. Their eggs must hatch and the alevins start to feed at the appropriate time for stream conditions in the spring. Thus an investigation to evaluate properly the effectiveness of a restocking programme must be carefully planned and executed.

4. CONCLUSION

In view of the complexity of the process of arriving at the optimal strategy for choice of stock for enhancement programmes, it is hardly surprising that past results have often been very disappointing. Indeed, it is perhaps surprising that any have succeeded at all. Clearly, some attempts have been more successful than others, presumably where perhaps as much by luck as by judgement, the choice of stock has been good.

Fortunately, things look good for improved performance in the future. The slowly emerging understanding of the complexity of the beast with which we are dealing, the development of techniques of manipulation of stock, and the great steps in the methodology and philosophy of monitoring are combining to put planning and execution of rehabilitation programmes on a proper scientific basis. We may not always get it right but we should at least find out if we have; and if we have not, we should hopefully have some idea why.

REFERENCES

Bailey J. K., Buzeta M. I. & Saunders R. L. (1980). Returns of three year-classes of sea-ranched Atlantic salmon of various river strains and their hybrids. ICES. CM 1980/M:9. 10pp.

Bams R. A. (1976). Survival and propensity for homing as affected by presence or absence of locally adapted paternal genes in two transplanted populations of pink salmon (*Oncorhynchus gorbuscha*). Journal of the Fisheries Research Board of Canada 33, 2716 - 2725.

Bilton H. T., Alderdice D. F. & Schnute J. T. (1982). Influence of time and size at release of juvenile coho salmon (*Oncorhynchus kisutch*) on return at maturity. Canadian Journal of Fisheries and Aquatic Sciences, 39, 426-477.

Browne J. (1984). Contribution of reared fish to the national catch in Ireland. Paper presented at AST symposium on salmon stock enhancement, April 1984.

Cross T. F. (1989). Genetics and the management of the Atlantic salmon. Atlantic Salmon Trust, Pitlochry, 74pp.

DAFS (1985). Freshwater Fisheries Laboratory, Pitlochry. Annual Review 1985. 31pp.

DAFS (1989). Freshwater Fisheries Laboratory, Pitlochry. Annual Review 1988-89 37pp.

Donaldson E. M. & Hunter G. A. (1982). Sex control in fish with particular reference to salmonids. Canadian Journal of Fisheries and Aquatic Sciences, 39, 99-110.

Gjerde B. (1984). Response to individual selection for age at sexual maturity in Atlantic salmon. Aquaculture, 38, 229-240.

Gray R. W., Cameron J. D. & McLennan A. D. (1987). Artificial reconditioning, spawning and survival of Atlantic salmon, *Salmo salar* L., kelts in salt water and survival of their F1 progeny. Aquaculture and Fisheries Management, 18(4), 309-326.

Laird L. M. & Needham E. (1984). Has salmon farming taught us anything about wild fish? Proceedings of the 15th Annual Study Course of the Institute of Fisheries Management, 33-39.

Pepper V. A. & Parsons P. (1987). An experiment on aquaculture potential of Atlantic salmon, *Salmo salar* L., kelts in Newfoundland, Canada. Aquaculture and Fisheries Management, 18(4), 327-344.

Piggins D. J. (1983). Annual Report of the Salmon Research Trust of Ireland for the year ended December 31 1982, XXVII

Piggins D. J. (1986). Annual Report of the Salmon Research Trust of Ireland for the year ended December 31 1985, XXX.

Riddell B. E., Leggett W. C. & Saunders R. L. (1981). Evidence of adaptive polygenic variation between two populations of Atlantic salmon (*Salmo salar*) native to tributaries of the SW Miramichi Rivers, N.B. Canadian Journal of Fisheries and Aquatic Sciences, 38, 321-333.

Ritter J. A. & Carey T. G. (1980). Salmon ranching in the Atlantic maritime provinces of Canada. In Thorpe J. E. (Ed) Salmon Ranching. Academic Press, London.

Saunders R. L. (1979). The stock concept - a major consideration in salmon restoration. North American Salmon Research Center, Report no. 3, 6pp.

Saunders R. L. (1981). Atlantic salmon (*Salmo salar*) stocks and management implications in the Canadian Atlantic Provinces and New England, USA. Canadian Journal of Fisheries and Aquatic Sciences, 38; 1612-1625.

Taggart J. B., Ferguson A. & Mason F. M. (1981). Genetic variation in Irish populations of brown trout (*Salmo trutta* L.); electrophoretic analysis of allozymes. Comparative Biochemistry and Physiology, 69; 393-412.

Verspoor E. & Jordan W. C. (1989). Genetic variation at the Me-2 locus in the Atlantic salmon within and between rivers: evidence for its selective maintenance. Journal of Fish Biology, 35, Suppl. A. 205-214.

Wilkins N. P. (1985). Salmon stocks - a genetic perspective. Atlantic Salmon Trust, Pitlochry, 30pp.

Youngson A. F., Martin S. A. M., Jordan W. C. & Verspoor E. (1989). Genetic protein variation in farmed Atlantic salmon in Scotland: comparison of farmed strains and their wild source populations. Aberdeen; DAFS Scottish Fisheries Research Report; No 42, 12pp.

STRATEGIES FOR THE REHABILITATION OF SALMON RIVERS - POST-PROJECT APPRAISAL

G J A KENNEDY & W W CROZIER

Department of Agriculture for Northern Ireland

1.INTRODUCTION

In the Report on Salmon Propagation in England and Wales (Harris, 1978) it was stressed that 'the need for monitoring to establish the success or failure of stocking programmes is fundamental to the proper management of the fisheries resource, and [for] the efficient and effective use of artificial propagation as a management technique'. However, the report noted that there appeared to be 'a general reluctance to monitor and evaluate the success or failure of artificial propagation and of post stocking programmes in terms of the resultant increase in the numbers of extra adult fish so produced'.

As discussed in an earlier paper on salmon enhancement (Kennedy, 1988), there is still a paucity of published information available on the effectiveness of rehabilitation schemes in terms of additional adult salmon returns or the cost-benefits of the work. As a direct consequence of this, stock enhancement schemes have been abandoned by some local fishery managers, and major differences of opinion expressed on the efficacy of some major national schemes (eg. see Thibault, 1983 and Rainelli and Thibault, 1985).

Many of the schemes undertaken to date have concentrated on the effectiveness of various techniques of juvenile stocking and habitat improvement, without having a clear view of how to quantify any resultant changes in runs. (We say 'changes' rather than 'improvements', as there is now evidence that stocking with inappropriate genotypes may in fact depress indigenous stock survival and overall returns in the long term (Thorpe, 1988)). This view of salmon enhancement is, to some extent, understandable, as there is frequently considerable pressure exerted on fishery managers to be seen to be doing something to improve local runs of fish in the face of real or perceived declines in local stocks. Stocking large numbers of juveniles, or habitat improvement and fish pass installation has proved to be a very satisfactory 'high profile' way of meeting these public pressures.

The problems commonly confronting fishery managers or scientists who are attempting to quantify the changes in salmon runs following a rehabilitation scheme on a river which still has a natural run can all be grouped under the heading 'lack of controls'. In every branch of science the need for control data is recognised as paramount when evaluating experimental results. However, rehabilitation schemes, whether high profile or not, are seldom carried out for experimental purposes, and smolt and adult salmon attributable to the enhancement work frequently cannot be distinguished from wild runs. Fluctuations in wild runs can readily mask any changes due to rehabilitation, and rod and commercial catch figures are not only at the mercy of salmon population dynamics, but also incorporate variation due to effort, environmental and non-reporting factors.

Appraisal of restoration schemes on extinct runs is much clearer, in that improvements in adult numbers following stocking can be correlated directly to the rehabilitation measures, eg. the Exploits River, Newfoundland (O'Connell, Davis and Scott, 1983); the R. Thames, England (Anon, 1985); the Jacques Cartier River, Quebec (Frenette, Dulude and Beaurivage, 1988); the Connecticut River, USA (Jones, 1988). However, even here the appraisal is not clear cut, as there is evidence that salmon runs will re-establish naturally in passable rivers when water quality improves eg. the R. Clyde, Scotland (McKay and Doughty, 1987).

The title 'post-project appraisal' allocated by the conference organisers for this paper therefore in many ways reflects the general historical approach to rehabilitation schemes, ie. let's do it, and then look for ways to evaluate it afterwards. However, in these days of cost-benefit analysis, has the time arrived when definitive methods of appraising the success of such work can be integrated at the design stage of rehabilitation work, and not considered as a 'post-project' afterthought?

Table 1. Published ranges of commercial exploitation for tagged wild and hatchery salmon from the rivers Burrishoole, N. Esk and Bush.

Source	River	Details	Marine exploitation rate
Anon. (1989)	Burrishoole	Hatchery reared microtagged grilse captured in Irish drift net fishery 1985-89.	70.0-85.2%
Shearer (1988)	N.Esk	Wild Carlin tagged grilse captured in net and coble fishery 1976-85.	35-62%
		Wild Carlin tagged MSW fish captured in net and coble fishery 1976-85.	39-63%
Crozier (1989, 1990)	R. Bush	Hatchery reared microtagged grilse from 1 + smolts captured in Irish drift net and N. Ireland's drift and bag net fishery	72.3-93.9%
Crozier & Kennedy (1987, 1989)		Hatchery reared microtagged grilse from 2 + smolts, captured in the Irish drift net and N. Ireland's drift and bag net fishery.	57.1-94.6%
		Wild microtagged grilse captured in the Irish drift net and N. Ireland's drift and bag net fishery.	65.3-89.0%

2. FLUCTUATIONS IN SALMON NUMBERS

Before any meaningful evaluation of the contribution of a salmon rehabilitation project can take place, the normal range of abundance must be quantified for the stock in question. Long, medium and short term trends in both overall numbers and in the proportions of grilse and multi-sea-winter fish have all been recognised (see Mills, 1989, for review). Measurement of the trends is in itself fraught with difficulty, since most figures are based on catch data - which are not necessarily good indicators of abundance (Lakhani, 1986; Shearer, 1986, 1988, 1989). Short term fluctuations in catch size from year to year may reflect local weather conditions and consequently fishing effort rather than run size. For example, there is evidence from recent microtagging studies that marine exploitation rates for R. Bush fish are inversely correlated with summer rainfall ie in wet years the adult fish are less vulnerable to netting as high river flows encourage rapid migration into freshwater, whereas in dry years the fish spend longer at sea before entering the river and are vulnerable to coastal netting for longer (unpublished data). The available data on commercial exploitation rates from the three index rivers reflect this variation from year to year (Table 1).

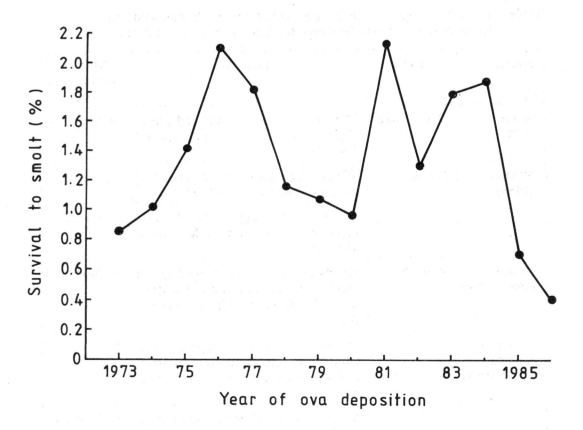

Figure 1. Ova to smolt survival for each ova deposition on the River Bush, 1973 - 1986.

Table 2. Details of annual smolt production and ova to smolt survival for the rivers N.Esk, Burrishole and Bush.

River	Years	Range of smolt production	Range of ova-smolt survival	Source
N.Esk	1964 - 1984	93,000 - 275,000	-	Shearer (1986)
Burrishoole	1970 - 1988	3,817 - 16,136	0.41 - 0.78	Anon. (1977, 1989)
Bush	1974 - 1989	10,694 - 43,958	0.40 - 2.13	Crozier & Kennedy (1989)

Marine exploitation rates also reflect variation in natural marine survival, and for wild R. Bush grilse these have varied from 29.7% to 37.7% (ie. for return to the coast prior to commercial fishing) (Crozier & Kennedy, 1989). The combination of natural and fishing mortality factors have resulted in variation in river returns of wild R Bush salmon from 6.26% - 12.47% over 16 years since the start of the project. Similar values have been reported for the R Burrishoole (5.2% - 12.0% for total adult river returns from 1970 - 1989) (Anon, 1989).

To discuss these percentage variations in absolute terms it is necessary to also consider the ranges of variation in freshwater production, both as smolt numbers and

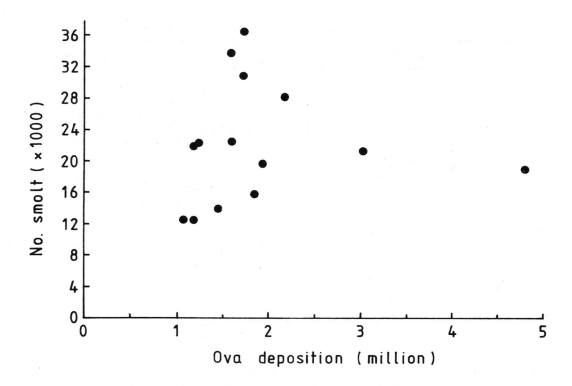

Figure 2. Total smolt production from each ova deposition on the River Bush.

percentage survival from varying ova depositions. Estimates of smolt numbers from the three index rivers in the British Isles have varied by up to over four fold (Table 2), due to variation in both ova deposition and ova to smolt survival. The interpretation of the relationship of ova deposition to smolt production is still equivocal. Some evidence indicates that the stock-recruitment curve is flat topped, and some that there is a mode of optimum ova deposition, above which smolt production is depressed (see Chadwick, 1985, Elliott, 1985 and Solomon, 1985, for reviews). Part of the reason for the difficulty in evaluating this work is the level of variation which has been experienced in annual ova to smolt survivals (Table 2 and Figure 1). This is apparently due to environmental and predation factors, but the precise causes have not yet been quantified. In the R Bush the variation in smolt production from the range of ova deposition experienced to date has produced a wide scatter of points on the stock recruitment graph (Figure 2).

The type of stocking/rehabilitation work carried out can also influence survival considerably, although there is conflict in the literature on the relative survival rates from the various techniques (see Kennedy, 1988, for review).

Prediction of either smolt runs or adult returns from known ova depositions and smolt releases respectively are therefore not yet possible, even in index rivers which have been carefully monitored over a number of years. The chances of being able to predict adult runs in a rehabilitated river with no database is therefore negligible, as the interaction of the potential annual variation in smolt production with both short and

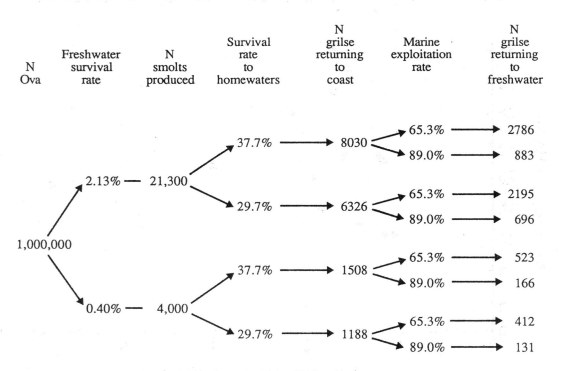

Figure 3. Potential grilse returns to the River Bush from an ova deposition of 1 million, as derived from the ranges of observed freshwater and marine survival rates, and the range of marine exploitation around the Irish coast on microtagged wild fish.

longer term fluctuations in sea survival can result in over an order of magnitude variation in adult returns from any one ova deposition (see Figure 3).

This problem has confounded the interpretation of every enhancement scheme to date where the enhanced rivers also have a run of wild fish (eg. Jones & Howells, 1969; Kennedy & Crozier, 1989). This has been exacerbated by the fact that many stockings have been carried out with relatively small numbers of ova or fry (Harris, 1978). There appears to be a failure on the part of many fishery managers to appreciate the high levels of mortality occurring in the wild and the low level of adult return occurring under normal conditions. (For example, from the survival figures quoted above for the R Bush, the expected adult return to freshwater per 10,000 naturally spawned ova is approximately in the range 2 - 33 fish over two years ie. both grilse and 2SW salmon). Returns to restored rivers have also frequently not lived up to expectations (eg. Cuinat, 1988; Jones, 1988), but the problems here have been further compounded by the lack of a native genotype with appropriate behavioural traits (Saunders, 1981; Thorpe, 1988).

How then is it possible to appraise the effects of an enhancement/rehabilitation scheme, where the potential increase in numbers of adult fish is much less than the unpredictable annual variation?

3. TECHNIQUES FOR THE APPRAISAL OF REHABILITATION PROJECTS

The techniques available for monitoring and appraising salmon rehabilitation projects have different degrees of applicability to enhancement schemes on rivers which already have a run of wild fish, compared to restoration schemes on rivers where the salmon run is extinct. A summary of the suitability and drawbacks of each technique to the two types of scheme is outlined below.

3.1 Adult traps

These are most effective for monitoring adult returns from restoration schemes, but provide only equivocal data in rivers where wild adults cannot be distinguished from enhancement fish. However, they can be used successfully in rehabilitation schemes using distinctively marked hatchery parr or smolts (Kennedy & Crozier, 1989) or on tributaries or upstream areas to which salmon previously did not have access - whether this is combined with a stocking programme or not (Anon, 1978; Taylor & Bauld, 1973). One of the main benefits of adult traps is the access that they provide to the adult fish, either for biological monitoring or to obtain broodstock for the development of a 'local' strain - genotypically suited to further stocking in that area (Cuinat, 1988; Frenette, Dulude and Beaurivage, 1988). Problems with adult traps arise mainly from the practical point of view, in that they require daily or more frequent servicing, clearing and policing during the adult run. Also, in large rivers it may not be feasible to attempt more than partial trapping of the run eg. in the restoration scheme on the R. Thames (Anon., 1985). This provides a relative assessment of the success of rehabilitation with time, but makes estimates of the total run difficult if a target spawning stock has been set for the restoration scheme.

51

3.2 Smolt traps

As with adult traps, these are also only effective for monitoring restoration schemes, as they provide only equivocal results in rivers where smolt production is also derived from natural runs (Kennedy & Crozier, 1989). However, these can also be used successfully in enhancement schemes on tributaries or upstream areas where fish either did not previously have access, or where electrofishing surveys indicated that juveniles were not present prior to rehabilitation due to lack of spawning gravel, water quality problems, insufficient natural recruitment etc. Smolt trap data is the only accurate method of assessing ova-smolt production figures for rehabilitated stretches. They also provide access to the smolts for biological monitoring and tagging studies. As with adult traps, the main problems are practical, in that they require daily or more frequent servicing, clearing and policing during the smolt run. Despite regular attention, the loss of data from overtopping during floods is a constant problem. Also, partial trapping only may be feasible on large rivers. As with partial adult traps this may limit their use to a relative time series assessment of the success of rehabilitation measures. Estimates of the total smolt run can be made using mark-recapture techniques, but these are time consuming and subject to a number of potential errors associated with tagging and handling stress (Kennedy, Strange and Johnston, in press).

3.3 Fish counters

The 'state of the art' of electronic fish counting, and an assessment of their value to salmon river management was the subject of a fairly recent Atlantic Salmon Trust workshop in Montrose (Holden, 1988). One of the conclusions was that the design and technology have now improved so that an acceptable level of accuracy can be achieved for counts of adult fish. While the counters themselves are relatively inexpensive and require less maintenance than traps, the structures on which they must be mounted are expensive. Choice of site is also critical, and their value to rehabilitation schemes is subject to exactly the same provisos as adult traps. A further drawback is that adult fish cannot be accessed for either biological monitoring or broodstock development.

3.4 Redd counts

The value and accuracy of redd counts for salmon river management has been the subject of considerable debate. Fox (1981) concluded that they were particularly useful in spate free rivers, where surveys of spawning areas could be used to detect redds for up to four months after spawning. The overview of the distribution of spawning from year to year was seen as a starting point for more intensive population studies.

This view would seem appropriate for rehabilitation schemes, where redds within the rehabilitated area would be a useful indicator of the distribution of adult spawning fish returning to areas where the run had previously become extinct, or to which fish did not have access prior to the scheme. However, this distribution map would act as a guideline only, as redd counts cannot be relied on as indicators of the number of returning fish due to counting inaccuracies and the cutting of multiple redds where gravel is not ideal (Jones, 1959).

3.5 Commercial catches

As outlined previously, commercial catch data is not very suitable for evaluating the success of enhancement/rehabilitation schemes due to fluctuations in catch data as a result of salmon population dynamics, and unpredictable variation in effort, environmental and non-reporting factors. Also, most commercial salmon fisheries exploit mixed stocks of fish, and specific returns to rehabilitation schemes cannot be distinguished from other landings without a smolt tagging programme. In the case of commercial fisheries which are very localised (eg. estuarine netting, freshwater traps) increases in catches or catch per unit effort (CPUE) may be detected following large scale enhancement schemes eg O'Connell *et al* (1983). However, the data from commercial catches is always equivocal.

3.6 Rod catches

The uses and limitations of rod catch data have been discussed by a number of authors eg. Ayton (1981), Gee and Milner (1980), Small and Downham (1985). All agree that it is virtually impossible to get accurate returns, and various methods of employing correction factors have been employed. CPUE is considered the best indicator of fishing success (Mills, 1989), and Hadoke (1972) considered that CPUE from a small number of carefully selected competent anglers was the best method of providing a time series comparison. However, all rod catch figures can give misleading results on spawning stock size, because the timing and proportion of the run moving into freshwater during the angling season can vary significantly from year to year (Mills, 1989). Therefore in enhanced rivers, where wild salmon cannot be distinguished from those resulting from rehabilitation measures, angler data, including CPUE, provide only equivocal results. Angling has been found to build up quite rapidly as a sport on restored rivers, and as such is a measure of the success of rehabilitation schemes in meeting social and recreational aims (Frenette *et al,* 1988). Angling success can also be quantified in terms of meeting these socio-economic objectives on carefully managed fishing beats on an enhanced river such as the R Bush - where hatchery reared ranched fish are readily distinguishable to both anglers and the fishery managers by their adipose fin clip.

3.7 Genetic marking

The application of genetic marking to monitor fish stocking programmes has been demonstrated in several recent studies (eg Garcia De Leaniz, Verspoor and Hawkins, 1989; Reisenbichler and McIntyre, 1977; Taggart and Ferguson, 1986) and depends on the differential occurrence of electrophoretically detectable allelic products between the native and stocked fish. These electrophoretic differences may either be natural (if the stocked fish fortuitously possess different allele frequencies at one or more gene loci) or can be artifically arranged by selective crossing of broodstock at the hatchery.

The inherent advantages of a genetic mark over other marking methods are that it is permanent for the lifetime of the individual, can be passed on to subsequent generations (allowing longer term assessment of the contribution of stocked fish) and should not affect the fitness or behaviour of the fish. Furthermore, the fish require no special handling to mark them (Taggart and Ferguson, 1984).

The simplest and most powerful application of genetic marking occurs when the stocked and native (ie. wild) populations are fixed (homozygous) for different alleles. In this case, every individual subsequently examined can be unambiguously classified as wild or stocked and in the first filial generation the degree of interbreeding between the two types can be measured by the number of heterozygous genotypes among sampled fish. However, for most management purposes it is not essential that individuals be unequivocally identified as wild or stocked. It is still possible to estimate the relative contribution of stocked fish if the same allele occurs at different frequencies in the two populations (see Pella and Milner, 1987 for details). In either case the baseline allelic frequencies in the wild and stocked population must be obtained before stocking.

Using these methods, a very good assessment of the contribution of stocked fish to the smolt run or adult returns can be made, provided facilities exist to at least partially trap runs, and to allow tissue sampling of fish. Electophoretic sampling need not involve sacrifice of the fish, as markers can be identified in tissues (such as adipose fin) that can be harmlessly sampled (Carmichael, Williamson, Schmidt and Morigot, 1986; Crozier and Moffett, 1989). It is not recommended that coastal or estuarine commercial catches should be sampled for genetically marked stocked fish, as the potential presence of fish from populations other than the two 'target' groups will render the assessment unreliable. Perhaps the ideal assessment of the success of enhancement stocking is obtained by combining genetic marking of stocked fish with electrofishing surveys of the stocked river, using the fry survey technique detailed below. This would provide an assessment of the survival and distribution of stocked fish throughout the system and at the same time local and overall estimates of the contribution of stocked fish to the total juvenile population.

3.8 Electrofishing surveys

Of all the techniques employed for the assessment of salmonid populations, electrofishing to quantify fry densities is without doubt the most commonly used. The rationale for assessment at this juvenile stage of the life cycle is twofold. Firstly, initial high and variable salmonid mortality rates have already occurred by the first summer of life in streams (Mills, 1989). Subsequent freshwater mortality rates are less variable (Egglishaw and Shackley, 1980; Symons, 1979), and estimates of smolt production can be made from fry density data (Gee et al, 1978; Mills, 1964). The success of rehabilitation measures in terms of the extent of natural spawning in opened or improved areas, or of the survival of stocked fry can therefore be quantified within the same year, and projections made for potential smolt and adult production. These projections are, of course, subject to the same limitations imposed on all the other assessment techniques by the unpredictable vagaries of smolt and adult survival. However, if it is assumed that fry arising from rehabilitation measures are likely to be subject to the same survival pressures as naturally spawned fry, then the relative improvement in stock can be assessed ie an improvement in fry numbers implies an improvement in adult returns beyond the levels which would be expected if no action had been taken (see Kennedy, 1988). Also, in rehabilitation schemes on rivers also containing a wild run of salmon, electrofishing is the only accurate method of identifying the extent of natural juvenile recruitment throughout the system. This is of fundamental importance to fishery managers who wish to pinpoint areas of suitable habitat which are devoid of resident salmon, and where rehabilitation/stocking can be undertaken.

On the other hand, electrofishing has its limitations, and what may be a very accurate population estimate of the fish within a stop netted section may be a very innaccurate picture when extrapolated to a longer stretch of river channel (Kennedy, 1981). A further problem is the fact that quantitative electrofishing can be very labour intensive, restricting the data to a limited number of sites. In our view, the time has now come when electrofishing should be recognised as a valuable management tool as well as a research tool, and that the objectives of the former do not require highly accurate fish density data for a small number of sites. Rather, what is required for freshwater management of salmon stocks is an approximately correct picture of juvenile densities over whole river systems, at low manpower cost. Sir Ernest Woodroofe commented on a similar conclusion drawn at a recent AST Workshop as follows (in Holden, 1988)

> '..... the time had arrived when managers should stop regarding every river system and every river [electrofishing] survey as part of a research study. It was necessary to have a series of indicators of resources - status surveys - not just numbers on a yearly basis.'

Electrofishing surveys had a central role in stock enhancement work which was carried out on the R. Bush over a four year period from 1983 - 1986 (Kennedy & Crozier, 1989). A semi-quantitative techique was developed for acquiring information on salmonid fry (summer O +) densities rapidly at about 150 sites over the whole catchment. This was used both to assess the status of juvenile stocks and the extent of utilisation of available nursery habitat prior to enhancement, and subsequently to assess the survival of stocked fry throughout the system. The continued sampling of unstocked areas provided control data for comparison with the enhancement areas. This type of control data can not be obtained from any other assessment technique in a river where recruitment is derived from both natural spawning and stocking or other rehabilitation measures.

The semi-quantitative technique is based on two man teams, each using a single anode backpack, to catch O + fry only, over five minute periods in shallow nursery habitat. Older fish are ignored and not captured by intent. Riffle sites are chosen at frequent intervals (200 m - 400 m approximately) over all the available nursery habitat in both the main river and the tributaries. In addition to catching fry, the teams make an estimate of their efficiency at each site in terms of the numbers of fry seen but not caught. This is applied as a correction factor for standardisation between different fishing conditions on different days in varying flows and habitat types. All fry captured are anaesthetised, identified as trout or salmon, and measured before being returned to the stream. The technique has been calibrated by sampling within stop netted sections prior to full quantitative electrofishing, and a high degree of correlation obtained between fry caught in five minutes and the actual population density ($r = 0.87$, $p < 0.001$; see Fig 4). However, no attempt is made in the analysis of results to produce population estimates from this technique. The corrected fry totals caught in five minutes at each site are simply categorised as absent (no fry caught); poor (1 - 4 fry caught); fair (5 - 14 fry); good (15 - 24 fry) or excellent (>25 fry). Each two man team is capable of sampling about 10 - 12 sites per day using this method, and a fry distribution map can be made available for the whole catchment relatively quickly.

From the annual distribution map produced by this method it is possible to identify the extent of areas giving consistently good survival, and other areas of poor survival. Previously undetected pollution problems can be pin pointed, permitting rapid follow up action - including possible restocking. Poorer than expected survivals in certain areas can also help to identify insidious water quality problems or habitat deterioration. The fishery manager can therefore avoid wasting further stocked fry in these areas until remedial action is taken. This rationale was applied in the R. Bush, where the electrofishing following the first year of enhancement stocking indicated good to excellent survivals in 55.2% of the stocked areas. Improved results were obtained the following year after elimination of unsatisfactory areas from the stocking programme, and good to excellent densities were found in 87.8% of the stocked area.

Long term monitoring of rehabilitated areas can be maintained at fairly low cost using this technique. In the R Bush, for example, semi-quantitative surveys have been continued throughout the catchment following the ending of the stocking programme. These indicate that many of the previously unspawned/stocked areas, particularly in

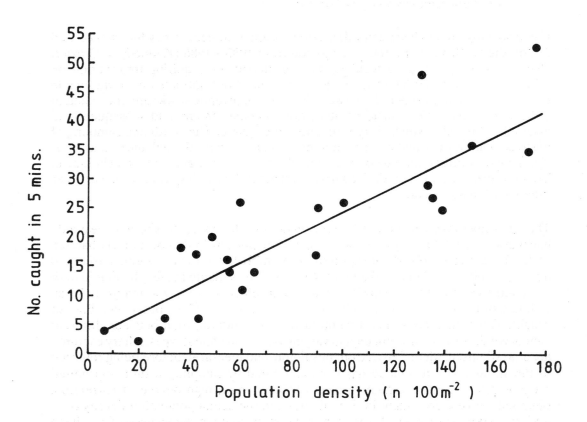

Figure 4. Relationship between numbers of salmon fry caught in five minutes using a single anode to the actual population density of salmon fry at various sites, as subsequently assessed fy full quantitative electrofishing.

the headwaters, are now utilised by natural spawners. For the fishery manager in any long term rehabilitation programme this form of annual monitoring permits the continuous re-assessment of the extent of natural colonistation of the river. This prevents wastage of resources through the stocking of areas now naturally spawned, and also helps to identify areas where nursery habitat may be suitable but spawning substrate is inadequate. Follow up remedial action can then be undertaken to introduce artificial spawning fords at appropriate sites.

4.CONCLUSIONS

Due to the paucity of hard information on the effectiveness of rehabilitation schemes, cost-benefit analyses have not been widely applied (Kennedy, 1988). Also, given the wide fluctuations in natural survival of salmon in both freshwater and the sea, it is hardly surprising that projections for returns from various rehabilitation schemes have frequently been highly inaccurate. A number of authors remain unconvinced of the value of salmon enhancement schemes as they feel that the scientific assessment has been inadequate to date. (eg. Thibault, 1983; Rainelli & Thibault, 1985). These authors have questioned the objectives of rehabilitation schemes in France in relation to the high costs for relatively low adult returns (eg see Cuinat, 1988)

The objectives of any rehabilitation scheme are always a complex mixture of scientific, economic and social. A number of authors considered that the concept of additional returns to the national catch is a major justification of enhancement schemes (Browne, 1981; O'Connell et al, 1983; Twomey 1982). However, all tagging studies to date have shown that salmon stocks from rivers throughout the British Isles are subject to interceptory fisheries both inside and outside national waters. For example, microtagging of R. Bush ranched smolts has indicated that 29% to 49% of returning adults are taken annually by nets in Republic of Ireland waters. Can the exploitation of a resource by users other than those developing the resource be costed as a benefit of a rehabilitation scheme?

The value of enhancement and river rehabilitation to the local economy through improved angling has been considered an important objective (Cuinat, 1988; Frenette et al, 1988; Leeming, 1989; Thurso, 1986). Although anglers remove relatively low numbers of fish compared to commercial exploitation, the value of these tends to be disproportionately high - although the precise value is the subject of considerable debate (£800 per fish on the R. Wye, Gee & Edwards (1980); £1000 per fish in Scotland, Gibbins (1987); >£250 per fish on the R. Tweed, Leeming (1989); IR£350 - IR£450 per fish in Ireland, Twomey (1984); IR£18 per fish in Ireland, Whelan and Whelan (1986)). Reported angler exploitation rates are also very variable both between and within rivers over time (eg R Bush, 0.06 - 0.17 (Crozier & Kennedy, 1989); R. Burrishoole, 0.06 - 0.16 (Anon., 1983); R. Spey, 0.04 - 0.10 (Shearer 1986); R. Wye, 0.25 - 0.47 (Gee & Milner, 1980)). The value of the variable surviving spawning stock can be assessed in terms of the cost of the fertilised eggs they represent (£37.50 per 1000 at 1990 prices).

By use of combinations of the appraisal techniques outlined earlier, a figure for the monetary benefits of a river rehabilitation scheme can therefore be derived. (Based on mean values for survival and exploitation, a model was developed in an earlier paper which estimated the value of adult salmon production per hectare of good nursery habitat in the R Bush at about £70,000 (Kennedy, 1985)). However, it is highly dependent on inputs, varying greatly between river systems and over time, and produces values which may not neccessarily accrue to those undertaking the rehabilitation work.

The social and conceptual aims of a rehabilitation scheme may be equally or even more intangible, but are considered by many to outweigh financial considerations. For example, Frenette *et al* (1988) summarised eight aims for the restoration of the Jacques Cartier River in Quebec - of which only two were concerned with valuation. They saw the scheme mainly as an important 'development focus' for the region, for recreational tourism, education programmes, visitors' centres, cultural and heritage benefits, conservation and a general 'collective pride' in the restored river. Appraisal of such esoteric concepts for a cost-benefit analysis is something which biologists may well have to come to terms with more frequently in the present era of developing environmental awareness.

REFERENCES

Anon. (1977). Annual Report No. XXII. The Salmon Research Trust of Ireland Inc., 43 pp.

Anon. (1978). Atlantic salmon review. Government of Canada, Fisheries and Oceans Resource Development Sub-Committee Report, November 1978, 55pp.

Anon. (1985). Salmon rehabilitation scheme. Phase 1 review. Thames Water, Rivers Division, Special Publication, 46pp.

Anon. (1989). Annual Report No. XXXIV. The Salmon Research Trust of Ireland Inc., 71pp.

Ayton, W. J. (1981). The significance of catch and effort, and the difficulty of finding indices for effort. Working Paper for Atlantic Salmon Trust Workshop, Windermere, October 1981, 8 pp.

Browne, J. (1981). First results from a new method of tagging salmon - the coded wire tag. Department of Fisheries & Forestry, Dublin, Fishery Leaflet 114, 6pp.

Carmichael, G. J., Williamson, J. H., Schmidt, M.E. & Morizot, D. C. (1986). Genetic marker identification in largemouth bass with electrophoresis of low risk tissues. Transactions of the American Fisheries Society, 115: 455-459.

Chadwick, E. M. P. (1985). Fundamental research problems in the management of Atlantic Salmon, *Salmo salar* L., in Atlantic Canada. Journal of Fish Biology, 27 (Supplement A): 9-25.

Crozier, W. W. (1989). Homewater exploitation rates on microtagged salmon returning to the R. Bush in 1988. Working Paper for ICES N. Atlantic Salmon Working Group, 5 pp.

Crozier, W. W. (1990). Homewater exploitation rates on microtagged salmon returning to the R Bush in 1989. Working Paper for ICES N. Atlantic Salmon Working Group, 6 pp.

Crozier, W. W. & Kennedy, G. J. A. (1987). Marine survival and exploitation of R. Bush hatchery salmon (*Salmo salar* L.) as assessed by microtag returns to 1986. Working Paper for ICES N. Atlantic Salmon Working Group, 10 pp.

Crozier, W. W. & Kennedy, G. J. A. (1989). The River Bush as an index river. Working paper for ICES North Atlantic Salmon Working Group, Copenhagen, March 1989, 10pp.

Crozier, W. W. & Moffett, I. J. J. (1989). Application of an electrophoretically detectable genetic marker to ploidy testing in brown trout (*Salmo trutta* L.) triploidised by heat shock. Aquaculture, 80: 231-239.

Cuinat, R. (1988). Atlantic salmon in an extensive French River system: the Loire - Allier. *In* Atlantic Salmon: Planning for the Future (eds D. Mills and D. Piggins), Proceedings of the Third International Atlantic Salmon Symposium, Biarritz, 21-23 October, 1986, 389-399.

Egglishaw, H. J. & Shackley, P. E. (1980). Survival and growth of salmon, *Salmo salar* L., planted in a Scottish stream. Journal of Fish Biology, 16: 565-584.

Elliott, J. M. (1985). Population dynamics of migratory trout, *Salmo trutta*, in a Lake District stream; 1966-83, and their implications for fisheries management. Journal of Fish Biology, 27, (Supplement A): 35-43.

Fox, P. (1981). The usefulness of redd counts for salmon stock assessment. Working Paper for Atlantic Salmon Trust Workshop, Windermere, October 1981, 6pp.

Frenette, M., Dulude, P. & Beaurivage, M. (1988). The restoration of the Jacques Cartier: a major challenge and a collective pride. *In* Atlantic Salmon: Planning for the Future (eds. D. Mills & D. Piggins), Proceedings of the Third International Atlantic Salmon Symposium, Biarritz, 21-23 October, 1986, 400-414.

Garcia de Leaniz, C., Verspoor, E. & Hawkins, A. D. (1989). Determination of the contribution of stocked and wild Atlantic salmon, *Salmo salar* L., to the angling fisheries in two Spanish rivers. Journal of Fish Biology, 35: 261-270.

Gee, A. S. & Edwards, R. W. (1980). Recreational exploitation of the Atlantic salmon in the R Wye. *In* 'Allocation of Fishery Resources' (ed. J. H. Groves), Proceedings of the Technical Consultation in Fishery Resources, Vichy, France FAO 20-23 April 1980, 129-137.

Gee, A. S. & Milner, N. J. (1980). Analysis of 70 year catch statistics for Atlantic salmon (*Salmo salar*) in the River Wye, and its implications for management of stocks. Journal of applied Ecology, 17: 41-57.

Gee, A. S., Milner, N. J. & Hemsworth, R. J. (1978). The effect of density on mortality in juvenile Atlantic salmon (*Salmo salar*). Journal of Animal Ecology, 47, 497-505.

Gibbins, H. (1987). The salmon: Too little too late? The Scotsman Magazine, 7(12), 8-10.

Hadoke, G. D. F. (1972). The salmon fisheries of the Foyle area. Foyle Fisheries Commission, Special Publication, 128 pp.

Harris, G. S. (1978). Salmon propagation in England and Wales. A Report by the Association of River Authorities/National Water Council Working Party. Published by the National Water Council, London, 62 pp.

Holden, A. V. (1988). The automatic counter - a tool for the management of salmon fisheries. Atlantic Salmon Trust, Pitlochry, 37 pp.

Jones, J. W. (1959). The Salmon. Collins, London, 192 pp.

Jones, R. A. (1988). Atlantic salmon restoration in the Connecticut River. *In* Atlantic Salmon: Planning for the Future (eds. D. Mills and D. Piggins); Proceedings of the Third International Atlantic Salmon Symposium, Biarritz, 21-23 October, 1986, 415-426.

Jones, A. N. & Howells, W. R. (1969). Recovery of the River Rheidol. Effluent and Water Treatment Journal, November, 70-76.

Kennedy, G. J. A. (1981). The reliability of quantitative juvenile salmon estimates using electrofishing techniques. Atlantic Salmon Trust Workshop on Data Acquisition, Windermere, 18 pp.

Kennedy, G. J. A. (1985). River pollution - how much does it cost fisheries? Advisers and Lecturers Conference, Loughry College of Agriculture & Food Technology. 15 pp.

Kennedy, G. J. A (1988). Stock enhancement of Atlantic Salmon (*Salmo salar* L.). *In* Atlantic Salmon: Planning for the Future (eds. D. Mills and D. Piggins), Proceedings of the Third International Atlantic Salmon Symposium, Biarritz, 21-23 October 1986, 345-372.

Kennedy, G. J. A. & Crozier, W. W. (1989). Salmon enhancement on the River Bush. Proceedings of the IFM Conference, Sept 11 - 14, Galway, 22pp.

Kennedy, G. J. A., Strange, C. D. & Johnston, P. (in press). Evaluation of Carlin tagging as a mark-recapture technique for estimating total river runs of salmon smolts (*Salmo, salar* L.). Aquaculture & Fisheries Management.

Lakhani, K. H. (1986). Salmon population studies based upon Scottish catch statistics: statistical considerations. *In* The Status of the Atlantic Salmon in Scotland (eds. D. Jenkins & W Shearer), ITE Symposium No. 15, 116-120.

Leeming, J. H. (1989). The Economics of the Tweed and its fisheries. *In* Tweed towards 2000 (ed. D. H. Mills), Tweed Foundation Symposium, 100-104.

McKay, D. W. & Doughty, C. R. (1986). The disappearance of salmon from the River Clyde, and their return : a historical perspective. *In* The Return of Salmon to the Clyde (eds. A. Holden and G. Struthers), Proceedings of an IFM Conference, University of Strathclyde, 15th November, 1986, 4-8.

Mills, D. H. (1964). The ecology of the young stages of the Atlantic Salmon in the River Bran, Ross-shire. Freshwater & Salmon Fisheries Research, Scotland, 32, 58 pp.

Mills, D. H. (1989). Ecology and management of Atlantic salmon. Chapman and Hall, 351 pp.

O'Connell, M. F., Davis, J. P. & Scott, D. C. (1983). An assessment of the stocking of Atlantic salmon (*Salmo salar* L.) fry in the tributaries of the Middle Exploits River, Newfoundland. Canadian Technical Report of Fisheries and Aquatic Sciences, No. 1225, 142 pp.

Pella, J. J. & Milner, G. B. (1987). Use of genetic marks in stock composition analysis. *In*, Population Genetics and Fishery Management (eds. Ryman, N. and F. M. Utter), University of Washington Press, Seattle, 247-276.

Rainelli, P. & Thibault, M. (1985). La surabondance de consommation de saumon autrefois : une surabondance veritablement ... fabuleuse. Cahiers de Nutrition et de Dietetique, 20 (4): 292-7.

Reisenbichler, R. R. & McIntyre, J. D. (1977). Genetic, differences in growth and survival of juvenile hatchery and wild steelhead trout, *Salmo gairdneri*. Journal of the Fisheries Research Board of Canada, 34: 123-128.

Saunders, R. L. (1981). Atlantic salmon (*Salmo salar*) stocks and management implications in the Canadian Atlantic Provinces and New England, USA. Canadian Journal of Fisheries and Aquatic Sciences, 38: 1612-1625.

Shearer, W. M. (1986). The exploitation of Atlantic salmon in Scottish home water fisheries in 1952 - 83. *In* The Status of the Atlantic Salmon in Scotland (eds. D. Jenkins and W. Shearer), ITE Symposium No. 15, 37 -49.

Shearer, W. M. (1988). Relating catch records to stocks. *In* Atlantic Salmon: Planning for the Future (eds. D. H. Mills and D. Piggins), Proceedings of the Third International Atlantic Salmon Symposium, Biarritz, 21-23 October 1986, 256-274.

Shearer, W. M. (1989). The River Tweed salmon and sea trout fisheries. *In* Tweed towards 2000 (ed. D. H. Mills), Tweed Foundation Symposium, 60 -79.

Small, I. & Downham, D.Y. (1985). The interpretation of anglers' records (trout and sea trout, *Salmo trutta* L., and salmon *Salmo salar* L.). Aquaculture & Fisheries Management, 16 (2): 151 - 170.

Solomon, D. J. (1985). Salmon stock and recruitment, and stock enhancement. Journal of Fish Biology, 27 (Supplement A): 45 -58.

Symons, P. E. K. (1979). Estimated escapement of Atlantic salmon (*Salmo salar*) for maximum smolt production in rivers of different productivity. Journal of the Fisheries Research Board of Canada, 36: 132 -140.

Taggart, J. B. & Ferguson, A. (1984). An electrophoretically-detectable genetic tag for hatchery-reared brown trout (*Salmo trutta* L.) Aquaculture, 41: 119-130.

Taggart, J. B. & Ferguson, A. (1986). Electrophoretic evaluation of a supplemental stocking programme for brown trout, *Salmo trutta* L. Aquaculture and Fisheries Management, 17: 155-162.

Taylor, V. R. & Bauld, B. R. (1973). A programme for increased Atlantic salmon (*Salmo salar*) production in a major Newfoundland river. International Atlantic Salmon Foundation, Special Publication Series, 4 (1): 339-347.

Thibault, M. (1983). Les transplantations de salmonides d'eau courant en France: saumon Atlantique (*Salmo salar* L.) et truite commune (*Salmo trutta* L.). Compte Rendu Sommaire de Seances Société du Biogeographié, 59 (3c): 405-420.

Thorpe, J. E. (1988). Salmon enhancement: stock discreteness and choice of material for stocking. *In* Atlantic Salmon: Planning for the Future (eds. D. H. Mills and D Piggins), Proceedings of the Third International Atlantic Salmon Symposium, Biarritz, 21-23 October 1986, 373-388.

Thurso, Lord (1986). The management of a rod and line and a commercial fishery. *In* The Status of the Atlantic Salmon in Scotland (eds. D. Jenkins and W. Shearer), ITE Symposium no.15, 55 - 59.

Twomey, E. (1982). The contribution of hatchery reared smolts to the Irish drift net fishery. Department of Fisheries & Forestry, Dublin, Fishery Leaflet No. 118, 9 pp.

Twomey, E. (1984). Evaluation of promoting natural propagation versus restocking. Atlantic Salmon Trust Workshop on Stock Enhancement, University of Surrey, 16 pp.

Whelan, B. J. & Whelan, K. F. (1986). The economics of salmon fishing in the Republic of Ireland: present and potential. Proceedings of the 17th Annual Study Course of the IFM, Univeristy of Ulster, Coleraine, 9-11 September 1986, 191-208.

MANAGING A RECOVERING SALMON RIVER - THE RIVER TYNE

A.S. CHAMPION

NRA: Northumbria Region

1. DECLINE AND FALL

In the early 1870s the River Tyne Fishery District returned net catches of salmon and sea trout that now seem scarcely believable. In his evidence to the Royal Commission of Salmon Fisheries in 1891 the Chairman of the Fishery Board opined that of the 121,600 killed in 1871 at least 110,000 were taken by the nets in the river. This seems unlikely in view of the fact that in 1873, the first year from which records are available, 163 drift net licences were issued for the sea and only 27 draft net licences in the river. The Chairman also reported that his rod fishery had declined from an average of 147 salmon in the 5 year period beginning 1880 to 43 in the period starting 1895 and, not surprisingly, attributed the decline to overfishing by the nets. During this period the total rod catch for the river varied from the highest figure of 3201 in 1885 to 123 in 1898. However, his statements regarding estuarial pollution are ambivalent in that he seemed to regard it as a temporary problem in low flows despite the fact that on his own admission most of the estuary was grossly polluted.

The Clerk to the Board was not an angler and would not be drawn into venturing an opinion on netting but detailed a horrific litany of pollution and dead salmon and smolts in the estuary. He attributed the total absence of salmon in the South Tyne to pollution from lead workings and in support of this supposition cited a case where gravel abstracted from the river was spread on a carriageway resulting in the early demise of the abstractor's hens from lead poisoning. There was no doubt in his mind that the decline of the salmon fisheries was a direct result of pollution.

The Commission noted that "the present polluted state of many rivers materially impedes the access of salmon to the upper waters and thus by limiting the available spawning area of the country must have a most prejudicial influence on the salmon fisheries of the country,....". However, they missed the point that whilst adult salmon can often successfully negotiate polluted estuaries during heavy spate conditions, smolt migration can be triggered by small variations in flow and then the migrants merely pass downstream to their doom.

This point was realised by the Board of Conservators for the Fishery District of the River Tyne which, in 1959, reported that in the Tyne "The floods ------- necessary to enable the smolts to reach the sea did not materialise and, as always happens, large numbers of these fish were killed on entering the tidal stretch -------. It is extremely improbable that they reached the sea in any numbers". That year, coincidentally was the first and only year in which no report was received of a salmon taken by rod and line.

The river net fishery was banned by byelaw in 1934 in an attempt to save the rod fishery but had long since lost favour with the markets because of the tainted tarry flavour of the fish. Despite a peak catch of 3361 in 1927 the rod fishery had ceased for all practical purposes in the early 1930s with an exceptional low of 15 in 1933 but 1959 was undoubtedly the nadir for the Tyne.

The sole glimmer of hope for later years was that some salmon were always present in the river and it now seems unlikely that the Tyne race of salmon was extinguished.

This paper is not about the rehabilitation of the Tyne as a salmon river, although some reference is made to how it was achieved, it is about how normal fishery management problems have been exacerbated by decades of neglect and by extremes of public opinion. Meanwhile therefore, suffice it to say that the River Tyne is now again a major salmon river as is clearly demonstrated by the rod catch statistics detailed in Fig. 1.

2. THE SEEDS OF RECOVERY

2.1 Water Quality

Northumbrian Water Ltd have spent £150m on the Tyneside Sewage Treatment Scheme which has involved intercepting all the effluents which used to discharge into the estuarial Tyne and subjecting them to primary treatment before returning the effluent to the low part of the estuary. The commissioning of the treatment works occurred in 1980 and this was the major factor in the rehabilitation of the river but because of the timescale and phasing of the scheme it is estimated that raw sewage from some 65,000 people will continue to flow into the upper part of the estuary until 1993. There have been mortalities of salmon and migratory trout during the drought conditions of the last two summers but even under these conditions the estuary is passable for fish at some stage of tide.

2.2 Kielder Scheme

The Tyne cannot be considered as a typical example of a recovering salmon river because of the overriding influence of the Kielder Scheme.

The construction of a reservoir with a capacity of 200 million cubic metres at the head of the North Tyne inundated 7 miles of salmon spawning and nursery area and prevented access to many miles of tributary. The latter was not considered of great significance to salmon populations since what little spawning gravel existed in these tributaries had been abstracted for local road building, however, it had a major influence on the mitigation scheme.

It was clear that if a fish pass was installed in the dam those fish that used it would find difficulty in spawning and it did not seem likely that they would provide the substance for a fishery in the reservoir. Consequently, it was resolved to build a hatchery instead of a fish pass and restock the Tyne system with 160,000 salmon parr/year. In the interests of rehabilitation this number has been exceeded and for the last 10 years an average of 250,000 parr/year have been introduced chiefly into areas not normally spawned by salmon. Survival has been high in some batches. Russell, (personal communication) by interpretation of microtag return data has demonstrated up to 2.03% recapture rate from net and rod fisheries. Moreover, the immediate vicinity of Kielder dam is stocked with hatchery parr because the natural spawning is unsuccessful due to an unfavourable temperature regime. Indications are that most of the returning adults in this immediate area are chiefly of hatchery origin.

Water is released from Kielder to allow abstraction at a number of points and to maintain a statutory minimum maintained flow, not only in the Tyne but also in the River Wear and the River Tees. The compensation flow from the dam has been set

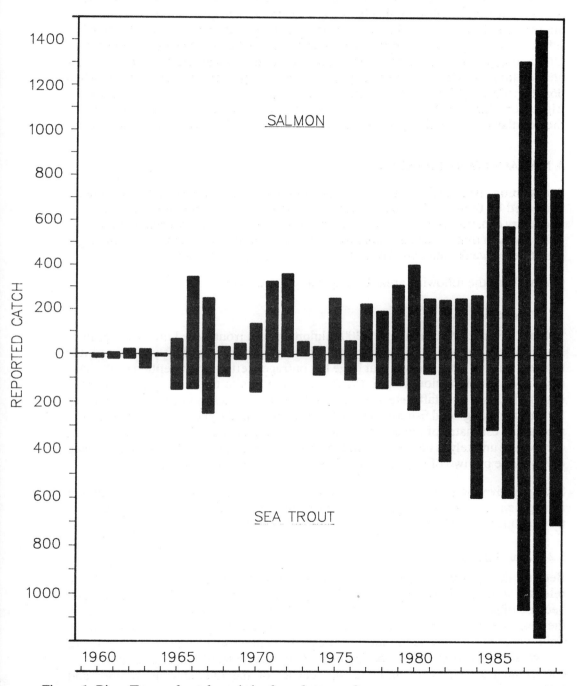

Figure 1. River Tyne rod catch statistics for salmon and sea trout.

at 1.25 cumecs in the summer and 0.625 cumecs in the winter and releases of 15 cumecs are also made for peak time hydro-electric power generation. Clearly the flow regime in the river is no longer natural and the behaviour of migratory fish is affected.

No scientific studies have been made on the movement of migrants in the river but it is apparent that if substantial releases are made after a spate salmon continue to migrate up river for an unknown but prolonged period once the flood water has subsided. During this period they continue to be catchable by anglers. Conversely, after a long period of compensation water releases only, an artificial increase in flow neither stimulates migration nor angling success except very late in the season when possibly the combination of minimal natural freshets with the release acts as the trigger for migration. However, a release invariably stimulates angling activity because the popular view is that high water equates with potentially high angling success.

3. MANAGEMENT PROBLEMS

Any salmon river carries with it the expectation amongst a minority that problems, perceived by them, will be put right to their satisfaction immediately regardless of budgetary constraints and cost to the management agency. A recovering salmon river differs only in that the usual problems are more numerous and the fisheries manager has at best a weak data base from which to argue the points raised.

On the Tyne the following areas have given rise to concern.

3.1 Water Quality

In both 1989 and 1990 some 200 - 300 salmon and sea trout were killed as a result of low dissolved oxygen in the estuary and stress related disease. Thirty years ago it is unlikely that the total run was that large but outraged letters and telephone calls have demanded instant action despite the fact that the loss to the river system has been negligible. Fisheries staff have been involved in many fruitless hours of work searching for and removing dead fish which have been reported and trying to convince the local media that estimates of thousands of fish by local anglers based on counts of 10 or 20 corpses are unlikely to be accurate and that the fish were not killed by dioxin and sheep dip to name but two of the popular opinions as to the cause of death.

Such negative media coverage does, however, have an advantageous spin off in that it heightens public awareness and increases the reporting rate of minor pollutions throughout the catchment.

3.2 Water Releases

Because the option to release water exists there is an expectation that water will be released to maintain or improve the fishing. Such pressure is resisted not so much because of the limited chance of success as explained earlier but because the water in the reservoir, by virtue of its potential use for hydroelectric power generation, has a finite value and its use for other purposes results in a loss of revenue which is not recoverable from anglers or riparian owners. It is designated for relief of pollution, encouraging spawners up into the top reaches of the river during October and November and any other reason which will improve the health of the fishery. It was not designated for improving the sport of anglers.

The artificial flow regime of the river is a potential source of future problems. It is already apparent that migrating salmon are unwilling to run the North Tyne above the confluence with the River Rede until the autumn and this may be connected with the lack of major freshets in the river below the dam.

It may be that the spawning grounds in the North Tyne will deteriorate through there no longer being sufficient floods to move them and they will ultimately become armoured and require machine working on a regular basis.

The releases of water from the reservoir also have a different temperature regime from the tributary streams despite the fact that water may be drawn from the surface layers. Generally, throughout the spring and summer the temperature of the water is lower than would be expected in the river but in the winter it is higher. Thus, in the immediate vicinity of the dam egg development is accelerated but the water is still too cold to initiate feeding and the resultant fry starve. The generation of hydropower undoubtedly extends this effect further down the river system but it is not yet clear how significant it is nor to what degree the growth rate and smoltification of parr are affected. It is generally agreed, amongst anglers, that the fly life has declined but there are no data to support or refute the claim.

3.3 Obstructions

Figure 2 shows on a map of the catchment the major artificial obstructions in the river system of the Tyne.

The first obstruction to the passage of migratory fish is believed to be the bridge footings at Wylam on the grounds that in the spring the bridge pool yields the best catches of salmon on the river. It happens to be the first pool above the head of tide and the head difference over the footings is at most 50 centimetres but the apron is shallow during low flows which do not occur in the spring. The case is not proven but in response to pressure plans were drawn up to concentrate the flow, a scheme which was opposed ferociously by the local angling club who claimed there would be an adverse effect on the flow through the pool and by the parish council which professed concern about increased danger to children playing on the apron. Any alternative scheme will be much more expensive.

Riding Mill weir was constructed as part of the Kielder Scheme. Salmon can only pass over a measuring weir which is less than one third of the width of the main weir. Initial problems of access were caused by the inclusion of a stilling basin of insufficient depth; these were solved by creating a rock basin downstream to back up the water against the face of the weir. However, some migrants still jump at the main weir and give rise to public concern regardless of the fact that they probably constitute less than 1% of the population.

Below Hexham Bridge gravel abstraction has lowered the river bed and a succession of works to protect the bridge foundations from undermining have formed a substantial weir upon which, through three decades, numerous devices have been installed to assist the passage of fish. They appear to work.

On the North Tyne, Chollerford Mill Dam has always been perceived as a potential obstruction but has not appeared to cause problems until recent years when the North

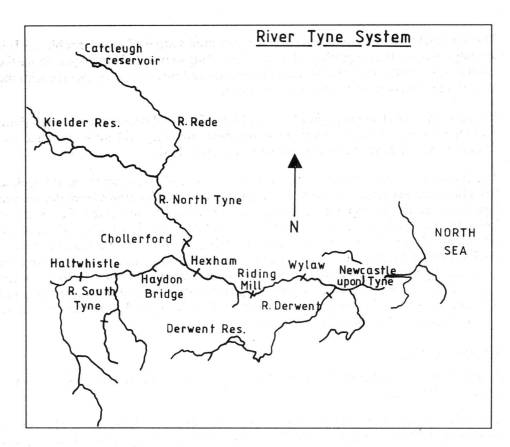

Figure 2.

Tyne has been used as the pipeline down which water has flowed on demand from Kielder Reservoir to Tyneside. As a result some migration of salmon has been possible in the Tyne despite minimum flows elsewhere. Public perception amongst some anglers and riparian owners upstream is that the fish pass should be improved to allow passage of fish at these moderate release levels. Realistically, the degree of improvements may not be significant and the investment is likely to be large and the beneficiaries few.

On the South Tyne, Haydon Bridge bridge footings have been exposed by lowering of the river bed downstream. They are level and pose an insurmountable obstacle except at moderate flow levels when the water is deep enough for fish movement. Fortunately, salmon only run the South Tyne on moderate to high flows so it is unusual for fish to be held up, but nonetheless angling interests upstream are insistent that something must be done about it and the pressure will increase when the major obstruction at Haltwhistle has been dealt with.

Below Haltwhistle Viaduct the bed level has been lowered by gravel abstraction. The footings create a fall approximately 130 centimetres high and above that the apron is shallow with a rapid flow. This is a serious obstruction and due to the advanced state of deterioration of the footings cannot be solved by the installation of a traditional fish pass. A rock wall across the river is now proposed to raise the river level downstream.

Other obstructions exist on the tributaries and various requests for the construction of fish passes have been received but of necessity have been allocated a low priority despite the fact that further spawning areas would become accessible.

3.4 Poaching

Clearly a river without a run of salmon required less bailiffing than a major salmon river but here again public perception is a major factor.

A poacher's haul of thirty salmon has an insignificant impact on a total population of say 5,000 but if publicised creates consternation amongst local fishery interests.

In the Northumbria Region it is accepted that total control of illegal fishing is not a practical target, nor is a minimal effort aimed at allowing the survival of sufficient spawning fish to ensure future runs. It is not possible to measure the level of illegal fishing and compile crime statistics to allow the setting of a target figure, so instead a philosophy has been developed based on the effect of deterrence provided by wide publicity to the successes of water bailiffs who operate not by seizing nets or by visible patrolling but through covert operations leading to prosecution of offenders. When poaching gangs are successful word of their success spreads through the criminal fraternity and illegal fishing activity rapidly reaches epidemic proportions as more individuals and gangs join in the bonanza. Fortunately, the opposite is just as true and experience has shown that the downfall of a well organised and hitherto successful criminal gang can for a short time stop poaching overnight and the resultant fear of detection limits the activities of most opportunistic poachers.

This philosophy is particularly relevant to the Tyne because as salmon runs have increased substantial poaching success has become easier, gangs have become larger and better organised and so water bailiffs have had to improve their response. Also, it is common practice to target the heaviest policing on those areas where salmon accumulate. In a river with few salmon those areas are not numerous but when large runs of salmon are the rule, good catches can be made throughout many miles of river. There are only two responses to such a scenario, to increase resources or to make more efficient use of those that are available.

On the Tyne both approaches were utilised. First "call-in" staff were nominated, trained and utilised at short notice to boost the strength of patrols, secondly the flexibility of the permanent bailiffs was increased by reorganisation of the structure to allow freer deployment of permanent bailiffs between river systems and crucially, better intelligence and informer systems were developed. Heightened public awareness plays a vital role in this aspect but it had to be developed through media interviews and articles and face to face contact with water bailiffs. This is one area where a developing salmon river differs from one with a more recent tradition of salmon fishing.

3.5 The Net Fishery

During the late 1960s monofilament drift nets first appeared in the region. By 1970 they were used by all licenced netsmen and it was apparent that the effective fishing effort had probably doubled. A Net Limitation Order was already in effect around the Tyne estuary and to the North but some 5 miles south of the Tyne, from which direction many salmon approach the river, no such Order was in existence. This omission was rectified in 1971 but it was not until 1976 that further steps were taken to protect specifically the residual stock of Tyne salmon. Agreement was reached with local netsmen for the imposition of a prohibited area one mile wide for a distance of 2 miles to the North and 4.3 miles to the South with the exception of two beach netting stations immediately to the South of the river in which netsmen were allowed to use 'T' nets, a type of fixed engine similar but very much more simple than the bag net in common use in Scotland. Despite claims to the contrary from anti-netting lobbies the rod catch returns shown in Figure 1 demonstrate the success of these measures. Local netsmen are satisfied because they are now benefiting from the increased production of the river and to complete the cycle many are prepared to turn informer against unlicenced netting.

3.6 Predators

During the last 20 years goosanders have become increasingly prevalent in the Tyne system. It is not known whether or not they damage the fishery by reducing the smolt run although throughout the major part of the river system the only available prey species are trout and salmon. It seems likely that now extensive natural spawning occurs in the river, density dependent mortality regulates smolt production and if that is the case the goosander population is unlikely to cause significant damage. However, the view of the angler and riparian owner alike is that the birds are a competing predator and should be eliminated. Since they are a protected species the traditional shoot to kill policy cannot be deployed and more requests have been made directly to fisheries staff and through the channels of the Regional Fisheries Advisory Committee to support control of this species by licence.

Cormorants have also caused similar concern especially as the presence of such a large body of water as Kielder Reservoir in the headwaters of the river has encouraged this species further inland.

Bearing in mind that the Tyne also contains substantial numbers of brown trout which undoubtedly prey on salmon parr and smolts and, in the spring, shoals of coal fish move into the estuary (to prey on smolts?) the significance of bird predation must be open to question.

Grey seals and mink also pose problems. The latter are easily trapped and the occasional population explosion is rapidly controlled by local gamekeepers; but the frequent occurrence of grey seals in the upper part of the estuary can ruin the fishing. Since the lower reaches of the Tyne are heavily populated, it is not possible to shoot the animals and other humane attempts to scare them away have failed.

3.7 Restocking

The true impact of the salmon parr introductions has never been assessed. Microtagging experiments indicate that overall in the order of 10% of the population could, in some years, be of hatchery origin but it does not necessarily follow that the population has been boosted by 10% and a comparison of the salmon and sea trout catch returns in Figure 1 demonstrates that the pattern of improvement for the two species is very similar although sea trout have not been stocked into the Tyne system for many years.

The Tyne does not experience a 0 + SW sea trout run, most maiden fish are 1 + SW and the bulk of the run consists of second spawners, so perhaps the potential for recovery of the population is marginally faster than for salmon but the observed figures do suggest that the stocking programme for salmon may not be as effective as is generally believed. Brood stock are selected from areas which are easy to fish so it is possible that such heavy stocking might ultimately affect the genetic composition of the stock and thus the continuation of the programme on the existing scale is open to question. Even so, public perception is that the level of restocking is of vital importance for future stocks.

3.8 Rentals

In 1980 the maximum cost of a day's salmon fishing on the Tyne was probably £5. In 1990 several beats on the river have been let for £30 per day to guests travelling from the south of England. Currently, the local riparian owners prefer to lease their water to people they know, but it seems ultimately inevitable that local angling clubs will be dispossessed of their rented water as the owners appreciate the profits available from letting to syndicates or high paying visitors. To some extent this has happened already on some of the lower beats where coarse fishermen have been excluded in order to give salmon fishermen the exclusive right of the fishery.

To date, there is little evidence of increased employment locally for gillies and although information is not readily available on where the visitors stay, it seems likely that most rent holiday cottages connected with the beats they fish rather than stay in local hotels.

Whilst it seems unlikely that licence evasion is prevalent amongst such visitors a greater level of enforcement is required to ensure that the National Rivers Authority is not defrauded of income. No estimates are available but to date it seems unlikely that the observed small increase in short term licences will equate with the increased cost of policing.

3.9 Licence Income

Unfortunately records of salmon licences issued prior to 1985 are not available but Figure 3 demonstrates the fluctuation in numbers of salmon licences issued for the Tyne. Undoubtedly the number of anglers has increased although the gross statistics only reflect this through the day licence figures, and although no effort figures are available the number of angler days has also increased. The licence income has not improved significantly from the rapid improvement of catches observed since 1985 apart from the overall increase in levels of duty imposed throughout the region.

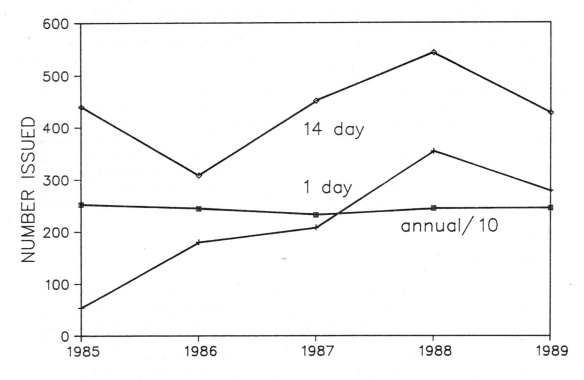

Figure 3. Number of salmon licences issued annually on the River Tyne, 1985-89.

4. CONCLUSIONS

The common denominator amongst all these problems, none of which are within the exclusive province of a recovering salmon river, is the gulf between the perception of many river users and the considered opinion of the fishery manager who must allocate a budget and prioritise future work on the river. On an established salmon river there may be a shortage of scientific information on which decisions can be based but there is usually a wealth of recent historical data that may not pass the test of scientific respectability but is nonetheless management information and can be deployed to aid in decision making.

On a newly rehabilitated river that information is absent and on the Tyne, where suddenly salmon fishing has become extremely valuable and the pressure from river users is in direct proportion, decisions must be made with a minimum of information regarding the future of a river which, as a result of the Kielder Scheme, is susceptible to manipulation for the benefit of a number of different interests. The potential cost of error is high and, because of the absence of similar experience from other schemes, the risk is difficult to assess.

Lastly, it will be apparent that to complete the job on the Tyne and safeguard future stocks substantial further expenditure is required. From where will the money come?

THE INTERNATIONAL IMPLICATIONS

MALCOLM WINDSOR AND PETER HUTCHINSON

NASCO

1. INTRODUCTION

For approximately 10,000 years the Atlantic salmon has migrated over its present range. But in the last 200 years, since the industrial revolution, its habitat has been damaged all over the North Atlantic, from Russia to Portugal and from Canada to New England. 10,000 years is hard to grasp so let us think of 10,000 years as 1 day. If we think of all the centuries since the last Ice Age 10,000 years ago as 24 hours then the damage to the salmon habitats all occurred in the last 20 minutes of the day. We do not really know the true extent of what we have lost. Forestry practices, hydro-electric schemes, impoundment, land drainage and pollution; these have all had a damaging effect on river systems but assessment of just how much has been lost is difficult. Now, in the past decade or so, at one minute to midnight on our clock, the process of restoration has begun and I would like to suggest to you that we can have some confidence that restoration efforts from now on will be supported by international cooperation rather than threatened as may have been the case in the past. Why do I say this? Simply because we can, for the first time in human history, have real confidence that all over the North Atlantic there is a genuine concern to conserve and restore the salmon. The mere fact that every North Atlantic nation with salmon interests has signed the NASCO Treaty shows that there is a real willingness to cooperate internationally. In doing so each nation has stated its desire to promote, among other objectives, the restoration of salmon rivers.

2. POLITICAL CHANGES

Many things have changed in the last decade, just one minute to midnight on our time-scale. In my view they have almost all changed for the better. The political climate is very different now. This change is international in nature and has crossed all frontiers in the Western world. I believe it will now happen, if slowly, in what was the Communist bloc as democracy takes root there. Politics have "greened". There are votes in conservation and the environment, so restoration of river systems now has a following wind and this means financial support. In New England, for example, we have seen massive financial support for the restoration of the salmon rivers there. On the Connecticut River alone it is estimated that $26 million has been spent on fishways and fishlifts at three dams. In France we see large efforts to make rivers accessible to salmon and this meeting will be a record of some of the progress made.

This change in the public climate is of fundamental importance and means that politicians want to keep up with internationally directed conservation trends because of the pressure of public opinion. This change is international in nature and we now see in Britain, for example, that many environmental quality standards including those concerning our seawater and our beaches seem to be laid down more by the European Community than by the British Parliament. To take another example, we are all aware of the damage done to fish resources by acid rain. But the subject has now reached high on politicians' agendas. Industry in the US causes problems of acidification in Canada and this has produced a strong groundswell of public opinion which has led to talks on the subject at Presidential and Prime Ministerial level between the US and Canada. The same subject occurred in talks between the Prime Ministers of Norway and Great Britain. The dumping of radioactive waste in the North Sea by the UK has now become a hot potato in European terms though in fact the practice has a long history. So I would suggest that the international changes in political climate are now very favourable to river restoration and that this is probably an irreversible shift in public opinion and in politics.

3. NEGOTIATIONS IN NASCO

Let us think now about the narrower world of international salmon politics. The main thrust of my remarks today lies in the changes that have occurred in international cooperation on the high seas and in the developments in international negotiations on salmon conservation issues. Let us briefly deal with interceptions. We all know that salmon are subject to a complex pattern of interceptions. During the last decades we have seen the Canadians intercepting US fish; the Norwegians intercepting Russian fish; and the Faroese intercepting Norwegian fish. The Greenlanders intercept fish of European and North American origin. And even the English intercept Scottish fish! In these circumstances those who spent precious resources to build fish passes, restore spawning grounds and reduce pollution must have wondered for whose benefit they were doing it. Now, however we see the development of an awareness in NASCO that those who take strong conservation and restoration actions deserve international support.

Look at the large US restoration effort and see how Canada has made a real effort to recognise this and to minimise its interceptions of US fish. Consider too how Greenland, recognising the need to see viable salmon populations, has reduced its interception of European and North American fish since the establishment of NASCO. Before NASCO's inception the catch at Greenland reached a peak of about 2500 tonnes, then there was an interim bi-lateral arrangement for a quota of 1190 tonnes. Now the NASCO quota is around 900 tonnes. Similarly in the Faroese zone the present NASCO quota of 550 tonnes is half the peak catch in this fishery. These are large reductions for countries that are very dependent on fish for their survival. Look too at the elimination of the international Northern Norwegian Sea salmon fishery beyond the economic zone of the Faroe Islands, which at its peak amounted to almost 1000 tonnes. The advent of the NASCO Treaty completely ended this fishery by international agreement. We have seen in the NASCO forum that countries can convince others of the strength of their arguments if they can show evidence that they are acting in accordance with the Convention. For example, a State of Origin can point to its conservation and restoration efforts as a powerful reason why an intercepting state should moderate its catches.

As many present will know the NASCO Treaty requires that each Party makes an annual declaration as to what steps it has taken to conserve and restore salmon stocks. This in itself encourages countries to take action and to declare what they have done and I think you will agree that we have seen much salmon legislation and regulation in the last few years since this requirement came into effect. Look for example at the recent measures in Norway where a total ban on drift netting, together with effort restrictions in the bend net fishery and prohibition of salmon fishing by all methods in 74 rivers, has been introduced.

If I may I would like to add that much of the other work being undertaken by international agreement in the NASCO forum will help to ensure that threats to wild stocks are understood and minimised. For example, NASCO has asked detailed questions of the International Council for the Exploration of the Sea (ICES) concerning salmon stocks. These have included quantification of the loss of salmon production due to acidification and reviews of the methods of restoring populations to acidified rivers. The factors leading to unreported catches have been reviewed and estimates of the level of unreported catches have been provided by ICES. The Council is presently considering methods of reducing the impacts of unreported catches.

The whole question of the genetic, disease, parasite and environmental impacts of salmon farming on the wild stocks is under study internationally. A Code of Practice for salmon aquaculture with the aim of minimising damage to wild stocks is close to being internationally accepted. Guidelines for the establishment and operation of gene banks for threatened stocks have been adopted in order to safeguard the genetic diversity of salmon stocks.

These steps can all help to ensure that damage is minimised or even eliminated though it has to be said that we live in times when constant vigilance is needed because of the new and unexpected threats that arise on our horizons. One such threat is the recent development of a fishery for salmon in international waters in the North-East Atlantic by vessels re-flagged in Panama and Poland so as to avoid the provisions of the Convention. As a result of the excellent spirit of international cooperation within NASCO the Council was kept fully informed of all the evidence concerning the existence of this fishery and was able to take swift diplomatic action to end the fishery.

4. NEW NASCO DATABASE

Perhaps one of the more significant areas of interest in relation to the subject of this meeting is that the NASCO Council has recently agreed that the process of building a database on the status of all North Atlantic rivers be started. What we intend to do here is to establish a complete database of every salmon river flowing into the NASCO Convention area. Each river will be map referenced and briefly described. It will then be placed in one of five categories:

Category 1: Lost

Rivers in which there is no natural or maintained stock of salmon but which are known to have contained salmon in the past.

Category 2: Maintained

Rivers in which there is no natural stock of salmon, which are known to have contained salmon in the past, but in which a salmon stock is now only maintained through human intervention.

Category 3: Restored

Rivers in which the natural stock of salmon is known to have been lost in the past but in which there is now a self-sustaining stock of salmon as a result of restoration efforts or natural recolonization.

Category 4: Threatened with loss

Rivers in which there is a threat to the natural stock of salmon which would lead to loss of the stock unless the factor(s) causing the threat is(are) removed.

Category 5: Not threatened with loss

Rivers in which the natural salmon stocks are not considered to be threatened with loss (as defined in Category 4).

We are about to start this major effort and when it is complete we shall have in effect a "Domesday Book" describing the state of the North Atlantic salmon rivers at the close of the twentieth century. By re-assessing these rivers perhaps every 5 or 10 years we shall see what progress is being made. How valuable it would have been to us today if some medieval "biologist" had constructed such a record. Then we really would know how many populations have been lost. The establishment of this new database will be a further step in giving confidence that the international community cares about restoration of salmon populations and it will enable us in the longer term to monitor the improvements in river systems.

5. CONCLUSION

Perhaps you will think me unrealistically optimistic, but even a hard-boiled pessimist would have to accept that both the national and international political climates have changed considerably. He or she would have to accept that those who promote the restoration of salmon rivers now have a real chance that their efforts will not be frustrated by increased pollution, by hydro-electric schemes without fish passes and by unacceptable levels of interceptory fishing on the high seas. Having said this, the evidence seems to show that restoration of salmon to damaged rivers is not an easy process. Once a stock has been lost it seems to me that it is extremely difficult to restore it. It is much easier and much less costly to conserve what you have. In every case restoration is slow and costly. But we can be reasonably sure that it will not in future be frustrated or negated by external factors. We can be sure that the international community will be aware of steps taken by each country with salmon interests.

Mr Chairman the fact that we are holding this meeting is heartening. It shows that the healing process has begun. And from where I sit I believe that the international community is now behind every one working in this field.

A COMPARISON OF TWO SALMON RIVER RESTORATION PROJECTS: THE DORDOGNE (FRANCE) AND THE JACQUES CARTIER (QUEBEC)

PIERRE DULUDE

Department of Recreation, Fish and Game, Quebec

GUY PUSTELNIK

Conseil Superieur de la Pêche, France

1. INTRODUCTION

Over a century ago, the Atlantic Salmon was found in abundance in both the Dordogne (France) and the Jacques Cartier (Quebec) rivers. Unfortunately overexploitation of stocks, habitat degradation and the construction of insurmountable hydro-electric structures, led to the total disappearance of this species in these rivers.

It was only at the end of the 1970's that real interest developed concerning these two rivers and that Atlantic salmon restoration projects were finally begun. Since then, numerous actions have been realised in both cases and the results raise interesting comparisons, as much as in the way these projects were orginally addressed as in the contexts and the way things were eventually carried out.

Within the framework of cooperation programmes signed between France and Quebec, the two governments agreed in 1985 to twin the Dordogne and the Jacques Cartier so as to promote the cumulation of these restoration projects notably, through scientific exchanges. As such, by the autumn of 1989, a joint document was prepared, entitled: *"The Restoration of Migratory Fish in the Dordogne (France) and Jacques Cartier (Quebec) Rivers: A comparative study of methods, achievements and obtained results"*, the object of which was to evaluate in a systematic manner, the overall performance of these projects after more than a decade of effort.

The following presentation gives a synopsis of an evaluation made of the different procedures, of the different elements taken into consideration, of the different analytical methods used as well as on the information obtained and how it was put to use. In the first part, we will deal with the various preliminary studies that were undertaken prior to the elaboration of the action plans. Then, after indicating the roles of the different interest groups and organisations and the monitoring methods that were subsequently set up, the results will be analysed, followed by a general discussion on the global direction that each of these restoration projects has adopted.

2. THE ORIGINS OF THE RESTORATION PROJECTS

As much as in the case of the Jacques Cartier as in that of the Dordogne, these two restoration projects originated out of an increased general awareness of the intrinsic value of salmon rivers. With the Dordogne, the project was inscribed in two national plans those being: The Salmon Plan (1976-1981) and the Migratory Plan (1981-1986). In the case of the Jacques Cartier, the project was initiated following popular outcry and pressures exerted, especially by fishermen, in an overall context where the restoration of salmon rivers was becoming an important preoccupation as much as for the state as for fishermen, although no specific policy had as yet been elaborated at this time.

A study project manager had been enlisted by the Conseil Supérieur de la Pêche (C.S.P.) in order to elaborate a preliminary study of the Dordogne; whereas for the Jacques Cartier, a mixed committee composed of representatives of sports fishermen and civil servants (The Jacques Cartier Restoration Committee, C.R.J.C.) was responsible for the elaboration of a summary feasibility study.

3. PRELIMINARY STUDIES

The elements that were considered were practically the same for both rivers, however the degree to which each element was analysed differs substantially. As such, for the Dordogne, systematic and exhaustive studies were completed, notably on the past history of the river, on water quality, on river morphodynamics as well as on the biology of the numerous fish species present. These studies, completed for the most part by the same individual, tried to respond to a complex, problematical situation, where amongst other things, the following aspects had to be addressed: the protection of a habitat currently being destroyed by gravel extraction; the construction of additional dam structures; the restoration of several migratory fish species and the protection of the river banks. Not only did these studies permit a rapid diagnosis of the situation, they also subsequently served as a solid base for following the evolution of the different known parameters as well as future actions, all the while allowing for the integration of the different limiting factors associated with other uses of the river.

On the Jacques Cartier, studies of the river ecology were directed more towards the identification of possible eventual obstacles to the restoration of a salmon population. Contrary to the Dordogne where the historical study was used to lay the foundation of the future action plan, on the Jacques Cartier the historical information served only to promote a favourable decision for the project by simply relating past abundance of salmon populations to future exploitation possibilities. As such, the problem of the Dery Gorge for example was never sufficiently analysed and was not identified from the start as a major limiting factor; whereas we know today that it does indeed constitute an almost insurmountable obstacle.

The summary studies carried out on the Jacques Cartier did not allow for the setting up of an exhaustive monitoring mechanism concerning water quality nor for the changing morphodynamics of the river, depriving the project of an important series of data concerning the evolution of the river.

Concerning the evaluation and the quantification of the potential numbers of "migratory fish", different methods were used. For the Dordogne, the carrying capacity was estimated sector by sector based on the description of different habitats identified by precise cartography, and by a global appreciation of feeding and spawning zones. The potential estimation takes into account all limiting factors related to the

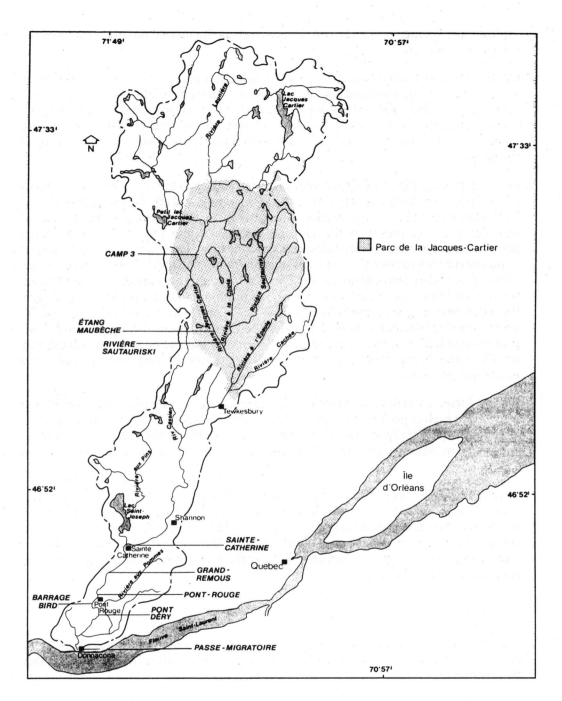

Figure 1. Bassin Hydrographique de la Rivière Jacques Cartier.
Catchment area: 1515km^2; length of main river: 161km;
Length of section accessible to salmon: 110km;
Number of municipalities 9; number of regional county municipalities 2
(Portneuf and de la Jacques Cartier); catchment population: about 30,000
(Donnacona is the biggest municipality with about 6000 inhabitants);
Difference in altitude - sources to mouth: 853km.

79

exploitation regimes of the various dams as well as the individual productivity of the different sectors.

On the Jacques Cartier, potential smolt production had been evaluated sector by sector based on a quantitative description derived from photointerpretation, to which theoretical production values were applied. Production values which may be readjusted in the light of new knowledge. Estimations of returning salmon runs are computed in function of the latest data on sea interceptions and are as such subject to change.

For both rivers, in spite of several tentative approaches to the socio-economic aspect of each situation, for the most part the social, economic and ethnographic context had hardly been taken into consideration. This discrepancy has become a shortcoming of considerable importance in the Dordogne valley where the involvement of the population in the restoration project remains quite low. The managerial context, such as that pertaining to the different types of exploitation and legal regulations, was also, more or less taken into consideration. On the Dordogne, the various uses of the river which could have interfered with salmon restoration had been studied, particularly the extraction of gravel, the influences of hydroelectric dams and the effect of the professional freshwater fishery. However, the estuary where fishing pressure, both professional and amateur, is greatest, unfortunately did not become the object of a detailed study in regards to the restoration of migratory fish and is considered today as a major problem.

On the Jacques Cartier, the principal interference elements with regards to salmon restoration such as pollution zones and the established sport fishery for other species, were only superficially appraised and were considered from the start as non-limiting factors. However, the absence of precise data warrants certain additional studies today.

Concerning legal regulations, analyses were conducted at the level of these two watersheds. Without ever dwelling on the underlying causes of the observed situations, these analyses, nevertheless, contributed to an appreciation of the relative complexity of the problem, particularly on the Dordogne where the number of intervening interest groups renders a coherent and comprehensive approach to regulations rather difficult.

4. ACTION PLAN

The studies completed on the two rivers provided sufficient information to allow for favorable decisions as to the acceptance of each restoration project. From this moment on theoretical action plans were developed.

On the Dordogne, the action plan came out immediately following the end of the study, and was issued by a single organisation having a "fishing" vocation, that being le Conseil Supérieur de la Pêche (C.S.P.). This plan, however, does take into account, to a certain degree, the compatibility between the different water uses. Based on an exhaustive initial context, theoretical opitmal improvements are proposed that do not integrate, at least at this stage, the usual technical, administrative, political or economic factors; the eventual implementation of this plan would effectively deal with these particular factors. This exhaustive approach is based on a static situation and possible future modifications or changes are rather difficult to incorporate.

On the Jacques Cartier, three different action plans were completed in succession in different periods by the Department of Recreation, Fish and Game (M.L.C.P.), the Jacques Cartier Restoration Committee (C.R.J.C.) and elected representatives. Each presented different objectives which were more or less complementary. We can also observe a clear evolution over time from a strictly salmon plan to a more global development centred around an essentially recreo-tourist use. Overall, the original proposals were modified, even curtailed in order to adjust to the social, political, technical and economic context. This procedure takes into account that the different actions may be readjusted, to a certain degree, in relation to the results obtained and the evolution of the overall situation.

Essentially, the actions plans are comparable for both rivers, that is they both propose more or less the same actions but are simply adjusted to each particular and respective situation. Water purification, the construction of fish ladders on dams, the adjustment of regulations, management and exploitation policies, the dissemination of information, and the need for further research are all common elements found in both plans.

Furthermore, when considering the biological aspects, both plans proposed at the start the possible participation of government fish hatcheries in their fry stocking programmes, and even in the development of a genetic strain of salmon adapted to each river.

5. GOVERNING AND COORDINATING BODIES

Once all the elements of the action plan were in place, it was then necessary to define the possible sources of financing and to identify the roles and mandates for each of the groups involved. This stage of concerted action often determines the way in which the project will evolve, either towards its successful completion or towards possible failure.

For the Dordogne, the Secretary of State for the Environment was the initiator of the restoration operation, which at the beginning was limited to migratory fish. To achieve its goals, it uses numerous delegated groups who then deal directly with specific problems or who then sub-contract out to associations that are sometimes created solely to follow and coordinate certain operations. According to the nature of each undertaking, the level of implication and the duration of the association structures, the functional working scheme is rather complicated for each group. In the end, the actions of each group to one another are not, for all pratical purposes, coordinated.

Recently, the Committee for the Restoration of the Dordogne River was created. Its mandate is to coordinate the overall programme and to serve also as interlocutor to the Committee for the Restoration of the Jacques Cartier. Furthermore, at the express demand of the Secretary of State for the Environment, a new association was created: MIGADO or roughly translated as the Association for the Restoration of Migratory Fish in the Garonne-Dordogne Watershed, in order to coordinate and channel the energies and actions of interested fishermen in the restoration programme, no matter what their status (amateur, professional) or area involved (fluvial, estuary or open sea).

Moreover, certain other associations also serve as interlocutors because of their technical specificity as for example the Association Connaissance de la Vie Fluviale. In fact the restoration plan allows for the interaction of numerous (over 30) groups and organisations involved, all capable of positive actions but who function more often than not, without real coordination.

On the Jacques Cartier, a restoration committee was rapidly created in order to answer the needs of the numerous initial promoters of the project and to serve as a privileged interlocutor to the government, especially to the Department of Recreation, Fish and Game (M.L.C.P.). At the beginning, exclusively corporative and composed of salmon fishermen, it rapidly enlarged to encompass municipalities, user associations and the general public. At the same time it affirmed its willingness to immediately enlarge its mandate to include and promote a multiple use development of the river, particularly in regards to recreo-tourist activities.

Following the acceptance of this approach at the Quebec Region Economic Summit (1983) and in the management plans of the two Municipal Regional Councils, Portneuf and the Jacques Cartier, the C.R.J.C. increased its potential autonomy without necessarily assuring the information or the coordination initially agreed upon with the M.L.C.P.

In fact, at this stage of development and because of various independent financial sources (federal, provincial, municipal governments), three responsible organisations intervened simultaneously and independently from one another on the Jacques Cartier: the M.L.C.P. for salmon restoration, the municipalities and the Department of the Environment for water purification treatment, and the C.R.J.C. for salmon restoration as well as for all other aspects (information, education, tourist development, etc...)

Considering a few years later that the reintroduction of salmon must remain the absolute priority in the restoration programme and that the C.R.J.C. was trying to develop well beyond its possibilities of self financing its activities, the M.L.C.P. reaffirmed its leadership in the salmon operation.

Today the role of the C.R.J.C. in regards to the salmon is limited essentially to the operation of the salmon fish pass at Donnacona. It does, however, maintain its role of coordinating and promoting other areas of activity related to the river. It foresees the possibility of eventually constituting the managing body responsible for the salmon resource.

6. ANALYSIS OF RESULTS

The application of the action plans led to the realisation of numerous interventions which appropriately were analysed after a period of ten years.

6.1 Chemical managements

On the Dordogne, in spite of several attempts, projects were few or so poorly organized that efforts to clean up the waters of the river have had little impact. In effect, even now during periods of high tourist affluence, the bacteriological quality of the water is incompatible with swimming and other nautical activities on many beaches. Overall, we are also witnessing an important increase in the levels of certain minerals (nitrogen, phosphorus) caused principally by agricultural practices and the high permeability of the heavily tilled soil in the valley. This increase, if it continues, will certainly have a negative effect on the quality of potable water and the overall biology of the river.

On the Jacques Cartier river, following discussions in 1980 with the Corporation for the Restoration Jacques Cartier, the three principal municipalities together decided to take advantage of the government programmes at that time, and accepted to take the necessary steps to treat their waste water. Today the quality of the water in the midsection of the watershed has greatly improved. Water treatment in the lower section of the river is now considered a priority, especially concerning the industries located at Donnacona and Pont-Rouge.

This active approach to the improvement of water quality corresponds to a collective affirmation on the part of the different municipalities on the importance of water quality in all development projects geared towards tourism and outdoor activities.

6.2 Physical Managements

6.2.1 Protection

On the Dordogne, the collective awareness of the dangers that gravel extraction posed for the equilibrium and the future of the river finally led to a complete halt to this type of exploitation in the lower sections of the river. Confirmation of this willingness to protect the river habitat was evident when two Departments enacted appropriate regulatory measures (Corrèze and Lot). Two other Departments of the Dordogne have as yet to follow this example (Dordogne and Gironde).

However, in spite of these regulatory measures, the Management Union of the Dordogne Valley (Lot Department) still continues to carry out somewhat disturbing management activities (island clearing) which are hardly compatible with an adequate protection policy. This example illustrates the difficulty of the populace to accept certain restrictions. The Jacques Cartier, not being menaced in any way by such practices, has never been the object of any particular protection policy.

6.2.2 Restoration

On the Dordogne, the extraction of gravel aggravated the process of river bank erosion and contributed to the drying up of certain ox-bow sections of the river which were once ideal reproduction zones for some fish species associated with calm water. Some restoration projects are currently underway: ox-bows are once again being flooded by channel digging; river bank protection, traditionally done by costly boulder riprap, is now being carried out experimentally by transposing gravel and natural vegetation.

These types of problems were hardly considered on the Jacques Cartier in spite of some problems with sand fill of the river bed due in part to river bank erosion and

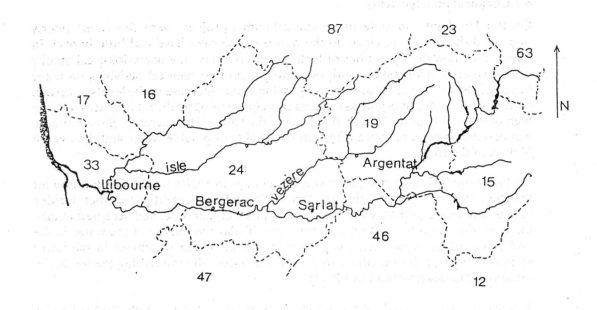

Figure 2. Bassin hydrographique de la Rivière Dordogne
Catchment area: 24,500km^2; Length of main river: 475km
Length of river accessible to salmon: about 350km from Bec d'Ambes
Number of municipalities (between Argentat and Castillon): 117;
Catchment population: winter 140,000 - summer 280,000)
Difference in altitude - source to mouth: 1727km.

landslides. This problem has been compensated for by the excellent quality of salmon spawning sites located in the tributaries, such as the Sautauriski river.

The dam sites at Bergerac, Mauzac and Tuilières are now equipped with mechanisms for allowing fish to migrate upstream. The shad, lamprey and sea trout are presently recolonizing the mid section of the Dordogne, right up to Carennac. This fact, in effect, confirms preliminary studies on distribution potentials and justifies the special and rather costly work carried out to adapt structures specifically for the shad. The trap located in the fish ladder at Bergerac allows for the live capture of mature salmon which are kept for hatchery purposes. The fish pass at Mauzac, however, still needs some additional modification in order to improve its attraction for shad.

The Beaulieu dam also needs to be modified to allow for salmon migration (foreseen for 1990) whereas the dam at Carennac, also in recreational use, will soon be the target of complementary work, which should improve the efficiency of its fish pass system.

On the Jacques Cartier, the fish ladder at Donnacona allows for the passage of salmon as well as for their capture in order to transport them to the spawning sites. The efficiency of this fish pass still remains to be confirmed during periods of high water. The actual manner in which this pass is operated tries to conciliate the need to maintain a permanent attraction for the public at the observation window and the need to capture and transport a sufficient number of spawners to the spawning sites. The actual trap system in use involves the handling of individual salmon in rather difficult conditions and does indeed cause increased stress to the fish. The actual transportation system by truck is too small and is poorly adapted to the increasing number of returning spawners and as such the acquisition of a new vehicle is projected in the near future. The present system necessitates numerous round trips, resulting in a situation where salmon must remain for long periods in the trap, an undesirable situation during the hot summer months. On the Jacques Cartier, modification of the dams located at Donnacona and Pont-Rouge (Bird's and McDougall) as well as to the fish-pass equipment are also projected.

However, the problem at the Dery Gorge at Pont-Rouge as well as that at Pageau's Fall at Tewkesbury still need further study which is also projected in the near future.

6.3 Biological Management

On the Dordogne, the allocation of a public hatchery at Castels (Dordogne Department) will eventually allow for an annual production of 200 000 smolt. Up to now, production levels have been very variable and low compared to the actual potential of this hatchery. Additional production of salmon fry are obtained from two other hatcheries located in the Corrèze Department, and another one in the Lot Department. Salmon smolts are also bought from a private hatchery located in the Lot Department. In 1990, additional production will be obtained from a private hatchery in Corrèze and from a rearing pond in Cantal.

Presently, fry production is inadequate (10% of actual demand, until 1989). Fry stocking is carried out mostly on the main river between Argentat and Carennac, according to a stocking plan developed from potential estimates. Recently trial fry stockings have been carried out in small tributaries which allow for easier control. The recolonizing has been carried out using at first small size fry and later with autumn parr or one year old and 2 year old smolts (Fig.3).

Since the beginning of the restoration project, eggs of different genetic sources have been imported in varying numbers. Since 1988, eggs coming from French stock have been a priority and a rearing station for spawners with a capacity of 120 fish (or 1 million eggs) has been completed by professional fishermen, Conseil Superieur de la Pêche and the Musée Aquarium de Salart.

Salmon are also bought live from professional fishermen in La Loire and are kept until spawning time, after which time they are reconditioned. These same holding tanks are also used to keep spawners that have migrated up the Dordogne river. Eventually these installations will be used as a gene bank.

Since 1985, the trapping station at Bergerac allows for controlling migrating salmon (Figure 4) as well as many other species (almost 30 species). We can note a rather

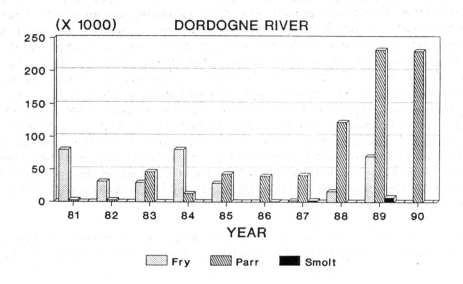

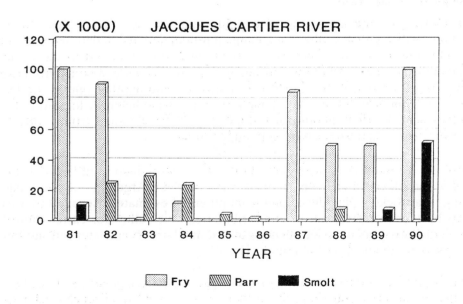

Figure 3. Atlantic salmon stocking 1981 - 1990.

small number of salmon arriving at Bergerac: on average about 25 per year and only 10 in 1989, as well as the important migration of shad (8000 between May and August 1989) and lamprey (more than 1000 for this same period). These remarkable migrations only mask the poor performance of salmon, and contribute somewhat to complacency as if this phenomenon is some sort of compensation.

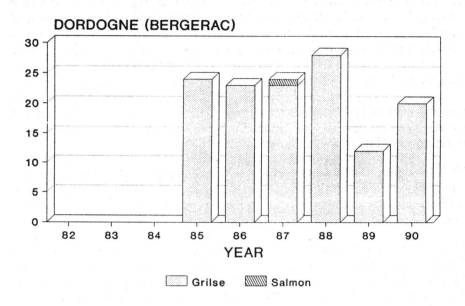

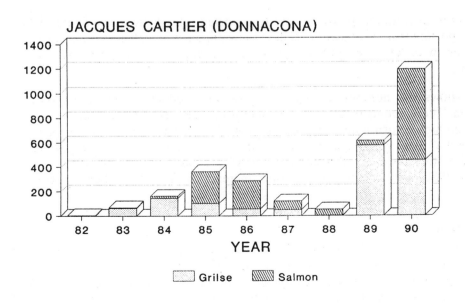

Figure 4. Adult returns in rivers.

Concerning other fish species, and in spite of some trials carried out locally with success on the protection of genetic strains of pike, the majority of managers continue, contrary to the action plan, to stock with imported fry, which entails the inherent risks of natural stock degradation, and the possible introduction of pathogenic agents.

In the case of the Jacques Cartier, the Department of Recreation, Fish and Game does not allocate any hatchery exclusively for this river and the number of available fry depends on provincial production. In effect, the fry stocking plan was adjusted in relation to provincial production between 1981 and 1989, and in every case, to much lower numbers than identified needs. Because of functional problems at the hatcheries, the real number of fry stocked has always been lower than the original number promised. In some years, the number of fish stocked was pratically zero. Moreover, the majority of fish available were small fry measuring 3 to 5 cm. Also stocked, but in smaller quantities were parr 1 + (7 to 8 cm) distributed by boat in the main river and over two years, ready to migrate smolts were also used. The stocking of fry is carried out in the principal tributaries as well as in the main river according to a general norm of 50 fish for every 100 m^2.

From 1990, for a period of 6 years, a new stocking plan has been approved whereby annual stockings will be maintained at 50 000 smolts and 100 000 fry, in addition to the use of incubators installed on various tributaries which are presently inaccessible to salmon.

The eggs initially used were from spawners captured at Tadoussac and originated from rivers along the North Coast and the Saguenay (rivers with similar conditions to those on the Jacques Cartier). Later on, fish returning to the Jacques Cartier were captured and used as early as 1985 in hatcheries for egg production (both migrating and reconditioned salmon).

Parallel to this procedure, spawners were transported principally to the Sautauriski river, an important tributary having excellent spawning sites, as well as to other sectors of the river in order to ensure adequate natural reproduction throughout the watershed.

Figure 4 shows the number of returning fish observed at the salmon pass at Donnacona. There seems to be a direct relationship between the incidence of fry stocking and high return numbers. This relationship is however not evident for the years 1989 and 1990 when over 600 and 1200 salmon respectively were captured whereas the stocking of fry was comparatively low. Natural reproduction of fish released in 1985 may explain this important increase in salmon numbers for these years.

6.4 Regulations

France, not having a national tagging programme has no such available data concerning the areas or zones where her salmon grow in the open sea. She has also not been involved in the international management of stocks. However, since 1987, fish have been marked with microtags on the Dordogne.

Concerning salmon, no precise agreement exists between the Ministère de la Mer and the Secretary of State for the Environment which inevitably, especially in the estuary and along the coast close the river's mouth, leads to confusion as well as to a lack of adequate protection, the importance of which, even though difficult to evaluate with precision because of a lack of information is believed to be considerable.

There does not seem to be any real coherence between the fishing regulations decided at the level of each Department whether it concerns exploitation methods or protection policies. Even if salmon fishing is halted in the four concerned Departments, maggot fishing in production zones still decimates the juvenile segment of the salmon population and the difference in the legal size limit for trout does not permit adequate protection for smolts. Following recommendations, maggot fishing had been prohibited in the Corrèze Department for a year, and then allowed once again because of fishermen demands. The legal limit for trout has been increased from 23 to 27cm throughout the Valley, but this decision is constantly being challenged by fishermen in most Departments (sometimes with success).

In the lower reaches of the Dordogne, and at the entry of the estuary, the different types of fishing gear that are permitted, and especially the number of fishermen who are authorized to fish, is creating important pressures on a number of fish species. The salmon, even though it is the object of ongoing research, is often captured, accidentally or not, in unknown quantities.

In 1990, the gill net fishing period for amateur fishermen with gear in the Lot Department was reduced to the period from the 7th of August to the 6th of October. Moreover, the gill net mesh size has been fixed at a maximum of 40mm in Gironde from the 1st of October to the 16th of January. Finally, the decision was taken to gradually phase out completely gill net fishing by amateurs in the Gironde Department.

The Dordogne river has been protected against new hydraulic installations, but only partially protected against physical degradation. Fish habitat is protected by law in Corrèze and in Lot.

Some sectors of the river (such as ox-bows, or areas located downstream from certain installations) have been put aside, but other vulnerable transit sites used by salmon (between Mauzac and Tuilères and downstream from Bergerac) still have no adequate protection.

Surveillance is assured principally by the Departmental Federations of AAPP who have at their disposal a small contingent of personnel supplied by C.S.P. and whose availability for the Dordogne is shared between their numerous other activities. This is especially the case in the Gironde Department where the Federation has only 4 agents. The need to increase the number of agents and the setting up of a special brigade is very evident.

On the Jacques Cartier, in addition to the general regulations presently in force in Quebec (prohibition of commercial salmon fishing in the major part of the St-Laurent Estuary, restrictions in sport fishing, daily catch limits, mandatory registration and tagging) the Department of Recreation, Fish and Game, in conjunction with the C.R.J.C. has applied the following regulations with the intent of further protecting salmon in the river as well as on certain fry production sites:

- The prohibition of fishing up to 300 downstream from the Donnacona dam from the 10th of June to the 15th of August (the period of upstream migrating salmon);

- The prohibition of fishing on the Sautauriski River where salmon spawners are released, following their transfer from the salmon pass at Donnacona;

- The prohibition of fishing on the Cachée and l'Epaule rivers situated inside the Jacques Cartier Park boundary and where fry are stocked;

- Mandatory fly-fishing between Donnacona and Pont-Rouge;

- The prohibition of fishing in the Dery Gorge.

The Department of Recreation, Fish and Game each year swears in a number of auxiliary conservation agents (up to 20) to aid the regular contingent.

Quebec also takes part in the task force of NASCO and is also involved in the international management of the salmon resource.

As we can see, in the case of the Jacques Cartier, the existing regulations are well adapted for safeguarding the salmon. They are flexible and constitute an excellent tool needed to realize the restoration of this species. The need to examine and determine the exploitation policy of the river, as well as designating a future manager for this resource, and the classification of this river for salmon are presently being studied.

6.5 Exploitation

On the Dordogne, no tangible results were obtained from the restrictions on fishing pressure in the lower reaches of the river, downstream from Bergerac and in the estuary where an important fishery (shad, lamprey, mullet) exist. The real impact of this fishery on salmon is still unknown except for several indications confirming that catches do occur by this established fishery. An extrapolation made from surveys, although somewhat disputed, does give an approximation of between 300 and 1000 salmon captured per year. Quite a lot still has to be done in this field.

Along the same lines, indications and several surveys have shown that there is a certain fishing pressure on parr (that had been stocked as fry) in the upper reaches of the Dordogne. An evaluation of the importance of these captures has still to be done.

On the Jacques Cartier, measures taken at the provincial level concerning commercial fishing (permits, quotas) has led to a notable decrease of the fishing pressure on the salmon resource. At the local level, the allocation of spawners is determined by the Department of Recreation, Fish and Game. In years of small runs, all fish are reserved for hatchery needs, or are transported to spawning sites where fishing is prohibited. In years of large runs, salmon are distributed in several river sections and the majority of grilse are released in that section of the river between Donnacona and Pont Rouge where sport fishing is permitted.

6.6 Research

6.6.1 Monitoring

On the Dordogne: based on an initial description in 1984 as well as other key points, a monitoring of the evolution of the river environment was completed. It was constantly updated over the whole length of the river by direct or indirect observations (by diving, or by boat) and transcribed on to maps. This mass of information, superimposed on the initial data allowed for the detection of changes occuring over time along the length of this waterway.

On the Jacques Cartier River, the monitoring of the river environment over time was not considered so necessary. No initial description of the Jacques Cartier was completed, nor was any effort made to amass any pertinent information. When data were eventually obtained their interpretation could not be fully appreciated since no comparison could be made with initial conditions. The monitoring of the environment is therefore only really considered when problems arise. As such, not having an adequate knowledge of the past history of the river, it is somewhat difficult to prepare for the future, and does lead to a great deal of subjectivity in the way decisions are made.

Overall monitoring of the physical environment, as well as water quality, was much more intense on the Dordogne than that on the Jacques Cartier. This monitoring was more efficient because precise descriptions were made from the start of the restoration plan.

6.6.2 Study of genetic stock

No additional information has been obtained for either river since the action plans were prepared.

6.6.3 Reproduction of threatened migratory species (shad, sturgeon)

In the case of Dordogne, for these two species, artificial spawning has been mastered, but much more research is needed when it comes to the feeding stage of the larva. Actually, reopening the dams downstream will allow the shad to increase their populations naturally. This is not the case for the sturgeon, which is now the object of complementary research under the authority of the CEMAGREF.

6.6.4 Specific salmon studies

The selection of genetic strains

The necessary equipment is in place on both rivers and rearing techniques have all but been completely mastered. The selection process has not yet begun on the Dordogne given the very few specimens available.

On the Jacques Cartier natural reproduction, without human intervention, has been favoured.

Policy and monitoring stockings

On the Dordogne, stockings are carried out mostly in the main river and fish are distributed by boat. Afterwards little control study is possible. No follow up of the stockings has been undertaken in a satisfactory manner because of the difficulties related to the size of the waterway. Only fragments of information allow us to affirm to a certain degree the survival of the fish stocked: parr have been observed in the

91

fishermen's catches in the stocked sectors. With limited means available and the absence of a satisfactory method, monitoring of the stocking results is very difficult. Recent actions have tried to improve, at the technical level as well as with the results, these monitoring difficulties.

On the Jacques Cartier, stockings are mostly carried out in the tributaries and the main river. In tributaries, surveys completed by electro-fishing allow us to affirm unequivocally the survival of the fish stocked. Because of technical difficulties with surveys on large rivers like the Dordogne, no satisfactory data could be obtained on the main Jacques Cartier River either, and partial information enables us only to affirm the survival of the fish stocked.

On the Jacques Cartier, the Department of Recreation, Fish and Game assures the monitoring of fry abundance as well as natural reproduction, which is much more important than that of the Dordogne. Most of the effort is concentrated on a few well known spawning sites and in tributaries where fry stockings are carried out. On these small tributaries, surveys with electro-fishing is easy and it is easy to evaluate fish survival, as well as the efficiency of the stocking. The stocking of tributaries was the direct result of the monitoring difficulties associated with stocking in the main channel.

Monitoring of downstream migrations
On the Dordogne, data collection is very difficult and very little is presently available. Smolt mortality registered at the turbines at Tuilières and Mauzac have been estimated at 13 and 5 percent respectively by Larinier in 1987.

Within the Jacques Cartier Park, information is collected from trout fishermen. The declarations of accidental catches of smolt by these fishermen gives a good picture of the chronology of the downstream migration.

Monitoring of upstream migration
On the Dordogne, where the number of migratory species and the large distribution in time of the different migration periods is an important problem, migrations are studied in a non exhaustive manner, based on the number of captures at the Bergerac trap. However, no appraisal is done of the actual number of spawners really present at the foot of the dam. There is also a probable negative influence on the migration due to the trap. Some indication of numbers is obtained by direct or indirect monitoring of the commercial fishing downstream. Complementary information is also obtained through the use of a video inside the fish pass at Mauzac. Today with its three dams now equipped with video control systems, the Dordogne possesses exceptional scientific apparatus for studying the different migrations.

On the Jacques Cartier, the migration, spread out over a period of two months, is evaluated based on the number of captures at the trap at the Donnacona fish-pass. The subsequent authorization of sports fishing downstream from the dam allows us to verify the presence of residual salmon below the pass.

A new problem, represented by the more and more frequent appearance of exotic Salmonidae (chinook and coho salmon, brown and rainbow trout) stocked notably in the Great Lakes Region, has arisen on the Jacques Cartier during recent years. Risk of interspecific competition with native species (Atlantic salmon and Brook trout) and the introduction of diseases and parasites are of major concern.

6.7 Economic benefits

A concise study has shown that in the French context and in the Dordogne valley in particular the direct economic benefits generated by the salmon resource should be shared between the professional freshwater fishermen and sports fishermen.

On the Jacques Cartier, based on the results of a provincial study on the economic impact of sport fishing, it is possible to evaluate the potential economic benefits that will be derived from salmon sport fishing in the valley.

6.8 Collective engagement

On the Dordogne, the Association Connaissance de la Vie Fluviale and its principal affiliate, the Aquarium Museum at Sarlat comprise the most active and dynamic group in the field of education and information related to the environment in the valley and in restoration activities. Since 1985 over 200,000 visitors have been informed of the various actions undertaken in the valley. Self financing, this association participates, with its own funds in migration research and in the production of salmon fry. This association uses these actions as a basis for developing more pedagogical activities and attractions: participation at spawning, during the transportation of salmon, open door days, etc... The Association Connaissance de la Vie Fluviale gives a regular account of the advancement of the different ongoing restoration procedures to the media. The Restoration Committee of the Dordogne River (CRRD) edits, at its own cost, in collaboration with the AAPP of Bergerac a journal called the FRY, in which different aspects of fishing and restoration in the valley are presented. This journal is circulated free of charge throughout the valley. The CRRD also organizes, in collaboration with Electricity of France an annual visit to the salmon pass at Bergerac (5,000 people have participated at these visits over the last three years).

In 1985, the Secretary of State for the Environment organized at Bergerac, a Franco-Quebec colloquium on restoration of salmon rivers, which was followed by the official twinning of the two rivers.

Presently, not all of those concerned are involved in the restoration project. In spite of the positive encouragement expressed by the many tourists who visit the valley for the restoration project, many locals remain sceptical. In the hopes of extenuating this negative opinion, a public programme regrouping the six Departments is presently being set up to deal with this problem.

In 1989, elected representatives of the valley formed MIGADO or the Association for the Restoration of Migratory Fish in the Garone and the Dordogne. They then took over the exploitation of the rearing station at Vitrac, created by the Professional Fishermen's Association and the Sarlat Aquarium Museum, and also took charge of the financial aspects of the fry production.

The Aquitaine, Midi-Pyrénées and Limousin Regions are now more involved finanically in the restoration plan, as well as the Departments Lot and Dordogne. Moreover, the CEMAGREF and the Conseil Supérieur de la Pêche have produced a brochure entitled "Welcome to Migratory Fish" which was circulated in large numbers.

On the Jacques Cartier, the very concept of the Jacques Cartier Restoration Corporation (C.R.J.C.) answered from the start the needs of all the interest groups involved in the restoration. This voluntary regrouping of elected officials, associations, user groups together constitutes an efficient concept for the integration and channeling of energies. The C.R.J.C., in order to extend this collective motivation to the general public uses different means:

- slogans: "A River For All", "A Common Pride", they convey and affirm an image of the willingness and conviction of the people of this valley to restore and to collectively take charge of their natural resource;

- a journal that disseminates information as well as the policy and goals of the Corporation throughout the whole valley;

- by pedagogical actions in schools (class discussions, activity booklets), and for the general public (information stands, conferences, posters, etc.);

- press conferences called on a regular basis by the Direction;

- mobile information activities such as a one day voluntary toll held on three bridges that span the river at various localities.

The Jacques Cartier Park, managed by the Department of Recreation, Fish and Game, is also a useful tool to reach out and instruct a vast public. This park offers a vast array of recreational and educational activities: canoeing, biking, museum films, animation, conferences, trails, and interpretation activities. Its personnel also participate with the transporting of salmon (by a special tank truck called "The salmon express"). Also during the spawning period, a special animated presentation is held concerning salmon reproduction on the Sautauriski river. On one particular day, 4000 people attended this presentation.

7. GENERAL DISCUSSION

The comparative analysis of the various actions undertaken on the two rivers brings to light fundamental differences concerning the overall decision procedures as well as the way in which things were eventually carried out.

We will try in this discussion mainly to centre on those points of each project which we believe would benefit from such a comparative analysis. The analysis that follows also tries to underline the possible improvements that can be applied to both projects.

7.1 Preliminary studies

If, indeed, both projects logically took into consideration basically the same elements of analysis, the resulting procedures reveal fundamental differences in concept.

On the Dordogne, almost all the studies that were completed were done so by the same person; human resources, as well as technical, mean the studies were nevertheless completed in an exhaustive and detailed manner in order to respond to a complex and multi-faceted situation which included, amongst other things, the protection of river habitat being destroyed by the excavation of gravel; additionnal dam projects; the restoration of several migratory fish species and river bank protection. The final document was conceived effectively as a tool for the rapid diagnoses and follow-up of future actions.

On the Jacques Cartier a minimum of key ecological information was collected for the purpose of trying to determine the most important limiting factors with regards to the restoration of salmon and to evaluate the eventual potential of this future population. The limited range of these initial studies is justifiable solely because of the fact that this project was not included in any well structured national plan and that from the start, extensive monitoring was at least undertaken.

The limitations of a policy of minimum initial investment used on the Jacques Cartier, even if in comparisons the means used (biologist, geographers, technicians, etc.) were more important than on the Dordogne because the availability of government job creation programmes are becoming more and more evident.

As such, the poorly developed historical aspect (compared with that of the Dordogne) and the limited use of photo interpretation were responsible, at least in part for not detecting the migration problems caused by Dery's Gorge and Pageau's Falls, that today necessitate new studies. The same is true in other fields (biological, hydraulic) where the need for new studies has become apparent. Unfortunately, the late acquisition of this information will not permit tracing the evolution of the river from the beginning of the programme (over 10 years ago).

For both rivers, in spite of several tentative approaches to the socio-economic aspects, geared mostly toward furnishing a positive argument for the restoration projects, for all intents and purposes, the social, economic and ethnographic aspects were hardly taken into consideration. This discrepancy is of considerable importance today in the Dordogne Valley where the involvment of the population remains low.

7.2 Operational methods

On the whole, the action plans for both rivers are comparable, that is to say that they prescribe essentialy the same actions. However, three fundamental differences do determine the evolution of each restoration process as well as the subsequent results: investment choices, regulations, and the fight against water pollution.

7.2.1 Investment choices

Up until 1985, the investment policies were the same for both rivers: the creation of a "salmon fish hatchery" in France, the use of government owned salmon facilities in Quebec; the construction of fish passes at Bergerac and at Donnacona, both equipped with trap systems.

The first returning salmon were observed on both rivers, and truck transportation systems were put in place. Whereas on the Dordogne, the priority for the construction of the fish passes at Tuilières and Mauzac was established as early as 1985 (they are built today), on the Jacques Cartier the decisions to install bypass systems at Dery's Gorge and Bird's dam are foreseeable, but not as yet formalized. These decisions have been put off until there is absolute proof that salmon will colonize the Jacques Cartier and because of the problems associated with the Dery's Gorge as well those at Pageau's Falls.

Presently, the necessary hydraulic studies have still to be undertaken, and the transportation of salmon goes on, even as the number of returning salmon increases. The crucial problem today is whether the Jacques Cartier will be considered as a river where the salmon will be able to migrate freely upstream (as in the case of the Dordogne) or will it constantly be saddled by the need to transport fish, diminishing as such the "wild" aspect of this river.

7.2.2 Regulations
Quebec has adopted the necessary regulations to assure the adequate protection of salmon once it has entered the St-Lawrence Estuary. The Jacques Cartier benefits from this favourable legal context and actual surveillance methods have proven to be sufficient to assure the protection of the migrating salmon.

Moreover, additional regulatory measures to protect the salmon once they have arrived in the Jacques Cartier river are easily adopted by the sole manager (M.L.C.P.) and have been so far well accepted by fishermen. This flexibility allows for delicate adjustments in managing the salmon runs (distribution of spawners according to spawning sites, and production zones; limitations of sport fishing zones, etc.)

On the Dordogne, the problem of salmon interception by the fisheries is not really taken into consideration: about 4,000 fishing permit holders, with all types of gear in the lower reaches of the river; and the intense maggot fishing pressure in the zones where young salmon are stocked. This phenomenon has not been well studied except for a small survey of commercial fishing (C.E.M.A.G.R.E.F.), and is possibly the reason for the low salmon returns observed at Bergerac.

Regulations on the Dordogne river also pose a problem of some consequence because of the fact that they are orientated and applied by the fishing federations in each of the four Departments concerned and that the social and biological contexts vary considerably from one Department to another. It is sometimes difficult to obtain a desired coherence.

7.2.3 Pollution
On the Jacques Cartier river, with the intention of developing a quality environment, and taking advantage of the programme offered by the Department of the Environment, whereby up to 95 percent financing of the cost could be obtained, the municipalities decided after only one meeting to treat all their waste water.

On the Dordogne, in spite of analyses that showed the mediocre, even deplorably poor quality of their water especially during the summer period, many municipalities, oblivious to this problem have not felt the need to treat their waste water, running the risk of one day losing the label "A clean river" which still is considered as a major tourist attraction for the Dordogne area. Undoubtedly a more interesting government programme (actually financing is limited to 40% of the cost) would entice more municipalities to restablish a healhier situation.

7.3 Governing and coordinating body

On the Dordogne, as on the Jacques Cartier, the situation is identical and is based on two preoccupations.

- permit and encourage multiple development all the time assuring that each development does not negatively impact on the restoration of the environment (and the salmon);

- obtain, in spite of this limitation, a grass roots involvement and maintain this motivation over time (do not create a gap between citizen and decision makers).

The first aspect is particularly evident on the Dordogne where the large number of actual and potential intervening groups, the eventual competition between them, the well guarded prerogatives of each, the absence of an established framework and the difficulty in coordinating, renders extremely difficult any coherence between actions and leads sometimes to projects that are incompatible with one another and with the salmon plan: construction of dykes for recreational purposes, dredging, motor-boating, maggot fishing, canoeing, etc.

On the Jacques Cartier, the creation of the Corporation avoided these stumbling blocks by assuring a link between each different intervening group (citizen, municipalities, governments) and coordinating the different actions. In reality, although the number of intervening groups is not as great as that on the Dordogne, the restoration project has had its share of difficulties, associated notably with a lack of communication, even coordination between those responsible. This discordance arose from many factors which included, financial difficulties, an absence of monitoring on the part of the different responsible groups and diverging perceptions of the restoration project. Presently the principle of cooperation between all groups has been clearly reaffirmed on the Jacques Cartier.

The promotion of exploiting the salmon resource constitutes an important point of diversion concerning the future management on both rivers.

On the Jacques Cartier, the restoration aims directly at promoting economic development based on the exploitation of salmon. The actual exploitation system in Quebec permits, by delegating management to associations, that the receipts from fishing rights (daily access rights) be directly reinvested in the river, or used for the functions or the development of the association.

On the Dordogne, the exploitation of salmon only results in national fishing fees that are not necessarily reinvested in the river. This inherent situation in the fishing activity in France which generates much less direct benefit at the local economy level than the Quebec system may explain the lack of motivation on the part of the population and their elected representatives for the restoration.

Moreover, the restoration of the Jacques Cartier does not hinge exclusively on the salmon. The C.R.J.C. has developed and marketed the concept of quality of life along the river (with the salmon as their emblem) on which it also promotes the tourist development of the valley. Within this framework, the various investments relating to the cleaning up of the environment have become priorities for the elected representatives.

The corporation plays an important role as a major source of information, and by promoting identifying slogans such as

- a river for all

- a challenge we can meet

- a common pride.

This notion of quality is not marketed in such an active and unanimous fashion in the Dordogne Valley.

7.4 Follow up and interpretation of results

There exist fundamental differences between the two rivers in the allocation of the amount of time and effort spent on the various aspects of each restoration project.

On the Dordogne, considerable initial energy was spent on various studies. Today the means deployed are clearly insufficient in regard to the actual needs for continuing the follow-up in an adequate manner. Inversely, on the Jacques Cartier efforts are geared principally towards carrying out an adequate follow-up as well as taking the necessary steps to reconstitute the salmon population, and organize its exploitation in the most efficient way possible.

As a consequence of these choices the Dordogne River today has at its disposal an environmental monitoring tool, whereas these precise descriptive documents are still wanting in the case of the Jacques Cartier (inadequate information on the sand deposits in the river bed, the hydraulic behaviour of certain dams, the monitoring of the various fish populations in the main river). However, considerably more effort has been spent on the Jacques Cartier for reconstituting the salmon stock.

If the numbers of observed returning salmon on the Dordogne are very low, as they have been for many years now, this very situation should in itself be cause enough to provoke those responsible to reflect on the most probable causes and the ways to remedy the situation:

- the insufficient quantity of fish stocked, and their survival in the river

- the interception of spawners during their migration.

On the other hand, the encouraging results obtained on the Jacques Cartier in regards to the number of returns, proves without doubt that the complete restoration of salmon in this river is possible. These results however should not detract from the importance of the studies that remain to be completed, nor as already stated from the possible risk that smaller than predicted salmon runs will occur and then be obliged to continue the artificialisation of the natural cycle (fry stocking and spawners transported by truck) which would inevitably tarnish the image of a "natural and wild river" that supports the Jacques Cartier project.

Moreover, the good results obtain through natural reproduction compared to the problems encountered with fry stockings, leads us to believe that the releasing of a sufficient number of salmon on the spawning sites is the most judicious choice, at least in the case of the Jacques Cartier. It seems then that in situations where quality salmon habitat is available and adequate measures are taken, notably at the level of the migration and the original genetic stock, that nature will resume its rightful place.

7.5 Comparison of approaches

In closing, it is appropriate to illustrate the procedures of a restoration project and to analyse in an overall manner the way it was applied in the French context as compared to the Quebec context.

The French approach appears more rational, at least concerning the appropriate studies and it favours the development of the restoration in a linear fashion process. The planning is more systematic, favouring as such a maximum of information with the hope of reducing the risk factor to virtually zero, all the while knowing that changes will be very difficult to make once the process has begun.

In Quebec, the approach appears more strategic. Planning is based on a notion of "calculated risk" to engage or not in an action with only a minimum of information. The follow-up is favoured and adjustments are easy to incorporate as the process develops.

Evidently, each of these approaches, generally well adapted to each particular problematic situation, as well as their social and political contexts, have their advantages and disadvantages. The French approach eliminates to a large extent the risk factor, but it's inflexibility significantly reduces the possibilities of intervening in cases where a new element is introduced or a sudden change is necessary, thereby putting in peril the completion of the restoration.

The Quebec approach, more opportunistic, allows for easy adjustments in regard to the evolution of the context or the results from monitoring, all the while stimulating continual interest in the project. However, the fact of minimizing from the start the analysis of certain problematic elements may constitute itself an important risk, as we have seen in the case of the "Dery's Gorge" and "Pageau's Falls".

Both methods would gain from being modified to a certain degree. For example, in Quebec, a more complete analysis of the principal problematic elements at the beginning would surely have avoided unwelcome surprises along the way. In France, the system should acquire more flexibility in order to facilitate the necessary adjustments.

Also, the role of the various intervening groups should be less hierarchical and become more interactive, much in the way it exists in Quebec. The number of intervening groups should also be maintained at a minimum in order to reduce the inevitable sources of conflict or interference between the different groups.

8. CONCLUSION

We conclude this report by reiterating the necessity, in a restoration plan of always keeping in mind certain concepts which will ensure the success of the project.

- time:

    The life cycle of salmon is spread out over several years, a restoration plan can only be undertaken on a long term basis (10 years) and it must adapt to the requirements of the fish (the opposite is not possible). It is also necessary to maintain over a long period, popular interest as well as the implication and cooperation of the different intervening groups, and at the same time, channeling their efforts in the same direction.

- people:

    A restoration plan cannot be realized without the local population and their elected representatives being concerned and feeling involved. Every restoration project should be based on the pride of realizing a collective challenge.

- means:

    In order to succeed in an acceptable time frame, it is indispensable that the restoration project be given the minimum of necessary means without which it would be unavoidably doomed to failure, and forgotten.

The restoration of the two rivers, Dordogne and Jacques Cartier is technically possible and the application of the three preceeding concepts can only be based on one thing: an expressed collective willingness.

May this document help the cause of these two superb rivers and that of any other project that is looking for some inspiration from past experiences.

BIBLIOGRAPHY ON THE JACQUES CARTIER RIVER

Alain, J. (1985). Plan quinquennal de fonctionnement. Corporation de restauration de la Jacques Cartier (document de régie interne), 19 p. + annexes.

Beaurivage, M. (1985). Inventaire de cours d'eau en période d'étiage estivale pour le choix d'un site d'un centre de reconditionnement des saumons noirs. Corporation de restauration de la Jacques Cartier, 21p.

Beaurivage, M. (1985). Planification du projet d'un centre de reconditionnement des saumons noirs. Corporation de restauration de la Jacques Cartier (document de régie interne), 93p.

Beaurivage, M. (1985). Résultats de la capture du Saumon de l'Atlantique de la rivière Jacques Cartier à la passe migratoire de Donnacona. Corporation de restauration de la Jacques Cartier, 19p.

Beaurivage, M. (1986). Résultats de la capture du Saumon Atlantique (*Salmo salar*) dans la rivière Jacques Cartier à la passe migratoire de Donnacona, saison 1986. Corporation de restauration de la Jacques Cartier, 57p.

Beaurivage, M. (1986). Evaluation préliminaire d'une ferme piscicole située en bordure de la rivière Cachée, à Stoneham. Corporation de restauration de la Jacques Cartier, 30p.

Beaurivage, M. (1986). Inventaire de cours d'eau le long de la rivière Jacques Cartier en fonction de l'établissement d'un centre de reconditionnement des saumons noirs et/ou d'un centre de recherche. Corporation de restauration de la Jacques Cartier (document de régie interne), 61p.

Beaurivage, M. (1987). Etude du comportement migratoire du Saumon Atlantique par télémétrie, aux rapides Déry et au barrage Bird sur la rivière Jacques Cartier. Corporation de restauration de la Jacques Cartier et Ministère du Loisir, de la Chasse et de la Pêche, 84p.

Bedard, L. (1986). Réglementation municipale en vigueur le long de la rivière Jacques Cartier. Corporation de restauration de la Jacques Cartier (document de régie interne), 17p.

Boivin, J. (1981). Inventaire ichtyologique par pêche à l'électricité, de cinq affluents de la rivière Jacques Cartier, en 1981. Ministère du Loisir, de la Chasse et de la Pêche, Service de l'aménagement et de l'exploitation de la faune, Québec, 19p. Rapport d'étape #1.

Boivin, J. (1982). Inventaire ichtyologique par pêche à l'électricité, de trois affluents de la rivière Jacques Cartier, en 1982. Ministère du Loisir, de la Chasse et de la Pêche, Service de l'aménagement et de l'exploitation de la faune, Québec, 19p. Rapport d'étape #2.

Boivin, J. & Georges, S. (1984). Prévision de retour en rivière des saumons atlantiques ensemencés dans le bassin hydrographique de la rivière Jacques Cartier, dans le cadre du projet de restauration. Ministère du Loisir, de la Chasse et de la Pêche, Service de l'aménagement et de l'exploitation de la faune, Québec, 15p. Rapport d'étape #5.

Boivin, J. (1984). Suivi des ensemencements du saumon atlantique dans trois affluents de la rivière Jacques Cartier, saison 1983 Ministère du Loisir, de la Chasse et de la Pêche, Service de l'aménagement et de l'exploitation de la faune, Québec, 21p. Rapport d'étape #6.

Boudreault, A. (1986). Potentiel salmonicole du bassin de la rivière Jacques Cartier, et caractéristiques des fosses à saumon sur le cours principal. Mandat réalisé par la firme Gilles Shooner et Associés. 22p. + 3 annexes.

Boutet, A. (1985). Eléments de repérage de la présence historique du saumon dans la rivière Jacques Cartier. Corporation de restauration de la Jacques Cartier (document de régie interne), 5p.

Cadoret, L. (1985). Mise en valeur du potentiel récréatif des rivières Sainte-Anne et Jacques Cartier. Université Laval, Québec, 149p.

Carriere, L. (1980). Etude biophysique de la rivière Jacques Cartier. Corporation de restauration de la Jacques Cartier (document de régie intern), 189p.

Chiasson, M. (1986). Schéma d'aménagement de la M.R.C. de la Jacques Cartier. 71p. (vol.1) et 81p. (vol.2) + annexes.

Côté, Y. (1976). Faune du Québec, brochure no 12. Le saumon, M.T.C.P. 1976.

Côté, Y. (1978). Inventaire des habitats à saumon et estimation de production par photographie aérienne. Ministère du Loisir, de la Chasse et de la Pêche, 12p.

Côté, Y. (1987). Essai de classification normalisée des substrats granulaires et des faciès d'écoulement pour l'évaluation de la protection salmonicole. Ministère du Loisir, de la Chasse et de la Pêche, 10p.

Côté, Y. & Gonthier, S. (1986). Colloque sur l'élevage et l'ensemencement du Saumon Atlantique. Ministère du Loisir, de la Chasse et de la Pêche, Québec, 324p.

Diguer, F. (1981). Etude socio-économique du bassin hydrographique de la rivière Jacques Cartier. Corporation de restauration de la Jacques Cartier (document de régie interne), 178p.

Diguer, F. (1982). Propositions préliminaires d'aménagement de la Jacques Cartier. Corporation de restauration de la Jacques Cartier (document de régie interne), 153p.

Dulude, P. & Vallieres, A. (1986). La réintroduction du Saumon atlantique dans la rivière Jacques Cartier: un premier bilan 1979-1985. Ministère du Loisir, de la Chasse et de la Pêche, 28p.

Frenette, M. (1987). Rapport de mission en France sur le projet de jumelage des rivières Dordogne en France et Jacques Cartier au Québec. Corporation de restauration de la Jacques Cartier (document de régie interne), 46p.

Frenette, M., Dulude, P. & Beaurivage, M. (1986). La restauration de la Jacques Cartier: un défi majeur et une fierté collective. Troisième symposium international du Saumon atlantique tenu à Biarritz en 1986. Corporation de restauration de la Jacques Cartier (document de régie interne), 28p.

Gagnon, R. (1984). La pêche récréative au saumon en 1981. Ministère du Loisir, de la Chasse et de la Pêche (Direction de l'analyse et de la recherche socio-économique), 66p.

Genois, L. (1978). Inventaire faunique de la vallée de la Jacques Cartier. Rapport annuel 1977-1978: section de l'animation de plein air. Ministère du Loisir, de la Chasse et de la Pêche, Service des parcs et du plein air, Québec, 31p.

Georges, S. (1982). Résultats des recaptures des saumoneaux ensemencés dans la rivière Jacques Cartier 1981-1982. Ministère du Loisir, de la Chasse et de la Pêche,

Service de l'aménagement et de l'exploitation de la faune, Québec, 11p. Rapport d'étape #3.

Georges, S. (1982). Résultats préliminaires de la localisation et la classification des fosses potentielles de Saumon de l'Atlantique, dans la rivière Jacques Cartier. Ministère du Loisir, de la Chasse et de la Pêche, Service de l'aménagement et de l'exploitation de la faune, Québec, 5p. Rapport d'étape #4.

Georges, S. (1984). Commentaires sur le rapport préparé par les consultants Pluritec intutilé: évaluation de la situation du saumon dans le cours inférieur de la Jacques Cartier. Ministère du Loisir, de la Chasse et de la Pêche, 14p.

Georges, S. & Brisebois, J.-L. (1984). Résultats de la capture de saumons atlantiques à l'embouchure de la rivière Jacques Cartier, saison 1983. Ministère du Loisir, de la Chasse et de la Pêche, Service de l'aménagement et de l'exploitation de la faune, Québec, 15p. Rapport d'étape #7.

Germain, H. (1984). Historique et inventaire du potentiel culturel et patrimonial du bassin hydrographique de la Jacques Cartier. Corporation Bibliothèque Nationale de Québec, 238p.

Groupe de Travail de la Rivière Jacques Cartier. (1979). Avant-projet de restauration de saumon dans la rivière Jacques Cartier. Direction régionale du Québec, Direction de la recherche faunique, Comité de restauration de la rivière Jacques Cartier, 64p.

Hydrotech Inc. (1986). Hydrologie de la rivière Jacques Cartier, 36p.

Lacasse, M. (1981). Le loisir relié à l'utilisation de la faune au Québec. Direction générale de la faune. Ministère du Loisir, de la Chasse et de la Pêche, 321p.

Landry, J. (1987). Schéma d'aménagement de la M.R.C. de Portneuf - Version de consultation. 253p.

Le Rouzes, G. (1979). Plan directeur de la vallée de Jacques Cartier: dossier d'inventaire (Principales composantes biophysiques du territoire-partie A). Ministère du Loisir, de la Chasse et de la Pêche, 153p.

Le Rouzes, G. & Berube, P. (1987). La qualité de l'eau de la Jacques Cartier. Ministère du Loisir, de la Chasse et de la Pêche, Direction régionale de Québec, 8p.

McGain, A. & Taillon, H. (1986). Etude de potentiel archéologique (vallée de la rivière Jacques Cartier) Corporation de restauration de la Jacques Cartier (document de régie interne). 172p. (vol.1) + 56 figures (vol.2).

Marcotte, G. (1984). Résultat de la capture de saumon atlantique à l'embouchure de la rivière Jacques Cartier: saison 1984. Etude bio-practo II. Corporation de restauration de la Jacques Cartier, 66p.

Menviq. (1986). Réseau-rivières 1979-1985; la Jacques Cartier. Compilation de données informatisées.

Ministere du Loisir, de la Chasse et de la Pêche. (1987). Réseau de rivières du patrimoine canadien: mise en nomination de la rivière Jacques Cartier. 28p.

Morneau, F. (1986). Cadre éco-géomorphologique du corridor fluvial de la rivière Jacques Cartier entre Donnacona et la rivière Caché. Corporation, 67p. + annexes.

Nettle, R. (1857). The Salmon fisheries of the Saint-Lawrence and its tributaries. Montréal, J. Lowell (ed.) 144p.

Paradis, H. & Saint-Michel, L. (1986). Analyse synthèse de la rivière Jacques Cartier (tronçon Sainte-Catherine-Tewkesbury). Corporation de restauration de la Jacques Cartier (document de régie interne), 10p. + cartes.

Piuze, H. (1985). Analyse synthèse de la rivière Jacques Cartier (tronçon Donnacona-Sainte-Catherine). Corporation de restauration de la Jacques Cartier (document de régie interne), 12p. + cartes (vol.2).

Repertoire des Municipalites du Québec, Edition 1987.

Sainte-Marie, L. (1983). Etude bio-practo 1. Corporation de restauration de la rivière Jacques Cartier (document de régie interne), 33pp. + 6 annexes.

Tremblay, D. (1987). Résultats de la capture du saumon atlantique (*Salmo salar*) dans la rivière Jacques Cartier à la passe migratoire de Donnacona. Corporation de restauration de la Jacques Cartier, 16p.

Vallieres, A. (1984). Résultats de la capture du saumon atlantique à l'embouchure de la rivière Jacques Cartier: saison 1984. Ministère du Loisir, de la Chasse et de la Pêche, Service de l'aménagement de la faune, Québec, 24p. Rapport d'étape #9.

Vallieres, A. & Pelletier, S. (1984). Analyse et interprétation de la lecture des écailles des saumons atlantiques (*Salmo salar*) de retour de la rivière Jacques Cartier, saison 1983. Ministère du Loisir, de la Chasse et de la Pêche, Service de l'aménagement et de l'exploitation de la faune, Québec, 12p. Rapport d'étape #8.

Vallieres, A. & Dulude, P. (1986). Travaux réalisés en 1985, dans le cadre du programme de restauration du saumon atlantique dans la rivière Jacques Cartier. Ministère du Loisir, de la Chasse et de la Pêche, Service de l'aménagement et de l'exploitation de la faune, Québec, 67p.

Vallieres, A. & Pelletier, S. (1986). Inventaire aérien des sites de frai du saumon atlantique (*Salmo salar*) dans le bassin de la rivière Jacques Cartier, Octobre 1985. Ministère du Loisir, de la Chasse et de la Pêche, Service de l'aménagement et de l'exploitation de la faune, Québec, 11p. Rapport d'étape #11.

Vallieres, A. (1987). Inventaire ichtyologique par pêche à l'électricité du bassin hydrographique de la rivière Jacues-Cartier. Ministère du Loisir, de la Chasse et de la Pêche, Service de l'aménagement et de l'exploitation de la faune, Québec, 23p.

Vallieres, A. (1987). Implantation d'oeufs de saumon atlantique (*Salmo salar*) au moyen d'une planteuse hydraulique dans la rivière à l'Epaule. Ministère du Loisir, de la Chasse et de la Pêche, Service de l'aménagement et de l'exploitation de la faune, Québec, 12p.

Vallieres, A. & Dulude, P. (1987). Travaux réalisés en 1986, dans le cadre du programme de restauration du saumon atlantique dans la rivière Jacques Cartier. Ministère du Loisir, de la Chasse et de la Pêche, Service de l'aménagement et de l'exploitation de la faune, Québec, 52p.

Vallieres, A. & Dulude, P. (1988). Travaux réalisés en 1987, dans le cadre du programme de restauration du saumon atlantique dans la rivière Jacques Cartier. Ministère du Loisir, de la Chasse et de la Pêche, Service de l'aménagement et de l'exploitation de la faune, Québec, 35p.

Vallieres, A. & Dulude, P. (1988). Introduction de saumons atlantiques à des fins de reproduction naturelle dans la rivière à l'Epaule, bassin de la rivière Jacques Cartier, en 1986-87. Ministère du Loisir, de la Chasse et de la Pêche, Service de l'aménagement et de l'exploitation de la faune, Québec, 26p.

BIBLIOGRAPHY ON THE RIVER DORDOGNE

Agence Financiere de Bassin Adour Garonne. (1978). Note sur la Consultation d'Electricité de France pour la régularisation saisonnière et journalière des débits de la Dordogne, à partir des réservoirs hydro-électriques, 6p.

A.F.B.A.G. (1977). Préparation des objectifs de qualité des eaux superficielles - bassin de la Dordogne.

A.F.B.A.G. (1975). Le Bassin de la Dordogne. Présentation géo-économique - approache des problèmes de l'eau. 41p.

Beldin, D.L. (1934). The spawning habits of the Atlantic Salmon. Transactions of the American Fisheries Society, vol.64, 211-218p.

Bethemont, J. (1977). De l'eau et des hommes, Paris, Bordas Etudes 280p.

Bouchard, B. & Clavel, C. (1978). Incidences des extractions de matériaux alluvionnaires et de l'aménagement des cours d'eau sur l'écosystème aquatique. Rapport de synthèse 1974-1978, Univ. de Clermont II, 13p.

Bousquet, B. (1979). Biologie et migration des smolts de saumon atlantique (*Salmo salar* L.) dans les bassins Loire-Allier et Adour-Gave d'Oloron. Thèse 3ème cycle I.N.T.P.

Bovee, K.D. (1978). The incremental method of assessing habitat potential for coldwater species, with management implications. American Fisheries Society, Special Publication no 11, 340-346p.

Bovee, K.D.: Probability of use criteria for the family salmonidae. Instream Flow Information paper no 4.

Bovee, K.D., & Milhous, R. (1978). Hydraulic simulation in instream flow studies. Theory and techniques. Cooperative Instream flow service group. 2625 Redwing Road, Fort Collins, Colorado 80526, 131p.

Burner, (1951). Characteristics of spawning nests of Columbia river Salmon. U.S.Fish and Wildlife Service, Bulletin, Vol.52, no 61, 91-110p.

Canyrt, M.A. (1976). Etude de la production et la qualité des jeunes saumons atlantiques (*Salmo salar* L.) de repeuplement élevés dans différents milieux. Thèse 3éme cycle, Biol. Anim. Univ. Toulouse, 126p.

Carter, W.M. (1968). Le saumon de l'atlantique du Québec. Ministère du Tourisme, de la Chasse et de la Pêche du Québec, 236p.

Cecpi, (1964 à 1976). Critères de qualité des eaux pour les poissons d'eau douce européen.

Cemagref Bordeaux, (1981). Etude hydrobiologique de la Dordogne. Etude no 3265p. Centre d'étude du machinisme agricole du génie rural et des eaux et forêts.

Document F.A.O. (1964 à 1976).Food and Agriculture Organization of the United Nation, CECPI, 1964.

Champigneulle, A. (1978). Caractéristiques de l'habitat piscicole et de la population de juvéniles sauvages de saumon atlantique (*Salmo salar* L.) sur le cours principal du Scorff (Morbihan). Thèse 3éme cycle. Univ. de Rennes.

Clavet, D. (1980). Approche géomorphologique dans la détermination du potentiel c'accueil salmonicole des rivières des principales régions physiographiques du Québec. Rapport no 52-53. Univ. de Sherbrooke, Québec.

Descamp, H. & Capblancq, J. (1988). Recherches sur le bassin Lot-Dordogne et herbier d'Argentat. C.N.R.S., Service de la carte de la végétation, Univ. P. Sabatier, Toulouse, 42p.

Dhomps, M. (1982). Etude comparative des herbiers de la Dordogne, entre Souillac et Siorac. Rapport I.B.D.

Dumas, J. (1978). L'élevage intensif des peunes saumons atlantiques de repeuplement. Bull. Scient. et Tech. I.N.R.A., 20p.

Dumas, J. (1980). La production extensive de juvéniles de saumon atlantique (*Salmo salar* L.) en lacs et étangs. *In* R.Billard, la Pisciculture en Etang, I.N.R.A. Paris 1908, 343-352p.

Dumas,J. (1981). Production extensive de jeunes saumons atlantiques (*Salmo salar* L.) d'un an,dans l'étang du Boucheron (Corrèze). Bulletin Français Pisciculture no 282 (3éme trim. 1981) 8p.

Dumas, J. (1981). Le programme de restauration du saumon dans la Dordogne: débuts prometteurs, 10p.

Dussart, B. (1979). Principes et applications de l'écologie. Théme Vuibert, Université, Série Biblogique, 2 vol., 100p.

Eaux et Forêts, (1975). Pêche fluviale, réglementation (1.2.75), 103p.

Gerking, S.D. (1953). Evidence for the concepts of home range and territory in stream fishes. Ecology, 34, 347. 65. 343-4.

Gibson, R.J. & Côté, Y. (1982). Production de saumoneaux et recapture de saumons adultes étiquetés à la rivière Matamec, Côte Nord, Golfe du Saint-Laurent. Québec. Naturaliste can. (Rev. Eccl. Syst.) 109: 13-25p.

Huet, M. & Timmermans, J.A. (1976). Influence sur les populations de poissons des aménagements hydrauliques de petits cours d'eau assez rapides. Trav. Stat. Rech. Eaux et Forêts, sér. D, n° 46, 27p.

Lamontagne, M.P. & Gauthier, J.P. (1972). Etude limnologique du lac de l'Achigan. Rapport Ministère des Richesses Naturelles du Québec, Service qualité des eaux, 65p.

Larinier, M. (1977). Les passes à poissons. C.T.G.R.E.F., Groupement d'Antony. Division: Qualité des eaux, pêche et pisciculture. Etude No 16, Paris, 136p.

Larinier, M. & Dartiguelongue, J. (1989). Bulletin Français de la Pêche et de la Pisciculture, numéro spécial 312.313, 1er et 2ème trimestre 89. Gestion des ressources aquatiques. Editeur: Conseil Supérieur de la Pêche.

Leopold, L. & Langbein, W. (1981). Les méandres des rivières: Les phénomènes naturels. Bibliothèque pour la science, diff. Belin.

Mathieu, B. (1979). La faune hyporheique - Ecophysiologie de la faune interstitielle hyporheique. Rapport D.E.A., 62p.

Milhous, R., Wegner, D. & Waddle, T. (1981). Users - Guide to the physical Habitat Simulation System. Cocp. inst. Flow. Serv. Group. US. Dept. of interior Washington, D.C., 20240.

Nisbet, M. & Verneaux, J. (1970). Composantes chimiques des eaux courantes: discussion et proposition de classes en tant que bases d'interprétation des analyses chimiques. Annales de Limnologie, 6 (2).

Peterson, R.H., Spinney, H.C.E. & Sreedharan, A. (1977). Development of atlantic salmon *(Salmo salar)* eggs and alevins under varied temperature regimes. Journal of the Fisheries Research Board of Canada 34: 31-43p.

Provencher, M. & Lamontagne, M.P. (1977). Méthode de détermination d'un indice d'appréciation de la qualité des eaux selon différentes utilisations. Rapport Ministère des Richesses naturelles service qualité des eaux. 225p.

Pustelnik, G. (1977). Contribution à la rationalisation de la description de l'habitat aquatique. Rapport D.E.S.S. Univ. Granche-Comté, 22p.

Pustelnik, G. (1979). Etude cartographique des herbiers de la Dordogne, entre Argentat et Mauzac. I.B.D., C.S.P., 15p. + ann.

Pustelnik, G. (1980). Caractéristiques générales de la vie piscicole dans la rivière Dordogne, 10p.

Pustelnik, G. (1980). Caractéristiques générales de la vie piscicole dans la rivière Dordogne, rapport I.B.D., 5p.

Pustelnik, G. (1981). Les saumons de la rivière Dordogne 1891-1981. Rapport Secrétariat d'Etat chargé de l'Environnement, 50p.

Pustelnik, G. (1982). Les saumons de la rivière Dordogne. Rapport Secrétariat d'Etat chargé l'Environnement, 54p.

Pustelnik, G. (1984). Hydrobiologie de la rivière Dordogne. Rapport Secrétariat d'Etat chargé de l'Environnement. Document Synthèse, 186p.

Pustelnik, G. (1984). Hydrobiologie de la rivière Dordogne. Cartographie écologique. Rapport Secrétariat d'Etat chargé de l'Environnement. Départment Corrèze, 56p. - Départment Lot, 67p. - Départment Dordogne, 68p. - Départment Gironde 42p.

Pustelnik, G. (1987). Etude écologique préalable à l'aménagement piscicole de la rivière Dordogne. Thèse 3éme cycle. Bordeaux III. 104p.

Rebouillat, J.-P. (1979). Données sédimentologiques sur les alluvions du lit mineur de la Dordogne, entre Brivezac et Pessac. Rapport Secrétariat d'Etat chargé de l'Environnement, I.B.D. Sarlat, 22p.

Roux, A.L. (1982). Cartographie polythématique appliquée à la gestion écologique des eaux. Ed. C.N.R.S. 112p.

Tinel, C. (1983). Eléments pour la réintroduction du saumon atlantique dans la rivière Dordogne. Thése Ingénieur. E.N.S.A.T. 69p.

Vibert, R. & Lagler, K.F. (1981). Pêches continentales, Biologie et aménagement. Dunod ed. 719p.

RESTORATION OF THE RIVER TAFF, WALES

G.W. MAWLE

National Rivers Authority: Welsh Region

1. INTRODUCTION

Over the past three decades, changes in industrial activity and increased pollution control have resulted in improvements in the quality of rivers in south-east Wales, U.K. Consequently the rivers are once again becoming suitable for migratory salmonids. This paper describes the strategy adopted for the rehabilitation of salmon (*Salmo salar* L.) on one river, the Taff, as an example of the work proposed or underway on several rivers in the area by the National Rivers Authority (N.R.A.). Although the paper concentrates on salmon, many of the comments apply also to sea trout (*Salmo trutta* L.).

2. THE CATCHMENT

The Taff is the largest of the three rivers which enter the Severn Estuary at Cardiff, the capital of Wales (Fig.1). It is short and steep, falling about 600 metres along its 60 kilometre length. Flows are highly variable, ranging during the last twenty years from 1.6 cumecs in extreme summer drought to 642 cumecs in winter floods: the median flow is 11 cumecs.

Iron and subsequently coal and steel industries were developed in the catchment during the 18th and 19th centuries. By 1921 there were 149 collieries operating in the catchment (Williams 1984), many in the headwaters of the Taff's tributaries. Heavy industry has since declined, but the catchment remains densely populated. Due to the steepness of the valleys, housing and industry extend in a ribbon development along the banks of the Taff and its tributaries (Fig.1). About 400,000 people live within the catchment, one eighth of the Welsh population. Many of the headwaters in remaining rural areas have been impounded for water supply.

3. HISTORY OF THE SALMON POPULATIONS

Prior to industrial development, the Taff had prolific runs of both salmon and sea trout supporting a variety of commercial fisheries (Mawle *et al*, 1985). However, by the time of the 1860 Commission into Salmon Fisheries in England and Wales (Anon 1860) the runs of salmon had been destroyed. The causes appear to have been the combined effects of overfishing, abstraction, obstructions to migration and pollution.

Over the next century salmon were rarely recorded in the Taff, which remained grossly polluted and ran black with coal solids for much of its length. Surveys in 1969 (Edwards *et al*, 1972) and 1978 (Winstone, 1978) found little evidence of salmonids in the middle or lower reaches although brown trout were present in the upper river.

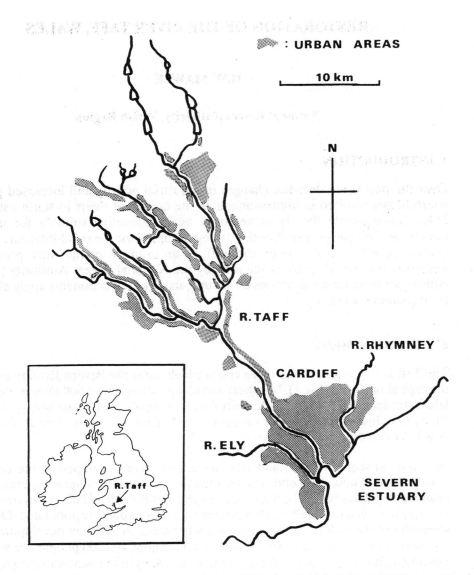

Figure 1. The Taff system showing its position within the British Isles and the extent of urban development within the catchment.

By the early 1980's, there had been major improvements in the water quality of the lower reaches due to economic recession and improved pollution control. It soon became evident from observations of fish at weirs, electrofishing surveys and anglers' catches that each year scores of sea trout and some salmon were once again entering the lowest reaches of the river in Cardiff (Mawle *et al*, 1985). The capture of a few juvenile salmon also indicated limited reproduction within the river.

In 1984, the NRA's predecessor (Welsh Water Authority) decided to assess the feasibility of further developing the salmon population and the associated fishery in the Taff.

4. FACTORS LIMITING REHABILITATION

Following reviews of the available information (Williams, 1984; Winstone, 1984), the Authority surveyed the catchment in detail to identify more closely the factors limiting development of the salmon population as part of a wider plan for management of the catchment (Bent *et al*, 1985). The investigation included water quality (Thomas *et al*, 1986), macroinvertebrate communities (Bent *et al*, 1986), fish distribution (Brown *et al*, 1986) and salmonid egg survival experiments (Brown *et al*, 1988).

Given the objective for rehabilitation on the Taff, i.e.

> to extend the migratory salmonid fishery into the larger tributaries and the main river downstream of the reservoirs with stocks being supported wholly or at least partly by natural reproduction,

the information collected in 1985 indicated that the following factors were likely to limit development of the population.

4.1 Pollution

Although greatly improved, water quality was still poor over much of the catchment. The main pollutants were suspended solids, ammonia and organic loadings (Table 1. Fig. 2). Their impact was firstly to limit the possible spawning and nursery area. Egg planting experiments indicated that successful spawning was likely to be confined to the upper reaches (Fig.2). In addition, poor water quality might inhibit or prevent salmon migration to the from the nursery areas (Thomas *et al*, 1986).

Table 1. The main sources of pollution in the Taff in 1985.

POLLUTANT	MAIN SOURCES
Suspended solids	Coal washeries
Ammonia	Smokeless Fuel Plant, sewerage system
Organic loading	Sewerage system, Gelatin factory

4.2 Obstructions

Five weirs on the main river are major obstructions for the upstream migration of adults, the four nearest the sea preventing access to any of the spawning areas (Fig.3). In addition, there are culverts and weirs on some of the tributaries.

Aside from the problems of chronic pollution, there is also concern about intermittent pollution caused by spillages of toxic chemicals or by failure of effluent treatment plants or the sewage system. Due to the urban and industrial nature of the catchment, such incidents may occur virtually anywhere. However, although there may be occasional fish kills, if fish are well distributed stocks are unlikely to be eradicated, particularly since at any one time part of the population will be at sea.

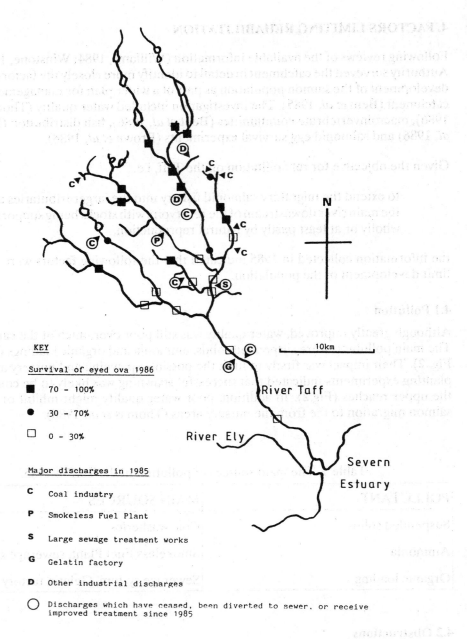

KEY

Survival of eyed ova 1986

■   70 - 100%

●   30 - 70%

□   0 - 30%

Major discharges in 1985

C   Coal industry

P   Smokeless Fuel Plant

S   Large sewage treatment works

G   Gelatin factory

D   Other industrial discharges

◯   Discharges which have ceased, been diverted to sewer, or receive improved treatment since 1985

Figure 2. The Taff system showing (i) the survival of eyed ova of brown trout (Salmo trutta L.) planted in egg boxes in 1986 (ii) the major discharges to the river in 1985, indicating where the discharges have since been changed, (adapted from Brown et al 1988).

4.3 Exploitation

The proximity of half a million people to the river means that stocks may be over-exploited, whether by legal or illegal means. There was evidence even in the early 1980s that salmon were being illegally taken in the sea off Cardiff by driftnets ostensibly used for sea fish. Fixed nets were also being set on the foreshore within and close to Cardiff Bay. Judging by activity off the nearby River Usk, such fisheries were considered likely to expand if Taff stocks increased.

In the lower reaches, angling pressure had increased from virtually nothing in the 1970s, particularly as the coarse fishery had also shown signs of improvement. Although the fishing rights are leased by angling clubs in Cardiff, there was little control and many anglers considered the fishing a free-for-all, giving little heed to regulations.

The urban development over much of the upper reaches means that the illegal removal of spawning adults, which are particularly vulnerable, is likely to be extensive.

4.4 Speed of recolonisation

The majority of salmon are thought to return to spawn in their native river (Mills, 1989). Tagging studies (Swain, 1982) show that some straying occurs. The capture of juvenile salmon in the Taff (Mawle *et al*, 1985) indicates that at least some strays remain to spawn. Nevertheless, unless straying is extensive, full recolonisation of the Taff by salmon is likely to take several generations, even assuming a low exploitation rate and free access to and from the nursery areas.

4.5 Future developments - Cardiff Bay Barrage

Subsequent to the studies in 1985, the local county council promoted the idea of constructing a barrage across Cardiff Bay for amenity purposes. The barrage would impound the rivers Taff and Ely and totally exclude the tide (Fig.3).

Such a development could impair or prevent the full rehabilitation of the salmon population. Possible effects include physical obstruction to migration and mortality of migrants due to the potentially poor quality of impounded water.

5. RATIONALE

The rationale for rehabilitation of the salmon population has two dimensions. Firstly, the regeneration of a fishery for migratory salmonids would enhance facilities for angling in an area where access to such fisheries is both limited and expensive.

Secondly, and perhaps more importantly, the return of salmon to the Taff is considered to have significant conservation value. Salmon are symbols of clean water. A breeding population of salmon in the Taff, so grossly polluted for so long, would be the clearest demonstration of its improved quality. It seems likely that most people value improvements in their local environment more highly than similar changes elsewhere. The Taff is part of the local environment for about half a million people. In addition, it might be considered to be the capital river of Wales. As the Thames is to London, so the Taff is to Cardiff. Though difficult to quantify, these factors suggest that the return of salmon to the Taff is likely to be highly valued by the local and Welsh populations, regardless of any fishery.

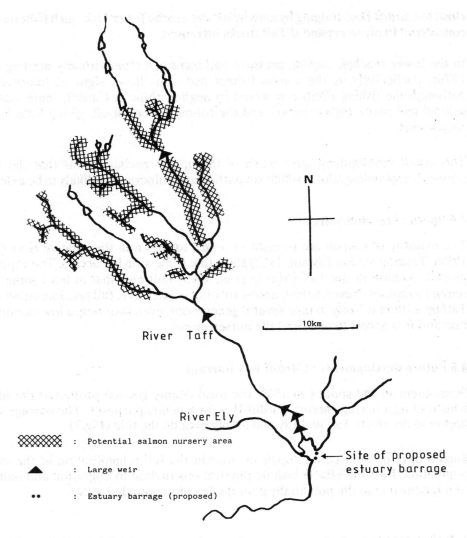

N

River Taff

10km

River Ely

▨▨▨▨▨ : Potential salmon nursery area

▲ : Large weir

•• : Estuary barrage (proposed)

Site of proposed
estuary barrage

*Figure 3. Potential salmon spawning and nursery areas in the Taff system
identified in 1985/6, showing the positions of four large weirs and the
site of the proposed estuary barrage.*

6. STRATEGY FOR REHABILITATION

6.1 Pollution control

Water quality is considered the primary constraint on the potential nursery area available. About 84 hectares of river were considered good or moderate nursery area based on the 1985 data (Fig.3). Given full utilisation, it is estimated that between 15,000 and 30,000 salmon or sea trout smolts could be produced annually, generating a run of between 350 and 750 adult salmon, depending on the balance between salmon and sea trout (Table 2). Improvements in water quality were considered desirable to realise the full potential of these areas. Tentative standards to be achieved for water quality in the nursery areas have been defined by both chemical standards and the macroinvertebrate communities present (Table 3).

Improvements in water quality were also considered necessary to safeguard the passage of adults and smolts to and from the nursery areas (Humphrey 1986). An appropriate criterion for safe passage was considered to be water quality meeting NWC Class 2 (Table 3). Achieving this standard throughout the middle and lower reaches should also permit limited smolt production in this area where a further 73 hectares of potential nursery area is available. Even a productivity of 100 smolts per hectare would generate 7300 smolts per year increasing potential smolt production in the catchment by between 25 and 50 per cent.

Increased powers under the Control of Pollution Act 1974 and the Water Act 1989 have permitted greater control over pollution. In addition there has been a further contraction of the coal industry in the catchment. As a result many of the worst effluents identified in 1985 have been diverted into the sewerage system, receive improved treatment or have ceased (Fig.2).

The beneficial impact of these changes is being assessed in 1990 by a detailed survey of chemical water quality and macroinvertebrate communities. Further egg survival experiments in the middle and lower reaches are planned for 1990/91.

Table 2. Estimation of the potential salmon and sea trout production of the
Taff based on the amount of suitable sursery area in 1985.

	ESTIMATE
Good/ moderate nursery area 1985	84ha
Potential average productivity	165-350 smolts ha^{-1} yr^{-1}
Potential production	14,000 - 30,000 smolts yr^{-1}
Assuming: (i) a ratio of 4 adult sea trout: 1 adult salmon (ii) 25% of adult sea trout are repeat spawners (iii) survival from smolt to returning adult is 5% for salmon and 15% for sea trout	
Potential average adult run	350 - 750 salmon yr^{-1} 1400 - 3000 sea trout yr^{-1}

6.2 Fish Passes

Fish passes have been constructed or are proposed for the four weirs nearest the sea. At least 65 hectares of good or moderate nursery area should be accessible to adult fish. The combined cost of these passes is estimated to be £180,000.

Table 3. Tentative Environmental Quality Standards (EQS) for potential
salmon nursery areas and the river downstream through which smolts
and adults migrate.

	EQS
Spawning and nursery area:	(i) Compliance with the European Community's Directive for Freshwater fish = salmonids.
	(ii) Support benthic macroinvertebrate communities intolerant of pollution ie. Groups I and II (Bent *et al* 1986).
Migration Zone:	Water samples comply with National Water council water quality class 2. ie. (i) Dissolved oxygen >40% saturation (ii) BOD ≤ 9 mgl^{-1} with a mean of <5 mgl^{-1} (iii) Non-toxic to fish as defined in Alabaster and Lloyd (1986).

6.3 Transport of adult fish

Given sufficient resources the four fish passes will be completed in 1991. Until then adult salmon are being captured by electrofishing or trap and trucked upstream of the main obstructions to suitable spawning areas to accelerate recolonisation. Radio-tagging has indicated that transferred adults remain in the nursery areas and pair up, though there is no confirmation as yet of successful spawning (Strange, 1988).

6.4 Artificial propagation

The objectives of stocking the catchment are twofold. Initially, the purpose is pump-priming to accelerate recolonisation. Earliest stocks, were with older parr and smolts (Table 4) to make the greatest use of the limited ova available. All these fish were microtagged and reported recaptures indicate that they have contributed significantly to runs in the Taff (Table 5). However, as adult runs to the river are enhanced providing more broodstock, stocking is being switched to younger fish as being potentially more cost effective. In each of the next four years it is intended to stock 100,000 fed fry per year over the nursery area identified (Fig.3). No stretch of river will be stocked in consecutive years to minimise intercohort competition. Electrofishing surveys will compare the performance of stocked fry in different areas within the catchment.

The presence of juvenile salmon in the Taff may also induce straying of adult salmon destined for other rivers (Solomon, 1973). Tens of thousands of adult salmon migrate past the Taff en route for other rivers further up the Severn Estuary. Even a small increase in the proportion of strays would significantly increase the number of salmon running the Taff.

Even assuming that pump-priming is successful, it is envisaged that some stocking with fry may continue in order to by-pass the most vulnerable stages in the life cycle (i.e.

Table 4. The number, life stage and origin of juvenile salmon stocked into
the Taff since 1986: all were microtagged except the fed fry.
(* Initial stockings for Cardiff Bay Barrage Monitoring Programme.)

YEAR	NO.	LIFE STAGE	ORIGIN OF OVA
1986	4,700	2 year old smolts	R.Shin, Scotland
1987	9,300	2 year old smolts	R.Shin, Scotland
1988	10,000	2 year old smolts	R.Shin, Scotland
	2,300	1 year old smolts/parr	R.Usk, S.Wales
1989	*10,000	2 year old smolts	R.Usk, S.Wales
	5,000	6 week old fed fry	R.Taff
1990	*7,200	2 year old smolts	R.Usk, S.Wales
	3,600	1 year old smolts/parr	R.Taff
TOTAL	51,800	Juvenile salmon	

adults on the spawning redds and ova in gravels choked by fine solids). Such stockings will only be made where densities of naturally spawned fry are known to be low, particularly upstream of those obstructions which remain impassable.

6.5 Control of exploitation

Enforcement of salmon fisheries legislation by the NRA has been increased both in the river and in coastal waters. In addition new fisheries regulations are being promoted.

In order to protect the salmon from the coastal fisheries, NRA guidelines prohibiting fixed engines in or close to the estuary have been in force since 1987. In addition, byelaws are being considered which will prohibit driftnetting for sea fish in the vicinity of the Taff to prevent the accidental or deliberate capture of adult salmon.

In Cardiff, the NRA has worked closely with the angling clubs to bring the river fishery under control, with considerable success. A significant rod fishery for salmon has developed (Table 5) with individual anglers catching up to 17 salmon in 1988. However, it was apparent that exploitation rates were likely to be high. In particular, the accumulation of adult fish below the weirs made their capture relatively easy. Consequently a club rule was introduced in 1989 making the weirpools sanctuary areas where no angling is permitted. The club also limits its members to taking two salmonids a day. In addition, the predominant method of catching salmon, spinning, can only be practised by anglers with a more expensive 'Salmon' permit and the appropriate NRA rod licence. Angling effort is thereby constrained to an extent by a price mechanism.

Table 5. The total number of adult salmon reported by anglers or
caught by other methods (principally electrofishing) since
1983: the number of microtagged salmon reported is shown in
parentheses.

Year	Declared Rod Catch		Other		Total	
1983	0		4		4	
1984	2		-		2	
1985	15		-		15	
1986	12		-		12	
1987	38	(1)	20		58	(1)
1988	114	(45)	9	(5)	123	(50)
1989	4	(3)	33	(9)	37	(12)
1990 (up to 19.10.90)	not available	(21)	11	(3)	>32	(23)

When the fish passes are opened and salmon have access further up river, similar constraints on angling will be required. The NRA is therefore considering promoting byelaws that will provide such constraints.

6.6 Habitat improvement

The NRA's Land Drainage department regularly undertakes repair works to flood defence schemes. The opportunity is taken where possible to put in structures to improve the physical habitat for adults and juveniles. Such structures include low blockstone weirs, groynes and salmon stones.

6.7 The Barrage - Fisheries protection

Various measures for fisheries protection have been included in the Parliamentary Bill authorising the barrage and a Memorandum of Agreement between the promoters and the NRA (Anon., 1990).

(i) Fish Passes

The Barrage must incorporate structures approved by the Ministry of Agriculture, Fisheries and Food in accordance with Section 9 of the Salmon and Freshwater Fisheries Act 1975 to safeguard both the upstream migration of adult salmon and the downstream passage of smolts and kelts.

(ii) Water quality

The water impounded by the barrage must contain at least 5 milligrams per litre of oxygen at all times.

(iii) Impact assessment

The return rate of hatchery reared smolts stocked into the lower reaches will be compared before and after impoundment. Ten thousand microtagged smolts will be stocked annually and returns monitored over a ten year period by trapping and anglers catches in the lower reaches. Captures in the high seas and coastal fisheries will also be monitored. Radio and acoustic tags will be fitted to adult salmon and, if possible, smolts to identify if and how migration through Cardiff Bay may be impeded by the Barrage.

(iv) Mitigation

The monitoring programme is unlikely to be able to demonstrate as statistically significant any reduction of less than 37 per cent in the return rate of tagged salmon. Consequently, the Taff will be stocked annually with smolts to counteract such a presumed loss in the salmon population, regardless of the results of the impact assessment. However, if a reduction of greater than 37 per cent is demonstrated as statistically significant at the 60 per cent probability level then mitigative restocking will be increased accordingly. The fish tracking studies may indicate that any impact of the barrage could be ameliorated by changing its mode of operation. Where practical such changes would be adopted in preference to compensatory restocking.

7. CONCLUSION

After an absence of over a century, salmon are once again returning to and successfully spawning in the Taff. Natural penetration by adult fish of the river is still limited by an obstruction to the lowest 20 kilometres. In addition, the distribution of the species has been enhanced by transporting adults to, and stocking juveniles into the middle and upper reaches. In 1991, on completion of a further fish pass, adult fish will have access to the greater part of the catchment. With the aid of stocking, full recolonisation should be achieved within ten years. Fishing, pollution and future developments will have to be closely controlled if the population is to be maintained.

The rehabilitation of salmon in the Taff, the 'capital' river of Wales, is indicative of the major environmental improvement which has been achieved in this area over the last three decades.

ACKNOWLEDGEMENTS

This paper summarises the work of a large number of people in the National Rivers Authority and its predecessor, the Welsh Water Authority over the last decade. The author would also like to acknowledge the contributions of his colleagues to the rehabilitation of the salmon population, particularly the NRA's Fisheries and Pollution Control sections. Prof. R. Edwards, Dr. R. Cresswell and D.H. Williams kindly commented on the draft manuscript. The opinions expressed are those of the author and not necessarily those of the Authority.

REFERENCES

Alabaster, J. and Lloyd, R. (1986). Water quality criteria for freshwater fish. Butterworths, London. 297pp.

Anon (1860). Commission into Salmon Fisheries in England and Wales 1860. Report and minutes of evidence. Chairman W. Jardine. HMSO, London.

Bent, E.J., Harris, G.S., Humphrey, N.C., Strange, C.D., Thomas, D.R. and Williams, D.G. (1985). Fisheries management in the Taff catchment: the acquisition of base-line data. Welsh Water Authority. Report SE/10/85.

Bent, E.J., Dack, J. and Wade, K. (1986). The environmental quality of the Taff catchment, 1985: Biology. Welsh Water Authority. Report SE/6/86.

Brown, H.J., Strange, C.D., Jones, G.O., and Apprahamian, M.W. (1986). The environmental quality of the Taff catchment, 1985: Fish populations. Welsh Water Authority. Report SE/4/86.

Brown, H.J., Charrett, D.J., Strange, C.D., Apprahamian, M.W. and Jones, G.O. (1988). A study of salmonid egg and fry survival in the R. Taff catchment. Welsh Water Authority. Report SE/88/7.

Cresswell, R.C. (1989). House of Lords. Minutes of Evidence taken before the Committee on the Cardiff Bay Barrage Bill (H.L.) Thursday 20th April 1989. p 62 - 71. Sharpe, Pritchard & Co., 3, Dean Farrar St., Westminster, London. SW1.

Edwards, R.W., Benson-Evans, K., Learner, M.A., Williams, P. and Williams, R. (1972). A biological survey of the river Taff. Journal of the Institution of Pollution Control 71: 144-166.

Mawle, G.W., Winstone, A. and Brooker, M.P. (1985). Salmon and sea trout in the Taff - past, present and future. Nature in Wales, New Series, 4, Parts 1 & 2: 36-45.

Mills, D. (1989). Ecology and management of Atlantic salmon. Chapman & Hall, London. 351pp.

Solomon, D.J. (1973). Evidence for pheromone - influenced homing by migrating Atlantic salmon *Salmo salar* L. Nature 244: 231-232.

Strange, C.D. (1988). River Taff Salmon radio tracking 1987/8. Memorandum to Dr. G.S. Harris 18th October 1988. Welsh Water Authority. 3pp.

Swain, A. (1982). The migrations of salmon (*Salmo salar* L.) from three rivers entering the Severn estuary. Journal du Conseil International par l'Exploration de la Mer. 40 (1): 76-80.

Thomas, D.R., Bradshaw, J., Inverarity, R.J., Charrett, D.J., and Price, H. (1986). The environment quality of the Taff catchment 1985: Water quality. Welsh Water Authority. Report SE/7/86.

Williams, D.H. (1984). The recovery of the River Taff from pollution with special reference to the period 1950 to 1984. Welsh Water Authority. Report. 33pp.

Winstone, A. (1978). A fisheries survey of the R. Taff below Pontypridd. Part 2 of unpublished M.Sc thesis. University of Wales.

Winstone, A. (1984). The rehabilitation of the River Taff as a migratory salmonid fishery - a preliminary report. Fisheries Technical Unit (South), Welsh Water Authority Report.

ATLANTIC SALMON RESTORATION IN THE MORELL RIVER, P.E.I. AND THE NEPISIGUIT, N.B., CANADA.

A.T. BIELAK, R.W. GRAY, T.G. LUTZAC, M.J. HAMBROOK AND P. CAMERON

Department of Fisheries and Oceans, Moncton, Canada.

INTRODUCTION

The aboriginal range and productive capacity of Canadian Atlantic salmon rivers has been reduced significantly since the arrival of white settlers on the North American continent. Watt (1988) reported an approximately 50% loss of habitat production capacity during the industrial revolution. He identified a further net loss, since 1870,

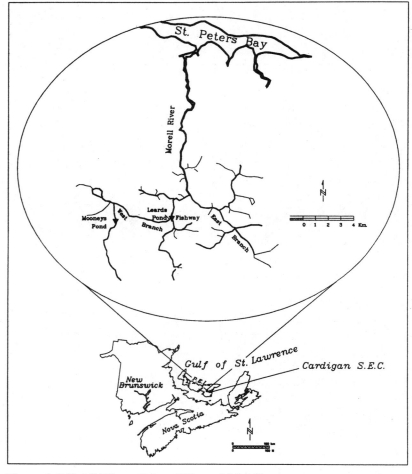

Figure 1. Morell River, Prince Edward Island.

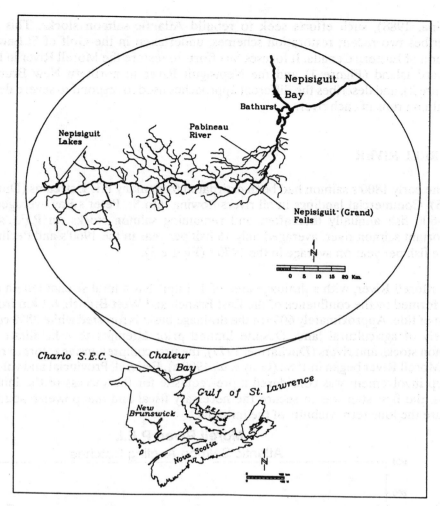

Figure 2. Nepisiguit River, New Brunswick.

of about 16% which he attributed to hydro power development, agriculture and acid rain.

Despite the effect of such reductions, and of additional depletions of stocks by various fisheries, Canada still boasts 400-500 Atlantic salmon rivers. These range in size from small streams, with less than 100 returns each year, to the vast Miramichi system in New Brunswick with an annual migration of about 100,000 salmon.

Attempts at mitigation of losses, and at colonization of new habitats, have been extensive. They have ranged from "low tech" stream clearing to "high tech" installation of fish passage facilities coupled with extensive stocking schemes (see papers by Beland, Bourgeois, Dulude, Legault, O'Neil, Pratt, Rideout, and Turgeon; in Bielak, 1990; Gray, 1974, 1981, 1986; Gray and Cameron, 1980; Cutting and Gray, 1984 *et al,* 1989).

In tandem with comprehensive management plans, first introduced by the Federal Department of Fisheries and Oceans (DFO) in 1984 (Muir and Bellefontaine, 1988;

Vezina, 1988), such efforts seek to rebuild Atlantic salmon stocks. This paper describes two recent restoration schemes, undertaken in the Gulf of St.Lawrence Region of Eastern Canada. It focuses on efforts to restore the Morell River in Prince Edward Island (Figure 1) and the Nepisiguit River in northern New Brunswick (Figure 2), and describes the different approaches used to respond to severe declines in salmon runs in each river.

MORELL RIVER

By the early 1800's salmon had been extirpated from many P.E.I. streams (Dunfield, 1985). Commercial landings in all rivers flowing into St. Peter's Bay averaged only 300-600 fish annually thereafter, and remaining salmon stocks on P.E.I.'s most important salmon river, averaged only 16 fish per year in the 1960's and declined to three fish per year on average in the 1970's (Figure 3).

The Morell River, with a drainage area of 171 km^2 has a total stream length of 140 km, formed by the confluence of the East Branch and West Branch, 6.4 km from the head of tide. Approximately 60% of the drainage basin is forested while 38% consists largely of agricultural land. Despite limited prior attempts to rehabilitate PEI's salmon stocks and rivers (Ducharme, 1977), the first comprehensive effort to restore the Morell River began in 1982 (Gray *et al*, 1990 a). Federal, Provincial and volunteer group involvement was considered a pre-requisite for the success of the initiative. Thus, the first step was to secure the necessary fiscal and manpower resources to ensure the long term viability of the initiative.

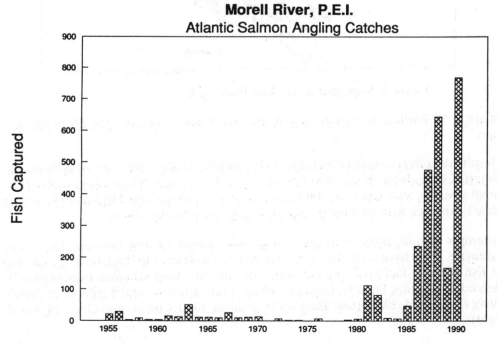

Figure 3. Note: Mandatory hook and release of MSW salmon introduced in 1984. Graph does not include released fish.

124

The eventual partners in the project included the following major players: the Federal Department of Fisheries and Oceans, the Canada Employment and Immigration Commission (CEIC), the P.E.I. Department of the Environment (Fish and Wildlife Division and the P.E.I. Conservation Strategy), the Morell River Management Co-operative, the P.E.I. Wildlife Federation, the P.E.I. Flyfishers Association and the Tignish and Cardigan Branches of the Royal Canadian Legion.

A clear set of enhancement objectives was developed (Table 1) and three major thrusts were implemented to deliver the programme:

a) Fish habitat improvement

b) Selective breeding of 'early-run' salmon

c) Development of semi-natural rearing ponds to rear high-quality salmon smolts.

The main elements of each strategy are detailed below.

Habitat Improvement

To prevent further degradation of the river, due to encroachment by industry, agriculture, road construction and forestry, Greenbelt legislation was introduced in the mid-1970's. It prohibited any development or forest harvesting within 60 metres of the stream, in a 44km section of the stream. Stream cleanup and habitat improvement were initiated in 1982-1983 on 12km of the West, and 4km of the East, branch of the river.

Initially those involved concentrated on eliminating sources of siltation, and barriers to fish migration. Efforts were then focused on habitat improvement and maintenance measures such as the planting of vegetation, placement of instream structures for cover, pool creation and bank stabilization. A total of 40km have been "reclaimed", to date, and the task remains a central and vital element of the restoration plan.

Selective breeding of early-run salmon

In order to develop an early-run salmon stock (returning between June and August and thus available for angling) it was necessary to import eggs from outside the province, since no such stock existed in P.E.I. A small number of early-run parentage Miramichi River-origin eggs were imported beginning in 1982 and subsequent years to the federal Salmonid Enhancement Centre (SEC) at Cardigan.

An aggressive selective breeding programme was implemented initially using returning multi-sea-winter (MSW) and 1-sea-winter (1SW) fish, some of which have subsequently been reconditioned (Johnston *et al*, 1987; Gray *et al*, 1987, 1990c) and spawned as many as six times to provide additional eggs. Recently, fresh sperm and fertilised eggs have also been imported from the Miramichi River in order to expand the gene pool. This was done in both 1989 and 1990. Details of the stocking regimes in the Morell River are summarised in Table 2.

Table 1. Enhancement objectives for the Morell River, P.E.I.

- to maintain the river as close to a wilderness river as possible;

- to improve habitat for fish and wildlife on the river and balance the multiple uses of the watercourse for fish, waterfowl, furbearers, canoeists, etc.

- to expand the populations of brook trout and salmon to a level where suitable harvest of both species were available for quality recreational pursuits;

- to improve fish passage at the Leards Pond fishway which had deteriorated over time;

- to develop and maintain an early-run salmon stock through an aggressive selective breeding program carried out by DFO at Cardigan SEC, so that salmon would be available to anglers in June, July and August, as well as in the traditional fall fishery in September and October;

- to implement a salmon kelt reconditioning program to maximise the use of scarce early-run genetic stock imported from New-Brunswick under the Fish Health Protection Regulations;

- to implement the stocking of high quality Atlantic salmon smolts reared under semi-natural conditions and release these at the best spawning and nursery areas in the river, so that returning adults would "home" to these areas thus maximising spawning success and the survivial of resultant juvenile stages;

- to evaluate each phase of the enhancement program annually and modify approaches and techniques as required;

- to explore opportunities and improve quality angling areas in freshwater as well as in the estuary and St Peter's Bay;

- to develop and recommend mechanisms whereby public conservation/ community groups could operate the enhancement project on a self financing basis with technical and scientific advice from the Department of Fisheries and Oceans.

Development of semi-natural rearing ponds

Traditionally, hatchery stocking of salmon smolts and fingerlings has been used to rehabilitate Atlantic salmon runs. However, the abundance of spring-fed ponds, coupled with the short rivers in P.E.I., presented an opportunity to experiment with semi-natural rearing of salmon smolts in ponds (Gray *et al*, 1990b). Yearling parr are stocked in a spring-fed pond and feed on natural food organisms. Their natural diet is supplemented by an artificial dry pellet diet during the growing season from May to November.

TABLE 2

DISTRIBUTION OF JUVENILE ATLANTIC SALMON IN THE MORELL RIVER, PRINCE-EDWARD ISLAND, 1978 - 90.

Year of Release	Genetic Stock	Rearing Location	Juvenile Stage at Release Parr 0+	Parr 2+	Smolt 1+	Smolt 2+	Total Number Released
1978	N.W. Miramichi	Cardigan SEC	14,943				14,943
1979	N.W. Miramichi Restigouche	Cardigan SEC	32,366				32,366
1981	N.W. Miramichi	Cardigan SEC				692	692
1982	Miramichi(EM)[1]	Cardigan SEC	34,700			3,645	38,345
1983	Miramichi (EM)	Cardigan SEC	9,000				9,000
1985	Miramichi Mixed[2]	Cardigan SEC Profit's Pond				10,428 10,997	21,425
1986	N.W. Miramichi(EM)	Cardigan SEC Profit's Pond				1,529 12,529	14,058
1987	N.W. Miramichi(EM)	Cardigan SEC Profit's Pond				3,055 22,250	25,305
1988	Miramichi Mixed	Cardigan SEC Profit's Pond		1,208	5,907	12,982	20,097
1989	Morell (HR) (1SW)[3]	Profit's Pond		1,560		20,650	22,210
1990	Morell Mixed (HR)	Mooney's Pond Profit's Pond		398 681		48,475 10,256	59,810

[1] EM = Early Migrating Stock
[2] MIXED = Both early and late migrating stock were taken for transfer because of the small number of eggs available
[3] HR = Progeny from previous hatchery stocking in the Morell River
  1SW = Grilse

Data: From Gray et al 1990a

TABLE 3

Survival of Atlantic Salmon from experimental groups of artificially (Cardigan) and semi-naturally (Profitt's Pond) reared smolts in the Morell River, 1985 - 87

| Year of Release | Rearing Location | Number Released | Recapture Location | | | Total # Recaptures | Sea Survival (%) |
| | | | Leard's Pond Fishway | | Sport Fishery | | |
			1 SW	2SW	1SW		
1985	Cardigan	10,428	102	10	43	155	1.5
	Profitt's Pond	10,997	618	56	237	911	8.3
1986	Cardigan	1,529	74	6	20	100	6.5
	Profitt's Pond	12,529	1,136	79	300	1,515	12.1
1987	Cardigan	3,055	79	7	7	93	3.0
	Profitt's Pond	22,250	1,326	77	136	1,539	6.9

Data: From Gray et al 1990a

Survival rates in the semi-natural rearing pond from stocked yearling parr to two year old smolts ranged from 58-61%. The major predators were herons, kingfishers, cormorants, and mink (Gray *et al,* 1990 a,b). Despite these mortalities, since juvenile salmon have been conditioned to a more natural environment, survival at sea is much higher compared with smolts reared in a traditional hatchery regime (Table 3).

As a result of the work on semi-natural rearing carried out at the original research facility, Profitt's Pond, north-western P.E.I., another semi-natural rearing facility, Mooney's Pond, was completed in 1989 on the Morell River system (Figure 1). It is capable of rearing some 80,000 salmon smolts annually, and is operated by the Morell River Management Co-operative. The original facility at Profitt's Pond will continue to be operated to produce high quality smolts for other rivers in P.E.I.

Results of enhancement efforts on Morell river

In 1986 the Morell River experienced the largest salmon return in decades. The Leards pond fishway on the West branch of the Morell passed 626 MSW salmon and grilse in 1986, compared to 15 in 1985 (Figure 4). In addition DFO angling statistics placed the number of salmon angled in the river at 236 grilse, with an unknown number of large salmon released as required by law. Of the grilse, 61% were angled during the summer between July 1st and September 30th. The significance of these results

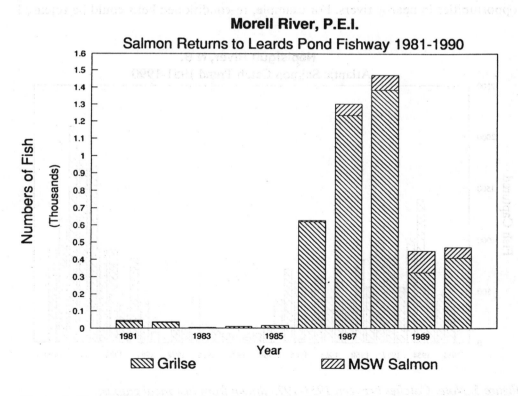

Figure 4. Note: A large proportion of smolts stocked in 1988 and 1989 were released downstream of Leards Pond and thus would not have "homed" back to the fishway in 1989 and 1990.

was not just the number of early-run salmon which returned in 1986, but the fact that they resulted from the release of a small experimental group of adipose-clipped smolts numbering only 21,425.

Angling catches and returns to the Leards Pond fishway since 1986 have generally shown an increasing trend (Figures 3 and 4). The availability of early-run salmon in the Morell created tremendous recreational opportunities as anglers fished a total of over 2,700 rod days in 1986 and almost 9,000 in 1990, compared with the annual average of 118 rod days from 1976-1980 when only late-run salmon entered the river.

In fact the whole experience has been so positive and returns so high, for what can basically be considered a rather short river with relatively few angling pools, that innovative methods of harvest of the "surplus" fish have been investigated in the last two years. An experimental saltwater sport troll fishery was initiated in St Peter's Bay in 1989. Secondly, although politically sensitive, a proposed terminal harvest fishery, based on surplus salmon, could prove viable. Several options are being studied for the disposal of surplus fish (primarily grilse which are more than 76% male), with the proceeds going to the Morell River Management Co-op to offset the cost of the operation of the semi-natural rearing ponds and the maintenance of fish habitat.

The sale of fresh or smoked fish has been discussed and other options include the use of surplus salmon in ways which would create additional recreational fishing opportunities in nearby rivers. For example, re-conditioned kelts could be released

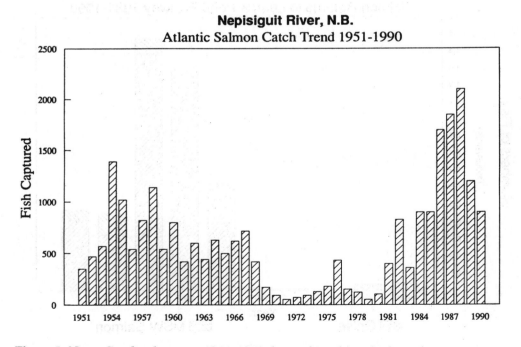

Figure 5. Note: Catches between 1951-1973 drawn from historical graphs;
for 1974-1990 data courtesy of Nepisiguit Salmon Association.
Mean captures 1959-1968 and 1969-1973 estimated to be 500 and 37 fish
respectively. (Baker 1990, Lutzac 1985). Totals since 1980 include released fish.

in newly-created or restored pools open to anglers on a daily fee basis with proceeds once again being used to fund operating costs, or the sale, to aquaculture interests, of salmon eggs from reconditioned kelts.

NEPISIGUIT RIVER

The Nepisiguit River in northeastern New Brunswick, with a drainage area of 2,330 km^2, is one of the largest rivers in the Province after the Main South-west Miramichi, the Saint John and the Restigouche. Historically the Nepisiguit was largely under private lease, and few fish entered the river until late June. Angling catches averaged some 800 salmon in the 1950's, dropping to 400-600 fish each year thereafter as interceptory fisheries took their toll (Figure 5).

In 1969 a toxic metal spill from a mine - generated by runoff from sulphide waste dumps following heavy rains - situated near the river caused massive mortalities of juvenile fish in the main stem, and non-entry into the river of adult spawners (Baker, 1990). Several years passed with minimal returns to a still-polluted river, until adequate waste treatment measures were implemented and a small autumn run entered the river in 1974. These returnees were, in all probability, fish which had survived in the tributaries unaffected by the spill. A large run of fish also returned in late September-October 1975, and there was a steady return of fish (mainly grilse) from late June to October, 1976.

The mainstem Nepisiguit flows for almost all its 128 km through mixed hardwood and conifer forest, north-east from the Nepisiguit Lakes to Bathurst where it empties into the Baie des Chaleurs. Only the lower 29 km of the main stem plus two small tributaries are accessible to salmon. An impassable 33m waterfall (Grand Falls) blocks passage to more than 400 km of additional salmonid rearing habitat (Figure 2). DFO began a stocking programme on the Nepisiguit in 1974 with 15,000 early-run Restigouche River-origin (Kedgwick River) smolts planted in the river (Table 4) The programme has continued since that time with a single hiatus in 1977.

Due to the cold northerly temperature regimes experienced at Charlo, coupled with limitations in groundwater supplies, smolt production possibilities proved limited and resulted in a growing emphasis on stocking of fall fingerlings. In 1976 a group of local anglers, with a vision of the 20-30,000 salmon which a completely accessible river could potentially produce, formed the Nepisiguit Salmon Association (NSA). With this goal in mind the NSA persuaded DFO to undertake a feasibility study for a fishway at Grand Falls, and planting of juvenile salmon above the obstruction. In 1978 some 170,000 autumn fingerlings from Charlo were distributed above the falls, this number rising to 225,000 planted both above and below the falls in 1979. A smaller number of autumn fingerlings (156,000) were similarly stocked in 1980, together with 27,000 wire nose tagged smolts planted near the falls.

The beginning of the new decade also marked a more formal beginning to the enhancement project with the collaborative efforts of DFO and NSA being enhanced by the participation of the Pabineau Indian Band and the Big River Community Improvement Association. The installation, in 1981, of a counting and broodstock collection fence, about 11 km from the river mouth and funded by the CEIC, was another milestone. The fence made the collection of early-run broodstock much

TABLE 4

DISTRIBUTION OF JUVENILE ATLANTIC SALMON IN THE NEPISIGUIT RIVER, NEW BRUNSWICK 1974-1990

YEAR	STAGE	MONTH STOCKED	NUMBER	STOCKING LOCATION	STOCK USED
1974	Smolt	--	15,000	--	Kedgwick
1975	Smolt	--	7,600	--	Kedgwick
	1+ Parr	--	6,250	--	Kedgwick
	Fall Fingerlings	--	63,000	--	Kedgwick
1976	Smolt	--	33,000	--	Kedgwick
	1+ Parr	--	5,000	--	Kedgwick
	Fall Fingerlings	--	78,210	--	Kedgwick
1977	No stocking	--		--	
1978	Fall Fingerlings	--	173,000	--	Nepisiguit/Rocky Brook
1979	Smolt	--	3,995	--	N.W. Miramichi
	1+ Parr	--	4,231	--	N.W. Miramichi
	Fall Fingerlings	--	225,480	--	Nepisiguit/Rocky Brook/Kedgwick
1980	Smolt	--	27,000	--	Nepisiguit/Rocky Brook/Kedgwick
	Fall Fingerlings	--	156,000	--	Nepisiguit/Rocky Brook/Kedgwick

Information courtesy of Bob Baker

TABLE 4 - (Cont'd)...

Year	Stage	Month	Number	Location	River
1981	Smolt	May	3,819	Pabineau Falls and Brook	Nepisiguit
	1+ Parr	May	16,310	Below Grand Falls	Rocky Brook/Kedgwick
	Advanced Fry	May	220,000	Above Grand Falls	Miramichi
	Fall Fingerling	October	550,000	Above Grand Falls	Kedgwick
1982	1+ Parr	October	2,980	Pabineau Brook	Kedgwick/Rocky Brook
	Fall Fingerlings	October	293,740	Big South	North West Miramichi/ Nepisiguit/Kedgwick
1983	Smolt	May	10,454	Below Grand Falls	Kedgwick/Rocky Brook
	1+ Parr	June	10,645	Big South	Kedgwick/Rocky Brook
	Advanced Fry	July	216,172	Headwaters	Miramichi/Rocky Brook
	Fall Fingerlings	October	298,453	Below Grand Falls	Nepisiguit/Kedgwick
1984	Smolt	May	10,752	Below Grand Falls	Kedgwick
	1+ Parr	June/October	18,667	Above Grand Falls	Nepisiguit
	Advanced Fry	July	65,576	Above/Below Grand Falls	Nepisiguit/Miramichi/Kedgwick
	Fall Fingerlings	October	261,141	Above Grand Falls	Nepisiguit/Kedgwick
1985	Smolt	May	10,650	Below Grand Falls	Nepisiguit/Kedgwick
	1+ Parr	June	11,153	Below Grand Falls	Nepisiguit
	Advanced Fry	July	30,000	Above Grand Falls	Nepisiguit
	Fall Fingerlings	October	316,618	Above Grand Falls	Nepisiguit/Kedgwick
1986	Smolt	May	72,937	Below Grand Falls	Miramichi
	1+ Parr	May	2,540	Pabineau Brook	Nepisiguit
	Advanced Fry	June	50,000	Pabineau Brook	Nepisiguit
	Fall Fingerlings	October	367,011	Below Grand Falls	Nepisiguit

TABLE 4 (Cont'd...)

Year				
1987	Smolt	May	10,706	Below Grand Falls	Nepisiguit/Kedgwick
	Yearlings	October	1,872	Below Grand Falls	Nepisiguit
	Advanced Fry	July	82,306	Below Grand Falls	Nepisiguit
	Fall Fingerlings	October	206,814	Below Grand Falls	Nepisiguit
	Eyed Eggs (Incubation Box)		150,000	Below Grand Falls	Nepisiguit
1988	Smolt	May	10,000	Below Grand Falls	Nepisiguit
	Incubation Box	June	300,000	Below Grand Falls	Nepisiguit
	Advanced Fry	July	141,000	Below Grand Falls	Nepisiguit
	Fall Fingerling	October	208,000	Below Grand Falls	Nepisiguit
1989	Smolt	May	10,000	Below Grand Falls	Nepisiguit
	Incubation Box	June	336,000	Below Grand Falls	Nepisiguit
	Fall Fingerlings	October	206,000	Below Grand Falls	Nepisiguit
	Fall Fingerlings	October	284,000	Below Grand Falls	Nepisiguit
1990	Smolt	May	10,800	Below Grand Falls	Nepisiguit
	Incubation Box	June	350,000	Below Grand Falls	Nepisiguit
	Fall Fingerlings	October	373,000	Below Grand Falls	Nepisiguit

easier. Brunswick Mining and Noranda Research formally joined the project in 1984, though their biologist had been studying the river since the spill in 1976, and informally assisting the NSA in the operation of the counting fence since 1981.

Biologists had also advocated the trial use of an incubation box system to expand the river's egg production, and funding from the industrial partner made this possible. Egg to fry survival rates proved phenomenal, for instance ranging from 96-98.1% in 1989 and 1990 (Baker, pers.comm.). The young salmon fry were 30-40% larger at the end of their first growing season than those produced through conventional hatchery trough incubation. The success of this initiative has led to increasing numbers of incubation boxes and eggs being placed in the river and tended to by NSA volunteers and CEIC/Industry/Private Sector/DFO-funded staff. (25,000 eggs were planted in 1985; 350,000 in 1989 and 1990).

Funding the project has always been "soft", requiring major efforts by the NSA each year to maintain it. DFO Gulf Region, despite providing a major material and advisory contribution to the project via its Charlo SEC, has been increasingly unable to contribute to the funding needed (approximately $130,000 in 1990) to fully operate[*] the project. In fact, because of growing fiscal constraints, the Department has even had difficulty in fully assessing the relative percentage returns of fish stocked at different developmental stages.

The stocking programme, which began using the progeny of a cross between early-run Miramichi and Restigouche stocks, and eventually used only early-run Nepisiguit broodstock, has proven successful, with continued improvement in angling catches and in salmon returns to the counting fence (Figures 5 and 6). Between 1981-89 and average of 30% of fish captured at the counting fence were identified as of hatchery origin, since most of the fish stocked from Charlo had been fin clipped.

Perhaps the most significant change has been in the timing of the run which enters the river about one month earlier than previously. Counts made at the fence show that only 17% of the fish trapped in October were hatchery fish while an average of 51% of the June return was a result of the enhancement programme (Baker 1990), and large fish are now commonly observed in the river on June 1st. Stocking of autumn fingerlings, since the programme was initiated, has proven very successful and the first returns resulting from the incubation box programme are eagerly anticipated in the early 1990s. While the results of the salmon enhancement efforts to date have been highly encouraging, it will probably be several years yet before spawning escapement is such that the river will be self-seeding on a sustainable basis.

The desire of salmon anglers to see salmon spawning above Grand Falls has lead to a backlash of sorts, with the formation of a strong Trout Protective Association which opposes any further introduction of salmon above the obstruction. This has in turn lead to the formation of the Nepisiguit River Fish Management Committee with representatives of both the trout and salmon fraternities, and various other interested

---

[*]   (Full operating costs include counting fence operations, broodstock transfer, electroseining to determine juvenile density, creel census, redd counts, juvenile stocking, habitat surveys and cleanup, water quality monitoring and the streamside incubation box programme.)

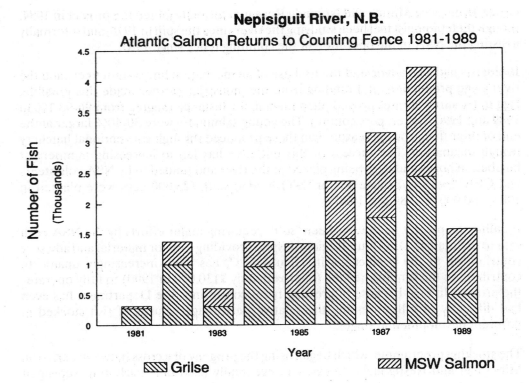

Nepisiguit River, N.B.
Atlantic Salmon Returns to Counting Fence 1981-1989

Grilse

MSW Salmon

Figure 6. Note: No count shown for 1990 due to counting fence wash-out.

parties including federal and provincial government departments. The Committee is currently working on a salmonid management and development strategy for the whole of the river, and will probably be expanded so that all interests are represented.

CONCLUSIONS

The Nepisiguit programme has been cited as a model for the rest of Canada (Gaudet 1989). The NSA - which was the first private sector group in the Maritimes to assume shared responsibility with DFO for a restoration project (Lutzac 1985) - was honoured as the Atlantic Salmon Federation (ASF)'s "Affiliate of the Year" in 1987, and in December 1990 was among the first five recipients of Canada's newly-instituted Recreational Fisheries Award. Without the energy and commitment of the NSA's volunteer board - which put in countless hours on the river, lobbied hard for programme support and secured ongoing funding from the CEIC, DFO and private sector organisations - and the guidance of knowledgeable and dedicated DFO biologists, it is unlikely that this project would have been possible.

As in the case of the Morell River restoration, where dedication was evident in both the "volunteer" and "professional" cadres, it is clear that a strong partnership between private sector groups and government can be a crucial factor in effective restoration efforts. This partnership is also important when one or the other of the participating bodies falters since others may be able to provide sufficient impetus to keep things going.

The involvement of the private sector also opens up alternative sources of funding opportunities and also enables the non-government organisations (NGO's) to act as third party sponsors for contract administration thus cutting through much of the red tape which seems on occasion to hinder timely and effective project management and delivery.

In each of the cases discussed above there has been opportunity for experimentation with new techniques and the ultimate potential for technology transfer to other NGO's. In the case of the Morell, if the terminal harvest initiative proves a success, lessons learned could be integrated into river-by-river management plans being developed in other areas. The incubation box techniques perfected on the Nepisiguit have already been shared with some 20 or so NGO's in New Brunswick and Quebec via a workshop co-sponsored in 1989 by the NSA, DFO, ASF and its N.B. Council, as well as Brunswick Mining and the Noranda Technology Centre.

It is probably fair to say that the approach taken in P.E.I., where all interested parties defined the enhancement objectives for the project at its outset, led to smoother programme delivery than on the Nepisiguit where tensions eventually surfaced between salmon and trout anglers with conflicting aims. In both cases, however, salmon have been restored to rivers where stock levels had fallen to perilously low levels, and the important early-run component boosted. It must be noted that in each case, although a stock from another river was used to provide eggs at the outset, "native" returns were used as soon as it was feasible to do so.

Eventually, production in the Nepisiguit will be limited by the natural carrying capacity of the river, and the need for a continued enhancement programme will come to an end. In contrast, on the Morell, it should prove possible to continue to boost production beyond the carrying capacity of the river via the use of semi-natural rearing ponds.

The methods used to restore severely diminished salmon runs differed in each instance. They evolved as a function of opportunities which presented themselves and as a result of the vision, skills, energy and knowledge of the principals involved. Full evaluation of the impact and success of each approach has proven challenging in times of fiscal restraint and possible changes in marine survival of salmon. However, even though various challenges remain to be met by those involved in both the Morell and Nepisiguit restoration projects, it is clear that the strategies employed have essentially proven successful, and both projects have resulted in substantially increased salmon returns.

ACKNOWLEDGEMENTS

The authors would like to acknowledge the assistance of Bob Baker, President of the Nepisiguit Salmon Association, and Daryl Guignion, Chairman, Department of Biology, University of PEI, for their collaboration in these enhancement projects. The assistance of Jim Conlon and Jim Ritchie of the Fish Habitat and Enhancement Division, DFO, Gulf Region, in the preparation of this paper is also acknowledged.

REFERENCES

Baker, R.W. (1990). Salmon Enhancement on the Nepisiguit River - A co-operative approach. Nepisiguit Salmon Association. 15p.

Bielak, A.T. (1990). (Editor.) Proceedings of the 1988 Northeast Atlantic Salmon Workshop. Special Publication Series No. 16, Atlantic Salmon Federation, St.Andrews, N.B., Canada. 156p.

Cutting, R.E. & Gray, R.W. (1984). Assessment of the Atlantic salmon stocks of the LaHave River, Nova Scotia. CAFSAC. Res.Doc. 84/40. 43p.

Ducharme, L.J. (1977). Atlantic salmon enhancement in the Morell River, Prince Edward Island, Fisheries and Marine Service (Maritimes Region). Technical Report Series: MAR/T-77-2. 19p.

Dunfield, R.W. (1985). The Atlantic Salmon in the history of North America. Canadian Special Publications in Fisheries and Aquatic Sciences. 80:181p.

Gaudet, E.G. (1989). Regional Director General's speech to Nepisiguit Salmon Association, October 1989. Typescript. Department of Fisheries and Oceans, Gulf Region.

Gray, R.W. (1974). Salmon development on the LaHave River. Atlantic Salmon Journal. 6:14-17.

Gray, R.W. (1981). Help for salmon in Nova Scotia. Atlantic Salmon Journal. 4: 20-24.

Gray, R.W. (1986). Biological characteristics of Atlantic salmon (*Salmo salar* L.) in the Upper LaHave River Basin. Canadian Technical Reports in Fisheries and Aquatic Sciences, No. 1437. 45p.

Gray, R.W. & Cameron, J.D. (1980). Juvenile Atlantic salmon stocking in several Nova Scotia and Southern New Brunswick salmon streams, 1971-79. Canadian Data Reports in Fisheries and Aquatic Sciences, No. 202. xi. 47p.

Gray, R.W., Cameron, J.D. & McLennan, A.D. (1987). Artificial reconditioning, spawning and survival of Atlantic salmon *Salmo salar* L., kelts in salt water and survival of their F1 progeny. Aquaculture and Fisheries Management. 18: 309-326.

Gray, R.W., Cameron, J.D. & Jefferson, E.M.J. (1989). The LaHave River: Physiography and potential from Atlantic salmon production. Canadian Technical Reports in Fisheries and Aquatic Sciences. No. 1701. iv. 58p.

Gray, R.W., Guignion, D.L & Hambrook, M.J. (1990a). Atlantic salmon enhancement of the Morell River, P.E.I. Atlantic Salmon Journal (submitted).

Gray, R.W., Hambrook, M.J. & Davidson, K. (1990b). Seminatural rearing of Atlantic salmon (*Salmo salar* L.) in spring-fed ponds in P.E.I. Canadian Journal of Fisheries and Aquatic Sciences, (In preparation).

Gray, R.W., Johnston, C.E., Hambrook, M.J. & Gallant, R. (1990c). Photoperiod and temperature induction of spring spawning in Atlantic salmon (*Salmo salar* L.) and survival of their F1 progeny. Canadian Journal of Fisheries and Aquatic Sciences. (in preparation).

Johnston, C.E., Gray, R.W., McLennan, A. & Paterson, A. (1987). Effects of photoperiod, temperature, and diet on the reconditioning response, blood chemistry, and gonad maturation of Atlantic salmon kelts (*Salmo salar*) held in freshwater. Canadian Journal of Fisheries and Aquatic Sciences. 44: 702-711.

Lutzac, T.G. (1985). assessment of the Nepisiguit River Salmon Stock in 1984. CAFSAC Research Document 85/101.

Muir, B.S. & Bellefontaine, N.A. (1988). Canadian Atlantic Salmon Management Program. (123-129): in R.H. Stroud (Editor). Proceedings of the Symposium on Present and Future Atlantic Salmon Management. Portland, Maine. Oct 1987. Marine Recreational Fisheries 12. Atlantic Salmon Federation, Ipswich, Mass.

Vezina, B.P. (1988). Historical overview of Atlantic salmon fisheries. Resource Allocation Branch, Atlantic Fisheries, Department of Fisheries and Oceans, Ottawa. 57p.

Watt, W.D. (1988). Major causes and implications of Atlantic salmon habitat losses. (101-111): *In* R.H. Stroud (Editor). Proceedings of the Symposium on Present and Future Atlantic Salmon Management. Portland, Maine. Oct 1987. Marine Recreational Fisheries 12. Atlantic Salmon Federation, Ipswich, Mass.

REHABILITATION OF THE ATLANTIC SALMON STOCK IN THE RIVER DRAMMENSELV, NORWAY

LARS HANSEN

Norwegian Institute for Nature Research,
Trondheim, Norway

1. INTRODUCTION

The River Drammenselv, south-east Norway, is one of the largest rivers in Norway. In the last century it was one of the major salmon rivers in the country, supporting a fast growing salmon stock consisting of fish spending 1-5 winters in the sea. Industrial pollution, river regulation and overfishing resulted in a serious decline in this stock, and 10-15 years ago the salmon in this river were close to extinction. This paper describes the historical situation for the salmon stock, and discusses the rehabilitation programme put into effect in 1979. I will also present some provisional results of the stocking programme with underyearlings and smolts, and the subsequent harvest of adult fish. Furthermore, specific problems related to the very recent introduction of the harmful parasite *Gyrodactylus salaris* are also discussed.

2. THE RIVER SYSTEM AND THE SALMON STOCK

The River Drammenselv system drains large areas of south-east Norway (drainage area = 17,140km^2) (Fig.1). The system is heavily affected by regulation for the generation of hydroelectric power, and a number of dams and weirs have been built. The Hellefoss waterfall, utilized to generate hydroelectric power, is located about 19km upstream of the estuary and is the lowermost waterfall in the system. Here the average annual water discharge is about 225 m^{3}s^1, but during the spring flood the discharge may exceed 1500m^{3}s^1. Before regulation and the construction of a dam, salmon could pass the waterfall when the flow was optimal. This dam is the first obstacle for the sea-run salmon to enter, and several salmon ladders have been built, but until recently they have been unsatisfactory. The best smolt producing areas are found more then 35km upstream of the estuary, above two other dams, where there is no natural salmon run.

Inside Svelvik the Drammen Fjord is the functional estuary of the river, and the salinity of the surface water varies between 2 and 5°/oo. Outside Svelvik the salinity increases and in the area where the fjord meets Oslo Fjord the salinity exceeds 20°/oo.

The Atlantic salmon in the River Drammenselv is a typically multi-sea-winter salmon stock spending 1-5 winters in the sea, and the majority of the adult salmon ascending the river vary between 2 and 20kg in size. The grilse, which are mainly males, are between 2 and 5kg in weight, whereas the size of the 3-SW fish varies between 5 and 12kg (mainly females). The size of the 3-SW fish ranges between 8 and 20kg and consist of approximately equal proportions of males and females. The 4 and 5-SW fish, which are males, are usually larger than 15kg, and individuals up to 30kg in size have been observed, although they are rare.

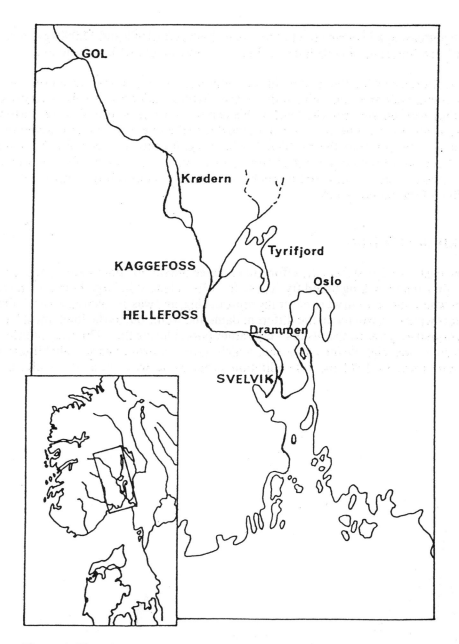

Figure 1. The River Drammenselv.

3. THE DECLINE OF THE SALMON STOCK

Catch statistics have been collected from the river system since 1876, and Fig.2 shows the nominal catch of Atlantic salmon up to the present time. From the beginning of this century, the catch declined and reached a low in 1978, when 400kg were reported caught. During this period commercial net fisheries were the most important gear in the river. The mean weight of the salmon in the fisheries is usually between 5 and 6kg, which implies that less than 100 fish were caught this year. From 1979 the catches again increased, and during the last few years between 10,000 and 13,000kg of salmon have been reported caught, and all salmon are now caught with rod and line.

The main reasons for the decline in the salmon stock were river regulation and the construction of dams and weirs in the system. Salmon ladders were also constructed, but they worked very poorly. During this century several pulp mills also started to operate, and the river became very polluted due to the release of fibres and chemicals. In the very recent years this problem has been significantly reduced. Finally, salmon have been heavily exploited in the Norwegian marine fishery and in the river for many years, and overexploitation of the stock may also have significantly contributed to the decline of the salmon stock.

4. REHABILITATION

In the past, very few systematic efforts to enhance the salmon population were carried out other than stocking unfed fry. These fry were released in large numbers in small areas where the salmon were naturally reproducing, and was probably a waste. Salmon ladders were constructed in the different dams and weirs, but as the lowermost ladder functioned very badly, the results were rather poor. During the 1970s the pollution by pulp mills was significantly reduced, which gave opportunities to rehabilitate the salmon stock. In 1978 the rehabilitation programme was initiated, involving the

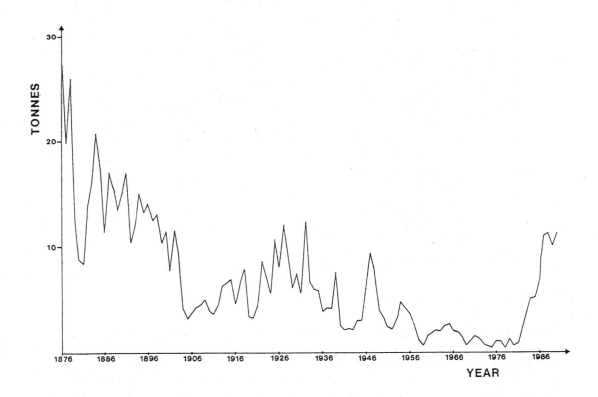

Figure 2. Nominal catches of Atlantic salmon in the River Drammenselv since 1876.

improvement of the two lowermost fish ladders, and the collection of broodstock for juvenile hatchery production. In 1979 a systematic stocking programme with fry and underyearlings, based on recognised biological principles, was started. All fish were stocked in optimal areas upstream of the natural salmon distribution area. In 1982 additional rearing facilities were available, and until present about 200,000 fed fry and 70,000 underyearlings were released annually. In 1990 a new hatchery came into operation, especially designed to support the salmon stock in the presence of *Gyrodactylus salaris*. At the end of the 1970s the commercial fishery in the river was banned, and angling then became the local legal fishery. Furthermore the management of the salmon stock was organised, and a board consisting of all parties involved was approved. This board is also responsible for the surveillance of the fishery.

5.EXPERIMENTAL STOCKING OF JUVENILES

5.1 Smolts

Smolts of the local stock are currently released at different sites into the River Drammenselv system as part of the rehabilitation programme. Groups of these fish are individually tagged with Carlin tags (Carlin, 1955). The first smolts were released in 1984. Over the first few years the smolts reared at the Research Station for Freshwater Fish, Ims, and transported by truck to the sites of release. In 1988 the local hatchery was expanded to produce smolts, and in 1990 a new hatchery came into operation.

The releases of tagged smolts have given an average total recapture-rate of about 7% of the number of smolts released, which equals an average production of about 400kg per 1000 smolts released. Of these about 65% are harvested in the marine and estuarine fisheries (Hansen, 1990).

5.2 Underyearlings

In September 1983 14,000 underyearlings (2.5g average weight) of Atlantic salmon of the local stock were released in the river, about 40 km upstream of the estuary where the conditions are excellent for salmon parr. In this area there is no natural run of salmon, but several other fish species are present, such as brown trout, whitefish, minnow, roach, pike and perch. All fish stocked had their adipose fin removed under chlorobutanol anaesthesia about 3 weeks prior to release. The fish were carefully stocked at a density of 1 individual per m^2. Returning salmon were recorded in the sport fishery downstream of the Hellefoss and in the salmon ladder in Hellefoss where all upstream migrating adults are controlled. The number of finclipped fish in the spawning stock downstream of Hellefoss was estimated using a mark-recapture procedure (Hansen *et al*, 1986).

The first returns of adult fish were recorded in 1986, when the grilse appeared. In 1987 the great majority of the returning salmon were 2 sea-winter fish demonstrating that the stocked fish mainly migrated to sea as 2 + smolts. The total estimated return to the river is shown in Table 1. In total, the estimated return to the river is 320 salmon, which is 2.3% of the number of underyearlings released. The total weight of the returns were 2,200 kgs or 0.157 kgs per fish released. Based on the data from the smolt releases the total marine exploitation rate of the stock is about 65% of the total number of salmon surviving to the adult stage. Using this figure it is then possible to estimate the total production of adult fish in this experiment as 914 fish (6.5%) of the number released) weighing about 6,300 kgs. This is equal to a production of 0.45kgs per underyearling released which is extremely profitable.

Table 1. Returns and weight of adult salmon to the River
Drammenselv of salmon released as underyearlings 1983.

Year	Number	Weight (kg)	Mean weight
1986	88	315	3.6
1987	210	1680	8.0
1988	14	150	10.7
1989	8	100	12.5
TOTAL	320	2245	7.0

This experiment was repeated in 1986 when 50,000 underyearlings were stocked in the same area. In 1989 and 1990 a total of about 350 adult fish from this group were recorded in the River. There was a high proportion of grilse returning in 1990, indicating that a relatively large proportion left the river as 3 + smolts.

6. EXPLOITATION

Salmon of the River Drammenselv stock are exploited in the marine fisheries in Norwegian home waters as well as by anglers in the river. Salmon from this stock are also caught in the long-line fishery operating within the 200 mile limit of the Faroes, and to a smaller extent at West Greenland. In total, the exploitation rate on the extant stock is around 65% (Hansen 1990). This exploitation will probably decline as a result of the regulatory measures recently introduced in Norway. However, the River Drammenselv stock was not heavily affected by the drift-net fishery. Exploitation rates in the sport fishery in the river have been estimated since 1985, and have varied between 33 and 53%.

7. PROBLEMS CAUSED BY *GYRODACTYLUS SALARIS*

The parasitic fluke *Gyrodactylus salaris* was observed for the first time on Atlantic salmon in Norway in 1975 (Johnsen 1978). The parasite, which is only about half a millimetre long, attacks salmon parr by attaching itself to the skin with its marginal hooks. The parasite causes heavy mortality of salmon parr (Johnsen and Jensen 1986), and it is probably imported to Norway from the Baltic (Bakke *et. al.* 1990), and has been spread to Norwegian rivers by stocking parr from infected hatcheries. It has now been recorded in 34 Norwegian salmon rivers.

In 1986 the fluke infected the salmon stock in the River Drammenselv, probably as a result of their being attached to rainbow trout that have escaped from fish farms in Lake Tyrifjord, about 45 km upstream of the estuary. This parasite will, in the future, have major effects on the natural production of Atlantic salmon in this river, and a serious decline in the parr population in the infected area has already been observed (Eken & Garnås 1990).

8. REHABILITATION STRATEGY

To enhance and to further rehabilitate the salmon stock in the presence of *Gyrodactylus salaris* is an enormous challenge, because the naturally produced parr will not survive the stocking of hatchery juveniles into uninfected areas as it is impossible to wipe out the parasite completely. Because adult salmon carry *G. salaris* upstream they will not be given access to spawning grounds far upstream. At present the salmon ladder in the third dam, about 35 km upstream of the estuary is now closed, and juveniles are stocked in the upstream area. However, experiments to disinfect the upstream migrating salmon using salt water have been initiated. Because underyearlings have given very promising results, efforts will be made to increase the proportion of those in the stocking programme, but smolts will also be released.

The exploitation in the river can be increased considerably, as natural spawning will be a waste due to the presence of the parasite.

ACKNOWLEDGMENTS

I am most grateful to Erik Fagerlid Olsen, Øivind Fladaas and the members of Østisiden Angling Club for their valuable support in this project. I am also indebted to the Atlantic Salmon Trust for financial support to attend the present meeting.

REFERENCES

Bakke, T.A., Jansen, P.A. and Hansen, L.P. (1990). Differences in the host resistance of Atlantic salmon, *Salmo salar* L., stocks to the monogean *Gyrodactylus salaris* Malmberg, 1957. Journal of Fish Biology 37: 577-587.

Carlin, B. (1955). Tagging of salmon smolts in the River Lagan. Report of the Institute of Freshwater Research, Drottningholm 36: 57-74.

Eken, M. and Garnås, E. 1990. Overvåking av lakseparasitten *Gyrodactylus salaris* på Østlandet 1989. Fylkesmannn i Buskerud, Miljøvernavdelingen, Rapport 7: 1-47.

Hansen, L.P. (1990). Exploitation of the Atlantic salmon (*Salmo salar* L.) from the River Drammenselv. Fisheries Research 10 (1-2): 125-35.

Hansen, L.P., Næsje, T.F. and Garnås, E. (1986). Stock assessment and exploitation of Atlantic salmon *Salmo salar* L. in River Drammenselv. Fauna Norvejic Series A 7: 23-26.

Johnsen, B.O. (1978). The effect of an attack by the parasite *Gyrodactylus salaris* on the population of salmon parr in the river Lakselva, Misvær in Northern Norway. Astarte 11: 7-9.

Johnsen, B.O. and Jemsen, A.J. (1986). Infestations of Atlantic salmon, *Salmo salar*, by *Gyrodactylus salaris* in Norwegian rivers. Journal of Fish Biology 29: 233-241.

DECLINE AND FALL OF THE RHINE SALMON OBSERVED IN THE LIGHT OF A POSSIBLE REHABILITATIONS.

S.J. DE GROOT

**Netherlands Institute for Fisheries Research,
IJmuiden, The Netherlands**

1. INTRODUCTION

In the framework of the International "Ecological Rehabilitation of the Rhine" programme, an initiative shared by France, The German Federal Republic and The Netherlands, a desk study was undertaken to evaluate existing information on the decline and extinction of the salmon (*Salmo salar*) in the River Rhine and also to study the possibility of reintroducing the salmon to the river system, that once was the largest salmon river in Europe (de Groot, 1989, 1990).

The length of the river from Constance to Hook of Holland is about 1114 km. The river basin is 185,000 km^2 (25,000 km^2 in the Netherlands). The average discharge of the river is 2200 m^3/s (575-13.000 m^3/s).

2. HISTORY

The oldest records mentioning the salmon of the Rhine date back to about 1100. According to toll and tax records, Dutch fishermen sold their catches in Koblenz (GFR). It is at present not possible to indicate the size of the stock in those days. However, from a study of the historian Van der Woude (1988), it is possible to derive some insight. Van der Woude studied the tax system on several products, the "ninth-pence". This tax was levied from 1650-1805.

During this period, twice the tax earnings dropped considerably, and after considering all possibilites, Van der Woude came to the conclusion that only a reduction in numbers of the salmon could explain the dip in earnings. The first decline, about 33% occurred in 1679 and again during 1680-1699 with another 33% compared to 1650.

From 1700-1805 the earnings were stable. Data on salmon catches for the first half of the 19th century are scarce. Only fragmentary data of some fishmarkets are available, (e.g. Geertruidenberg 1798-1810, 3,555 (1810) - 18,415 (1799) salmon per year.

Still in the 19th century, salmon fisheries, contributed largely to the economy and food supply. However, the impression exists that the salmon stocks were already on the decline. This became more evident around 1870, when the Rhine-states held the Mannheimer Convention to discuss e.g. the decline of the Rhine salmon. A salmon Treaty (Zalmtractaat) was formulated to improve the salmon fisheries. The treaty was ratified in 1886 by the Dutch government. However, after an initial rise in the Dutch salmon catches the decline continued. On a national level, the Salmon Commission was installed. the impressive final report of its findings was published in 1916. It is still a major source of our knowledge on the now extinct species (Anon., 1916).

3. SIZE OF THE POPULATION

It was possible to combine data from different sources on the Dutch salmon catches for the years 1863-1957 (Table 1, Fig. 1). The highest yearly catch was made in 1885 (104,422 salmon) Kühn (1976) traced catch data of the German part of the Rhine for the years 1875-1950. Also his data show a peak for 1885 (about 130,000 salmon). Kühn's data combined with those for the Netherlands provide us with a fairly complete picture (Fig. 2). The commercial salmon fisheries came to an end in 1932 for the Netherlands, those for Germany (GFR) in 1950. Now and then salmon are caught in the lower reaches of the Rhine and Meuse (Larsson, 1984).

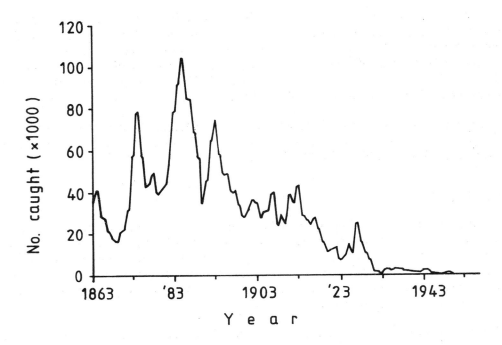

Figure 1. Dutch salmon catches 1863-1957

4. FLUCTUATIONS IN CATCHES

The grilse (1 seawinter (s.w.), or Jacobszalm, 61-67 cm) entered the Rhine in spring and summer. But most fishes entered the river from June-August, 85% were males. The 2SW salmon, small summer salmon (kleine zomerzalm) entered the Rhine and Meuse from May-July (83-91 cm, 7.5 kg). When they entered they were not mature, but became so during their upstream migration in the German part of the river. Large multi-seawinter fish entered from September-October. They had lengths of 103-115 cm., 5-15 kg. These large fish, if caught after the 1st of April, were referred to as large summer salmon. The kelts were mainly caught in April when they returned to the sea. Fig. 3 shows the fluctuations in the various categories for 1903-1919. Fig. 4 shows the average monthly catches 1911-1918.

Table 1. Total Dutch salmon catches 1863-1957

Year	Number	Year	Number	Year	Number
1863	35350	1895	48486	1927	25565
1864	41800	1896	49470	1928	14854
1865	28500	1897	39850	1929	9658
1866	27500	1898	41633	1930	5987
1867	20900	1899	33454	1931	1268
1868	17430	1900	27598	1932	1079
1869	15500	1901	31891	1933	611
1870	21600	1902	37336	1934	2642
1871	23142	1903	34686	1935	2300
1872	32015	1904	27541	1936	2868
1873	58255	1905	3098	1937	2311
1874	79107	1906	31564	1938	1920
1875	56852	1907	40544	1939	2016
1876	42383	1908	23557	1940	982
1877	44300	1909	29657	1941	1169
1878	49649	1910	24447	1942	1200
1879	38807	1911	39376	1943	1913
1880	41736	1912	34580	1944	2315
1881	44376	1913	43594	1945	456
1882	55079	1914	28298	1946	230
1883	78609	1915	27425	1947	233
1884	92116	1916	24161	1948	347
1885	104422	1917	28346	1949	900
1886	84230	1918	21032	1950	327
1887	84509	1919	14559	1951	94
1888	68048	1921	12039	1953	29
1890	34555	1922	13480	1954	27
1891	46091	1923	6520	1955	17
1892	65481	1924	9111	1956	2
1893	75175	1925	14586	1957	2
1894	57458	1926	9670		

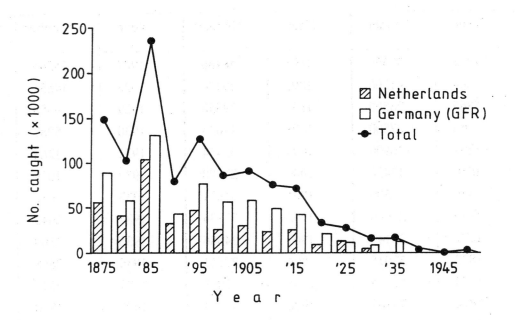

Figure 2. Total Dutch and German (GFR) salmon catches in the Rhine 1875-1950 (Dutch data Fig.1 and Kühn, 1976).

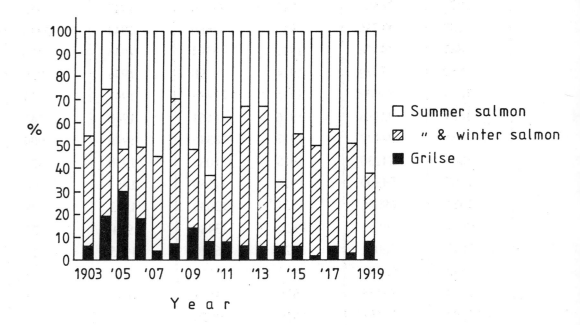

Figure 3. Dutch salmon catches 1903-1919 for the various market categories.

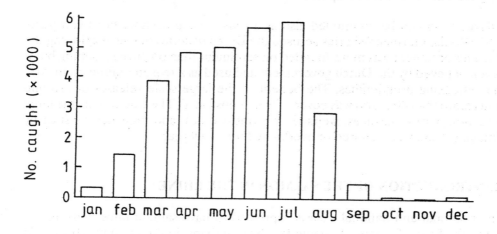

Figure 4. Average monthly landings of salmon 1911-1918.

5. CAUSES FOR THE DECLINE

From medieval times man has influenced the course of the Rhine, for either protection of villages, shipping or gravel dredging. The spawning areas in the various tributaries, all in Germany or Switzerland, or France, were affected by human activities. The multiple activities led to the removal of shallows, banks and islands, confining the main stream into a deepened part of the river. Although efforts to improve the flow of the Rhine are often associated with the last hundred years, a considerable amount of work had been carried out in The Netherlands during the 16th and 17th century to change the course of the various Rhine arms in the freshwater delta-area of the river (Van der Ven, 1976).

Also dredging of gravel in the spawning streams, the closing of old river loops, destroyed spawning sites and nursery areas. Weirs, dams and barrages built into the river hampered or blocked the up- and downstream migration of fish.

Around 1900 most of the tributaries of the Rhine were affected and became less, or unsuitable for salmon. Examples are: the Thur, Wutach, Aare, Reuss, Limat - Switzerland; Wiese, Elz, Dreisam, Ill, Rench, Neckar, Main, Nahe, Ruhr - Germany (GFR). Large weirs have been built on the Rhine below Basel since 1930. But still some rivers retained their value as salmon rivers, e.g. Kinzig, Sauer, Kill, Salm, Ruhwer, Dhron. However, the once largest salmon-river in Europe, changed into an average salmon-river, comparable with the present-day Tweed. The Mosel became the most important contributor to the Rhine salmon stocks, next to Sieg and Lahn.

Till about the 1920's and 1930's pollution of the main river played an unimportant role, notwithstanding that from medieval times it already played an important part in some of the smaller rivers. This was due to the river being glacial in origin. A rain-fed river is far more quickly affected by pollution. However, after 1930 pollution became more and more evident, but it is not the cause of the overall decline of the salmon although it may have speeded up its extinction during the last twenty years.

The fisheries should be mentioned also as a cause of the decline. For many years (1870-1940) the German fisheries accused the Dutch fisheries of over-exploiting the stocks. This argument was more founded on sentiment than on pure reasoning but it was even believed by the Dutch government and used as a reason to fund up to 80% of the restocking programmes. The benefit of the large scale releases of juvenile salmon (more than 80 years) was never fully demonstrated. The true causes, the large construction works, barrages, weirs (Rheinkraft-werke), and indicated as such by Fehlmann (1926), were ignored or overlooked for many years.

6. REINTRODUCTION OF THE SALMON IN THE RHINE

An international and national wish is expressed to have salmon once more in the Rhine in the form of a natural population. Not, perhaps, in the same numbers as in the past, but in enough numbers to demonstrate that the water quality has sufficiently improved due to the measures taken.

However, before reintroduction should be contemplated basic information is needed, such as:

1) Are there still sufficient spawning and nursery areas for salmon in the upper reaches of the river, non-polluted and protected?

2) Do the fish migrating downstream have enough and suitable resting places (the same for upstream migration)?

3) Is there any sign of a detrimental influence of detergents and other substances on the sense of smell? This may affect the memory of the outwardbound fish, or wipe out the possibility of their recognizing olfactory clues for homing to the native stream, by affecting their sense of smell (Bardach, 1965).

4) Most fish passes are built empirically; can they be improved by taking account of the specific behaviour of the fish?

5) What is the consequence of the large construction-works in the Rhine-Scheldt-estuary, to what extent do they block or hamper migrating salmonids?

6) What lessons does history provide us with to understand what happened to the salmon. Were the fluctuations in numbers the same as in nearby rivers (Elbe, Thames, Tweed etc.)?

Fluctuations may be caused by specific factors in the Rhine proper, but also climatic factors over a far wider area may have played their role (Shearer, 1988).

REFERENCES

Anon, (1916). Verslag van de Staatscommissie voor het zalmvraagstuk met bijlagen. Deel I: 1-91, Deel II: 1-271, 's Gravenhage, Algemene Landsdrukkerij.

Bardach, J.E.M., Fujiya, M. & Holl, A. (1965). Detergents: effects on the chemical senses of the fish *Ictalurus natalis* (le Sueur). Science, 148 (3677): 1605-1607.

Fehlmann, W., (1926). Die Ursachen des Rückganges der Lachsfischerei im Hochrhein. Beilage zum Jahresbericht der Kantonsschule Schaffhausen auf Frühjahr 1926, Schaffhausen, Buchdrückerei Meier und Cie, p.112.

Groot, S.J. de, (1989). Literature survey into the possibility of restocking the River Rhine and its tributaries with Atlantic salmon (*Salmo salar*). Publs. Reps. project "Ecological Rehabilitation of the River Rhine", nr. 11-1989, 56 pp, 14 tabs, 15 figs.

Groot, S.J. de, (1990). Is the recovery of anadromous fish species in the River Rhine a reality? 1. The Atlantic salmon (*Salmo salar*). De Levende Natuur, 91(3): 82-89. In Dutch with English summary.

Kühn, G. (1976). Die Fischerei am Oberrhein Geschichtliche Entwickelung und gegenwärtiger Stand. Hohenheimer Arbeiten, Heft 83, Stuttgart, Verlag Eugen Ulmer pp 1-193.

Larsson, P.O. (1984). Remote straying of salmon (*Salmo salar*) from the Swedish west coast and possible effects on sea ranching operations. Aquaculture 38: 83-87.

Shearer, W.M. (1988). Long term fluctuations in the timing and abundance of salmon catches in Scotland. ICES C.M. 1988/M:21.

Ven, G.P. van de. (1976). Aan de wieg van Rijkswaterstaat- Wordings- geschiedenis van het Pannerdens Kanaal. Gelderse Historische reeks part 8. Zutphen. De Walburg pers: 1-438.

Woude, A.M. van der. (1988). De contractie fase van de seculaire trend in het Noorder Kwartier nader beschouwd. Bijdr. med. Gesch. Ned., 103: 373-398.

THE EFFECTIVENESS OF TWO PHYSICAL IN-STREAM WORKS PROGRAMMES IN ENHANCING SALMONID STOCKS IN A DRAINED IRISH LOWLAND RIVER SYSTEM

M.F. O'GRADY, J.J. KING AND J. CURTIN(*)

Central Fisheries Board, Dublin, Ireland.
(*) Office of Public Works, Newtown, Trim, Ireland.

1. INTRODUCTION

The R. Boyne is one of Ireland's largest salmonid catchments. It drains an area of about 2,500 km^2 in the central and eastern part of the country, discharging to the Irish sea at Drogheda 50km north of Dublin city (Fig. 1).

An arterial drainage scheme was carried out on this catchment over the period 1968 to 1985 by the Office of Public Works. All main channel areas and tributary catchments above Navan were drained (Fig. 1). Since 1983 a post-drainage enhancement programme has been in progress. This exercise was funded by the Office of Public Works. The programme took the following format: a detailed biological survey of all drained channels was carried out. Information was compiled on physical, floral, faunal and fish stock regimes. These data in conjunction with hydrological information and physical records of an engineering nature (gradient, channel base widths, sinuosity, etc.) gave one an overview of the catchment. It facilitated the selection of areas with a potential for enhancement at reasonable cost and illustrated the extent to which channel morphology could be manipulated to suit salmonids without impeding the drainage function of the channel.

The overall cost of this rehabilitation programme is likely to be about IR£0.75m. It was decided therefore that specific enhancement exercises should be carried out initially on a pilot basis and monitored thereafter for three years to ensure their cost effectiveness before large scale works were undertaken.

This paper deals with two such pilot programmes. The nature of the sites in question are described. The works programme carried out is outlined and quantified. Data on the changes affected in the three year post-works period, in hydraulic, floral, faunal and fish stock terms, are presented and discussed. The relative cost-effectiveness of the programme is illustrated.

2. SITE SELECTION PROCEDURE

The survey data compiled on the drained areas of the R.Boyne main channel indicated that the most productive areas which support mixed salmon parr/adult trout populations are shallow (0.7m) relatively fast flowing (30-100 cm/sec) areas with a rubble or broken bedrock substrate. They have a complex hydraulic regime created by the relatively uneven bed resulting in the creation of riffles, gullies, back eddies and shallow "broken" glides. The gradient values in such areas was generally within the range 20cm to 25cm per 100m. The rock/rubble substrate here is heavily colonised

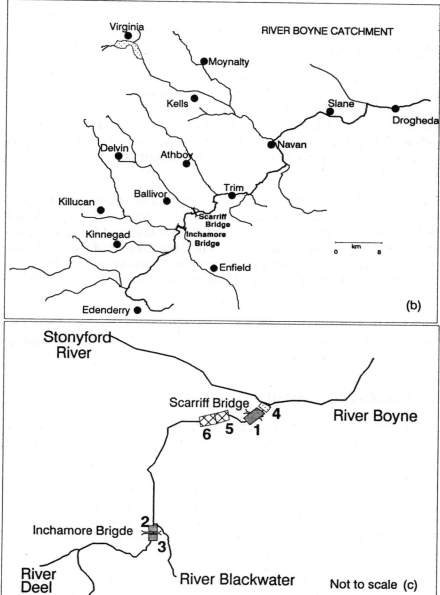

Figure 1. (a) River Boyne catchment in relation to Ireland.
(b) River Boyne catchment
(c) Site locations of the experimental and control zones.

by mosses and also supports limited stands of charophyte and macrophyte species (Section 5.2). There is an abundant and diverse macro-invertebrate fauna in such areas with plecopteran, ephemeropteran, *Hydropschye*, chironomid, simulid larvae and some Gasteropoda being common. Fish stocks are dominated by 1 + year old and older trout and 1 + year-old salmon parr. There are no significant gravel deposits in such areas, the salmonids present being recruited into such areas from the tributary catchments.

There are two extensive channel types in the main R.Boyne channel which differed significantly in physical, hydraulic and therefore biological terms from the productive zone outlined above. They are deep (1.0-2.5m) and shallow (0.5-1.0m) uniform glides.

In the deep glide areas incident light reaching the bed is inadequate to allow any plant growth. Apart from marginal vegetation, plant life is confined to isolated colonies of moss growing on top of occasional boulders which were ≤0.7m below summer water level. Such colonies covered <0.001% of substrate area. Qualitative faunal samples taken here indicated the presence of very few macro-invertebrates - only an occasional *Gammarus* and *Hydropschye* larva were present. In addition, there was very little hydraulic diversity in such zones.

The shallow uniform glide areas, in contrast, had a rich flora dominated by a range of macrophytic species and a rich and diverse fauna similar to that described previously for the shallow productive salmonid areas. Despite the rich flora and fauna, salmonid numbers were significantly lower in such areas than those present in the previously described productive areas which have a more complex hydraulic regime. Both the productive and barren areas described, had been drained in the same period (1972 to 1974).

Pilot zones were selected for enhancement in both the relatively unproductive shallow and deep glide areas as described above with the objective of increasing their capacity to support both salmon parr (1 +) and adult trout.

3. THE PILOT WORKS PROGRAMME

The works programme was designed to mimic, as far as was possible, the physical conditions of the productive shallow zones where good salmon parr/adult trout stocks had been recorded (Fig 1, Site 4).

The estimated minimum annual discharge (Q as m^3/sec) values were reviewed for a sixteen year period (1975-1990) at the nearest gauging station on the Boyne before works commenced. Q(T) values with a return time of less than 2 years were calculated from this data base. Subsequently, alterations in bed level with introduced rubble were made so that they would function best at such levels.

Three deep glide areas were selected in the middle reaches of the Boyne in 1987 (Fig 1). One of these was not altered i.e. it was maintained as a control zone (Site 3). The other two channel lengths (experimental zones) were altered physically by the introduction of large quantities of rubble placed in discrete mats across the full channel width (Sites 1 and 2). These stone mats were constructed with quarried limestone. Most of the individual stones had a diameter in the range 22cm to 38cm.

Three stone mats were constructed at intervals within each of the two experimental areas which were 163.5m and 243m respectively in length. Mean channel width per site varied between 13.0 and 17.0 m. The rubble mats were 12 m in length and were built to a height which reduced channel depth at summer levels to within the range 0.5m to 0.7m in depth over the surface area of each mat. Between 120 and 200 tonnes of rubble was required to construct each of the six mats. In addition ten large boulders (circa 0.7m in diameter) were placed randomly on the deep river bed areas between mats.

A continuous shallow glide area 400m long in the middle reaches of the R. Boyne was also selected for pilot works (Fig. 1). The mean channel width throughout the section was 18.0m. The upper half of this zone was maintained as a control zone (site 6). A total of 160 tonnes of rubble was introduced into the lower reaches (site 5). The rubble was arranged in the form of four mid-channel structures approximately triangular in shape ('V-shaped' structures). Stone size used was as previously described for the rubble mats. These structures were built up to low summer level as observed in 1987. They were designed to constrict the flow to either side of the channel at summer levels thereby increasing velocities over discrete lengths of channel. Following the construction of these islands, a single layer of rubble was placed on channel bed areas downstream of their location where flow velocities had, from visual observation, been increased as a consequence of channel constriction. In addition numbers of boulders were placed randomly on the bed in sections between the islands to create a more complex hydraulic regime.

4. MONITORING PROCEDURES

All of the experimental and control zones were examined prior to and on an annual basis after enhancement works were completed (1987 to 1990).

To investigate the effect of the rubble mats and V-shaped structures on the hydraulic regime, data were compiled on water depth and flow velocity at selected transects in the experimental and control zones. At all sites, measurements were taken along a graduated rope transect placed perpendicular to the direction of flow and secured firmly at each bank. Depth and velocity were measured, where possible, at 2.5m intervals along the transect. Depth was measured using graduated metal poles attached to a base plate which rested on the channel bed. Flow was measured using an OTT-'Z-200 flow meter attached to the metal poles. All flow readings were taken at a depth (D) of 0.6D as recommended by Leopold *et al* (1964). When recording, the operator always stood to the side and downstream of the instrument as recommended by Modde & Platz (1990). In the uniform control areas, transects monitored were spaced at a distance of 10 or 20m apart. They were more closely spaced on the rubble mats and along the V-shaped structures examined.

Summary mappings of the vegetation in the V-rubble area were compiled based on the methods outlined by Caffrey (1985). This involved use of graduated transects placed perpendicular to the channel to construct a scaled map of the section of channel under examination and the extent of cover of the major macrophyte elements present in the site. The level of precision used in compiling the mappings was set at a compromise level between a painstaking measurement of the dimensions of each macrophyte bed encountered and a simple indication of macrophytes present and their abundance. The mappings give a realistic indication of the extent of the major macrophyte elements present. Where material could not be identified in the field, samples were collected for laboratory examination and expert identification. Species lists were compiled both from the mappings and from the listing of species present in amounts too small to indicate on the mappings. On the rubble mats, the abundance of individual plant species was recorded semi-quantitatively using the classification of dominant (D), abundant (A), common (C) and present (+) as outlined by Caffrey (1990).

Observations on the macro-invertebrate communities at these sites, pre-works, are confined to qualitative samples - dredge samples from deep (> 0.7m) areas and pond net sweep samples from shallower zones. The attached fauna on large individual stones was also examined. Additional comment on the rate of colonisation of rubble mats by invertebrates was provided by Lynch & Murray (pers. comm.). This area is currently the subject of a detailed study which will be published at a later date by Lynch & Murray (pers. comm.).

Quantitative data on salmon parr and trout populations was compiled annually for each of the experimental and control zones. An electrofishing depletion technique was used (Zippin, 1958). Stop nets were employed to entrap the fish within the relevant section while fishing. All salmonids captured were measured and scaled. In 1990, the salmonids examined were also weighed. The productive unaltered shallow section (site 4) was only electrofished once (1988) on which occasion the salmonids present were measured, scaled and weighed. Some salmon fry (0 + year old) were observed at most sites. These numbers could not be quantified. The presence of other fish species was noted. Their numbers were not quantified.

5. RESULTS

Changes resulting as a consequence of the enhancement programme are presented here in physical, hydraulic, floristic, faunistic and fish stock terms. Comment is also provided in relation to the effects of the introduced structures on the drainage function of the channel.

5.1. Depth and Flow Regimes

(a) Rubble Mats:
A longitudinal profile of water depth and flow velocity along control sections and rubble mats is presented in Fig. 2. The depth and velocity at each point is the average of values measured across that transect at 2.5m intervals, discounting values within 2.5m of either banks. The range of values recorded at each transect is also presented in Fig. 2. Data presented were compiled in low flow conditions in July 1989. The control area upstream of Inchamore Bridge (site 3) is a deep unproductive glide with a poor gradient. The control area upstream of Scarriff Bridge (site 6) had a slightly higher gradient. The water was notably shallower and water velocities were higher than at Inchamore (Table 1). The velocities recorded over the rubble mats at each site far exceeded those in the control areas upstream. In terms of depth the rubble mat areas mirrored the regime in the 'natural' shallow productive areas (Fig. 2). The

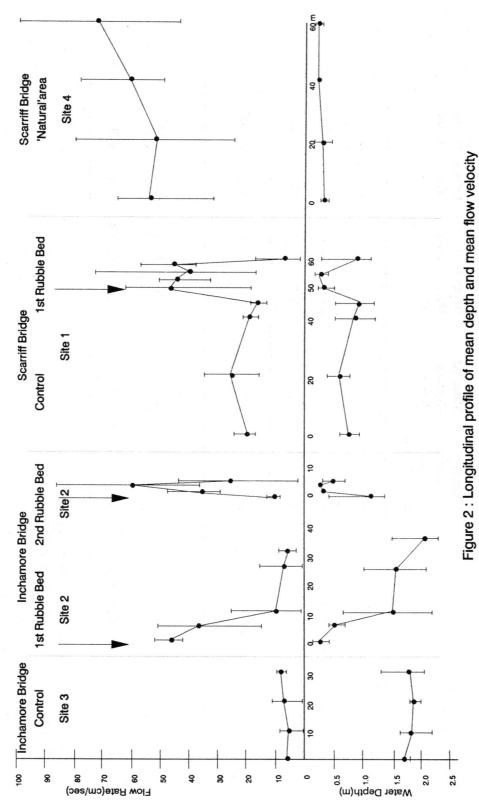

Figure 2 : Longitudinal profile of mean depth and mean flow velocity
at control and rubble mat sites on River Boyne,July 1989
Range values indicated by bars.
X-Axis = Distance(m) between transects at discontinuous series of sites.

TABLE 1. Data on channel depth, gradient and flow velocity in relevant transects at the experimental, control and productive shallow unaltered sites.

Site No., Location and Type	Channel gradient (Pre-works as cm/100m)	Mean (x) Channel Width (m)	Depth (cm) Mean (x)	Range	Velocity (cm/sec) Mean (x)	Range
1 Scarriff, Rubble mats(+)*	5.0	17.0	34	20-50	45.5	3-73
2 Inchamore, Rubble Mats (+)*	2.5	13.0	39.9	18-70	46.2	14-69
3 Inchamore, Control *	2.5	14.0	176.7	130-220	7.5	0-14
4 Scarriff, Productive Unaltered Shallow zone	22	16.5	24.8	15-40	55.3	25-100
5 Scarriff V-Rubble Experimental (LHS) (Sub-section) ** (RHS)	5 5	18 18	53.8 81.8	40-85 63-95	29.25 35.8	16-49 9-53
6 Scarriff V-Rubble Control **	6	17.5	91.5	63-109	11.3	0-26

(+) Measurements recorded on the rubble mats
*   Data of July, 1989 - low summer flow
** Data of July, 1990 - high summer flow

160

velocities achieved over the rubble mats were similar to those recorded in the natural unaltered shallow zone (site 4). This latter area had a good gradient which would, in addition to shallowness, have contributed to the elevated velocities recorded (Table 1).

The influence of the rubble mats on the in-stream hydraulic regime was very localised. The high flow rates recorded over the rubbled areas showed a rapid fall off immediately downstream of the mats. The depth and velocity regime between mats mirrored the regime in the upstream control area. Comparison of the two experimental mat sites indicates that the depth of water upstream of the rubble mats did not influence the recorded velocities across the beds. These velocities were a product of water depth over the bed. Depth and velocity over the rubble mats were very similar at both experimental sites (1 and 2) (Fig. 2).

(b) V-Rubble Structures:
A major feature of the V-rubble area (control and experimental) was the presence of extensive macrophyte beds in the channel. Some of the submerged macrophytes such as the mosses and *Callitriche* grew closely appressed to the bed of the channel. Others, such as *Potamogeton* spp. and *Sparganium emersum*, formed large streaming beds which trailed upward in the water column, with some trailing on the surface. These beds, along with such emergent macrophytes as *Sparganium erectum* and *Scirpus lacustris* created barriers to water movement in the channel and contributed to in-stream hydraulic diversity.

Channel width and gradient were similar at the V-rubble experimental and control sites (Table 1). Depth and flow rates (D/F) along a series of transects are presented in plans of the control and experimental sites (Figure 3 (a) and (b)). These results were compiled during a short period of elevated water levels in July 1990. A more uniform depth regime was present in the control zone with a majority of depths greater than 80cm. Low flow velocities were recorded, ranging from 0 to 26 cm/sec. The zero values were recorded downstream of macrophyte beds. The experimental area generated a more diverse regime in terms of depth and flow. The V-shaped mats of rubble in mid-channel and the loose rubble deposited between it and the channel's left bank served to deflect much of the flow along the right hand side of the channel. This created a degree of scouring which, together with the rubble, created a diversified depth regime (Fig. 3 (b)). The depth/flow transect 2.5m upstream of the front of the V-rubble structure gave similar values to the control transects. Macrophytes played an important role in the experimental section, functioning with the V-shaped rubble mats to create a fast-flowing run on the right-hand side of the channel. On the left side of the channel a relatively shallow depth regime was created. The widespread small stands of emergent macrophytes here tended to slow water velocities. However, flow rates were comparable to the maxima recorded in the control zone. The rubble layers placed along the banks downstream of the V-rubble structure caused a constriction in the channel and served to accelerate the water velocity (Fig. 3).

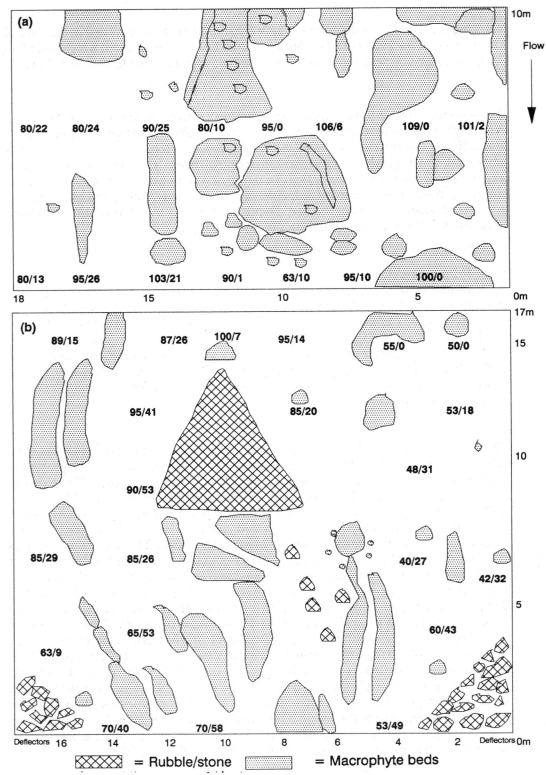

Figure 3. Scarriff Bridge V-rubble area: plan of depth/water velocity regime in (a) control and (b) experimental areas, July 1990.

5.2. Flora

(a) Rubble Mat Areas:

Data relating to the floral composition and abundance at control sites and on rubble mats are presented in Table 2. These results were collected in July 1989 and August 1990.

The deep control area upstream of Inchamore Bridge (site 3) and the 'natural' shallow area downstream of Scarriff Bridge (site 4) represent two extremes in terms of floral composition and abundance while the experimental rubble mats, via. colonisation from drift material, showed many of the features of the flora in the natural shallow area.

Table 2. Composition and abundance of instream flora at control and rubble mat sites on R. Boyne. (D = dominant; A = abundant; C = common; + = present; after Caffrey, 1990)

Site/Year	Deep control Site 3 1989,90	Rubble mat Site 2 1989	Rubble mat Site 2 1990	Rubble mat Site 1 1989	Rubble mat Site 1 1990	Natural shallow area Site 4 1989,90
Sagittaria	+					
Sparganium erectum	+	+	+	+	+	+
S. emersum	+	+	+			+
Scirpus lacustris	+					+
Potamogeton perfoliatus					+	+
P. crispus		+	+			+
Polygonum comphibium		+	+			
Callitriche	+				+	+
Apium		+	+	+	+	C
Rorippa	+			C	C	
Ranunculus		+	+	+	+	C
Zannichellia			+			+
Filamentous algae	D	D	D	A	A	+
Chara			+		+	A
Aquatic liverworts			+	+	C	A
Aquatic mosses	+	C		+	+	D
Lemna trisulca			C	+		

163

The deep control area upstream of Inchamore Bridge carried a sparse instream flora with occasional small stands of *Sparganium* spp. and *Sagittaria*. These plants can cope with the light-occluding properties of deep water via. the growth of emergent leaves or leaves which can trail at or just under the water surface. Small local stands of *Callitriche* and *Rorippa* were recorded close to the banks. The fringing bankside flora consisted mainly of *Phalaris* and *Glyceria maxima* with, in places, an understorey of *Alisma*, *Myosotis* and *Mentha*.

Floristically, the most prominent feature of the rubble mats was the dominance of filamentous algal genera (Table 2). These were found throughout the rubble mats but were most prominent on the large stones and boulder filled parts of the Inchamore mats. These boulder-filled areas, were otherwise largely devoid of macrophyte cover. This may be due to the large water-filled spaces between the rubble material which would be slow to fill with finer material due to the large size of the interstices and the scouring force of the high water velocities. Where the top of the mats contained a finer grade of rubble the relatively smaller interstices had begun to fill, to form a rough but continuous surface. Some limited colonisation by *Apium* and *Rorippa*, both broad-leaved macrophytes which can exhibit a low growth form and strong rooting systems, took place on the rubble mats. Small amounts of aquatic mosses were recorded on the rubble mats as were limited quantities of *Ranunculus* spp. Isolated small stands of *Sparganium erectum* were found on the rubble mats where pockets of sediment had deposited between the large stones. The localised stands of *Scirpus lacustris* were recorded where the mats had a compacted bed. Small amounts of *Potamogeton crispus* and *Polygonum amphibium* recorded at Inchamore in shallow back waters at one edge of the rubble mat were not characteristic of the instream flora. The more substantial development of some species and the greater floral diversity on the Scarriff mats compared to those at Inchamore (Table 2) may be due to the greater amount of downstream drift from the well vegetated areas upstream of Scarriff Bridge. In the case of Inchamore, a long section (1.3km) of deep, unproductive channel lies upstream of the rubble mat zone.

The natural shallow area downstream of Scarriff was characterised, physically, by low water levels and high water velocities. The instream flora was dominated by aquatic mosses. The other prominent components were aquatic liverworts, *Ranunculus* spp. and *Chara* spp. (Table 2). The mosses formed extensive carpets on the river bed which was firm and compacted with a well-developed calcified crust, characteristic of productive, hard-water sites. Large beds of *Chara*, to $0.25m^2$, were common.

The results for 1989 indicate that the flora at that time was transitional in type between the flora of the deep-water sites and that of the shallow fast-flowing area. These areas were examined again in August (1990) and the rubble mat flora exhibited some changes (Table 2). The mats at Inchamore showed increased floral diversity with *Zannichellia*, *Lemna trisulca*, *Sparganium emersum*, aquatic liverworts and *Chara* spp. being recorded. Some of these plants were characteristic of the natural shallow water flora. In addition, the extent of moss colonisation had increased. Large areas of the bed were, however, still devoid of any macrophyte cover.

(b) V-rubble structures:
A diverse flora was recorded at both the control and experimental sites. The relatively low water velocities facilitated the development of large stands of *Sparganium*

164

Flora Coding

1. *Sparganium erectum*

2. *Sparganium emersum*

3. *Scirpus lacustris*

4. *Potamogeton gramineus*

5. *Potamogeton perfoliatus*

6. *Potamogeton crispus*

7. *Elodea*

8. *Chara*

9. *Rorippa*

10. *Apium*

11. *Myosotis*

12. *Phalaris*

13. *Zanichellia*

14. *Glyceria maxima*

15. *Mosses*

16. *Oenanthe*

17. *Ranunculus*

19. *Callitriche*

20. *Sagittaria*

▨▨▨▨ = Rubble/stone

▒▒▒▒ = Macrophyte beds

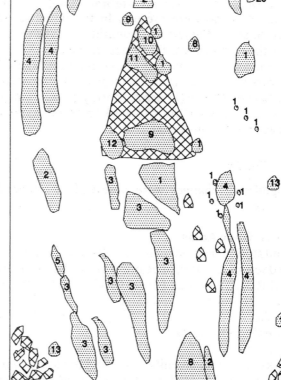

Figure 4. *Scarriff Bridge V-rubble area: plan of macrophyte distribution in (a) control and (b) experimental areas, July 1990.*

165

emersum and *Potamogeton perfoliatus* (Fig. 4 (a)). These occupied large 3-dimensional spaces in the water column. A substantial understorey flora was also developed, consisting of *Chara, Ranunculus, Elodea* and *Apium*, among others. Aquatic mosses formed an extensive part (not shown in Fig. 4 (a)) of this understorey. Within the control area, but downstream of the area represented in Fig. 4 (a), large stands of emergent *Scirpus lacustris* were recorded in 1990. These stands were not present when the V-shaped rubble structures were installed downstream.

The percentage of floral cover was lower in the experimental area. The more diverse hydraulic and depth regime has been referred to above. The elevated flow rates thus achieved may have favoured the floral changes observed. *Potamogeton perfoliatus* with its relatively broad-leaved form was largely replaced by the finer-leaved *P. gramineus* in the sections examined. Similarly, *Scirpus lacustris* was recorded with predominantly submerged leaves, offering less resistance to flow, rather than as an emergent. The shallow water on the left side of the channel favoured the substantial growths of filamentous algae recorded. The experimental area also carried an extensive moss cover.

5.3. Macro-Invertebrate Fauna

Pre-works in 1987 samples from all of the deep glide areas in question indicated the presence of a very poor invertebrate fauna - only occasional *Gammarus* and *Hydropsyche* larvae were present. In the initial six month period, post-works, the presence of some Baetiid, Ecdyonurid and *Hydropsyche* larvae and *Gammarus* was noted on the rubble mats. Two years after works, in 1990, the presence of a significant range of macro-invertebrate species was noted. Significant differences were observed in the diversity of invertebrates at the two rubble mat sites by 1989 with site 1 at Scarriff having the higher value (Lynch & Murray, pers. comm.). The very poor fauna observed in the deep glide areas prior to works had remained unchanged by September 1990 in the unaltered control zone.

5.4. Fish Stocks

Very significant changes were observed in salmonid stocks following the works programme.

5.4.1. Deep Glide Areas

Salmonid stock density values were estimated in the two experimental and one control zone in deep glide areas, once pre-works (1987) and annually thereafter from 1988 to 1990 inclusive. The works were carried out at the two experimental sites in September 1987 (Site 2) and May 1988 (Site 1) respectively. Consequently, there was a seven month difference in the post-works period when both sites were electrofished in 1988 and thereafter (Table 3).

Pre-works (1987) no juvenile salmon were recorded in the control and experimental zones. Brown trout populations were also at, or close to ($\leq 0.5 \times 10^3/m^2$), zero at all three sites. Post-works (1988 to 1990) major increases were evident in the stock densities of both salmonid species in the experimental zones. Trout and salmon parr numbers remained at zero level in the control area throughout this period (1988 to 1990) (Table 3).

Table 3. Salmonid stock densities recorded in both experimental (altered) deep (1 & 2) and shallow (5) glide areas, their respective control zones (3 & 6) and an unaltered shallow productive area (4).

Site and Location	Year *	Salmonid stock densities No./m^2 & 95% C.I. () - g/m^2		Period Post-works (months)
Rubble Mat Areas		**Salmon Parr**	**Trout**	
1 Scarriff Experimental	1987	0	$0.5 \times 10^{-3} \pm 0$	-
	1988	0.02±0.001	0.006±0.002	5
	1989	0.05±0.002	0.04	17
	1990	0.04±0.01(2.2)	0.06±0.006(13.74)	29
2 Inchamore Experimental	1987	0	$0.2 \times 10^{-3} \pm 0$	-
	1988	0.02±0.002	0.01±0.002	12
	1989	0.03±0.004	0.01±0.005	24
	1990	0.01±0.003(0.35)	0.01±0.002(2.14)	36
3 Control at Inchamore	1987	0	$0.2 \times 10^{-3} \pm 0$	-
	1988	0	0	-
	1989	0	0	-
	1990	0(0)	0(0)	-
4 (Unaltered shallow area at Scarriff)	1988	0.09±0.04(3.1)	0.03±0.003(9.1)	-
V-rubble Areas				
5 Scarriff V-rubble Experimental	1987	0.03±0.01	0.006±0.001	-
	1988	0.1±0.005	0.02±0.003	5
	1989	0.01 **	0.02±0.001	17
	1990	0.03±0.01(1.38)	0.03±0.004(5.34)	29
6 Scarriff V-rubble Control	1987	0.04±0.006	0.008±0.002	-
	1988	0.05±0.007	0.006±0.009	5
	1989	0.08±0.007	0.01±0.005	17
	1990	0.05±0.01(2.05)	0.02±0.004(3.94)	29

* Works were carried out at experimental sites 1 and 5 in April 1988 and at site 2 in September 1987.

** Minimum density estimate

At experimental site 1 there was a very significant increase in salmon parr numbers by September, 1988 only five months after works (from 0 to 0.02/m^2). Trout stocks had also increased substantially (from 0.5 x 10^{-3}/m^2 to 0.6 x 10^{-2}/m^2) although they still remained small relative to numbers recorded in the unaltered productive area of the R. Boyne main channel previously described (site 4) (Table 3). In 1989 a further significant increase was evident at site 1 in terms of both salmon parr (0.05/m^2) and trout (0.04/m^2). In 1990 a further increase was evident in trout numbers (0.06/m^2) and a slight fall in the salmon parr value (0.04/m^2).

In summary, the results for experimental site 1 were encouraging. Twenty-nine months after enhancement works the salmonid carrying capacity had increased from zero to 0.04 or 0.05 salmon parr/m^2 and from 0.5 x 10^{-3}/m^2 to 0.06/m^2 for trout. The figures achieved are significant for a number of reasons. All of the salmon parr were 1 + year-old fish (Fig.5). As the stock estimates were carried out in September each year the numbers of parr encountered is probably close to or slightly less than the pre-smolt "output" of the channel section. Some 0 + year-old parr were present each year. However, estimation of their numbers was impossible. A proportion of Boyne salmon do smoltify as one year-old fish. Very few Boyne smolts (< 0.1%) exceed 2 years of age.

At experimental site 2 a very similar trend was observed to that already described for site 1 with significant increases in both salmon parr and trout numbers post-works. The stock density of 1 + year-old salmon parr fluctuated between 0.03/m^2 in 1988 to 0.01/m^2 in 1990. There were no parr present prior to works. Trout numbers post-works increased from 0 to 0.01/m^2 in 1988 and remained at that level in both 1989 and 1990. This is a relatively substantial figure given the stock structure in question (Fig. 6).

The difference in stock density values recorded between sites 1 and 2 for salmon parr and trout is also reflected in standing crop values expressed as g/m^2 - 15.94 and 2.49 at sites 1 and 2 respectively for the combined salmon and trout values (Table 3).

A significant difference is evident between the standing crop values recorded for both salmon parr and trout at experimental sites 1 and 2 with site 1 supporting larger numbers of both species. This is despite the fact that site 2 was developed seven months earlier than site 1 (Table 3). Two factors may have played a role in creating these differences. Firstly, the extent of shallow bed area, as a percentage of total bed area, created in each of the two zones was different. It constituted 22.0% and 14.8% of total bed area at sites 1 and 2 respectively. The second important difference was the fact that site 1 was located downstream of a kilometre length of relatively shallow (mostly ≥0.7m) productive water while the channel upstream of site 2 was deep (≥1.5mm) and unproductive for 1.3 km. As a consequence it is likely that invertebrate drift levels to site 1 were very significantly higher than those to site 2. In addition a greater number of fish were present in areas adjacent to site 1 than site 2, a factor which may also have influenced colonisation rates.

Data indicate that 29 months after works the stock density of all salmonids at site 1 (0.1/m^2) was close to those recorded in the naturally productive area which was not altered physically post-drainage (site 4) (0.12/m^2). While values are very similar, the actual salmon/trout balance at the two sites was different with salmon parr numbers being lower (0.04/m^2 vs. 0.09/m^2) and the trout figure being higher (0.06/m^2 vs.

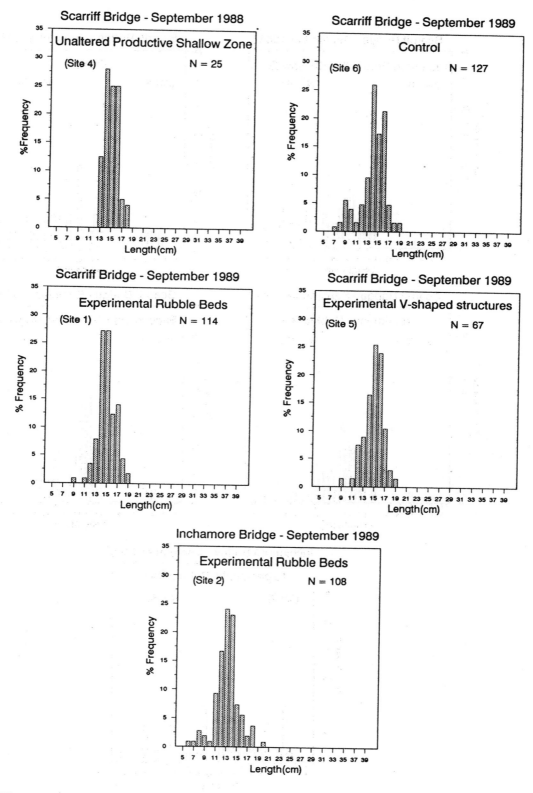

Figure 5. % Length frequency distribution of salmon.

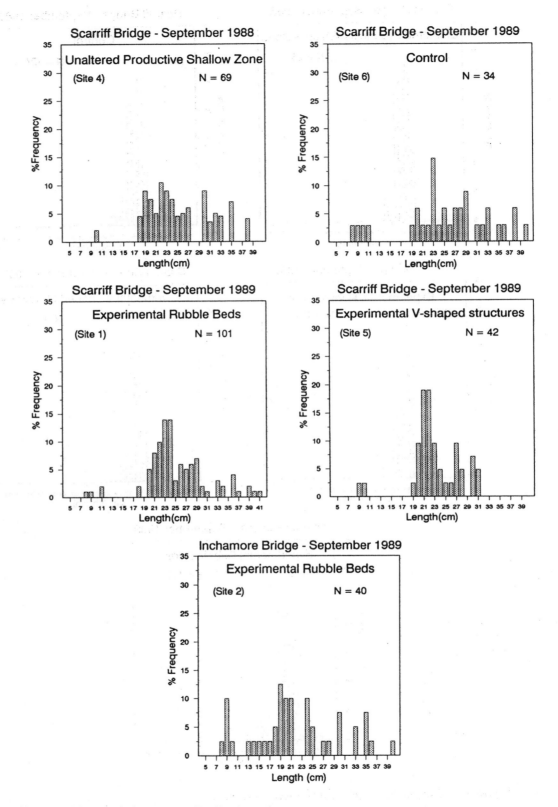

Figure 6: % Length frequency distribution of trout.

$0.03/m^2$) at site 1. In terms of salmonid biomass values higher weights are evident at site 1 than at the unaltered productive site (No. 4) ($15.94 g/m^2$ vs. $12.2 g/m^2$). This is a consequence of the greater numbers of trout being present at site 1 (Table 3).

5.4.2. Shallow Glide Areas

The changes evident in fish stocks from 1987 to 1990 in the experimental (site 5) and control (site 6) zones are illustrated (Table 3). Pre-works (1987), relatively moderate stocks of 1 + year-old salmon parr and poor trout numbers were present in both areas. Following physical alterations in 1987 the salmon parr numbers in the experimental zone rose initially ($0.1/m^2$ in 1988), subsequently fell ($0.01/m^2$) in 1989 and in 1990 returned to the recorded level ($0.03/m^2$) prior to works. A more stable pattern was evident in the control zone with parr stock densities only fluctuating between 0.04 and $0.08/m^2$ over the four year period (1987 to 1990) (Table 3).

In the experimental zone trout numbers rose sharply (0.006 to $0.02/m^2$) only five months after works. They remained relatively stable thereafter up to 1990 only fluctuating between 0.2 and $0.3/m^2$. In the control zone the trout stock density values were low in 1987 and changed little in 1988 (0.008 and $0.006/m^2$ respectively). They increased sharply in 1989 ($0.01/m^2$) and improved again in 1990 ($0.02/m^2$) (Table 3).

These results suggest that the works programme at site 5 was not successful in terms of increasing salmon parr numbers after 1988 and was only moderately successful in improving the trout carrying capacity of the zone 29 months after alterations were introduced.

Observations suggest that changing summer water levels over the period (1987 to 1990) may have been responsible for the pattern of results observed.

The low flow regimes which persisted in 1989 and 1990 changed the depth and hydraulic regimes in both zones. However, these are inadequate to illustrate the full extent of change. Minimum low summer water levels fell by 11cm in 1989 and 1990 compared to the two previous years. In summary a significant area of the shallow rubbled bed in the experimental area was actually exposed or too shallow to support 1 + year-old salmonids in 1990. In contrast, in the control zone the reduction in water levels resulted in the growth of mid-stream stands of emergent *Scirpus* spp. Visual observation also suggested a general increase in the biomass of macrophytes in this area as a consequence of lower water levels in 1989 and 1990. Further comment is provided in relation to these changes in the discussion.

5.4.3. Non-Salmonid Species

Salmonids were not the only fish species observed. By September 1990, large numbers of gudgeon (*Gobio gobio* L.) had colonised the rubble mat areas. Visual observation suggested the presence of a gudgeon stock which was larger than that observed in other parts of the R. Boyne system. This may have been due to the extensive quantities of filamentous algae on the rubble mats. Kennedy and Fitzmaurice (1972) have noted that algal material was a significant dietary item for gudgeon in a number of Irish waters. Numbers of eels (*Anguilla anguilla* L.), perch (*Perca fluviatilis* L.), stoneloach (*Noemacheilus barbatulus* L.), minnow (*Phoxinus phoxinus* L.) and a few three-spined sticklebacks (*Gasterosteus aculeatus* L.) were also present in all of the experimental and control zones. Quantitative data were not compiled for any of the non-salmonid species.

6. A COST BENEFIT ANALYSIS

The works programme involving the creation of rubble mats at site 1, has proved, after three years, to be the most successful of the enhancement programmes described here. To put the costs and benefits of this exercise in perspective the following scenario is presented. Consider the cost of constructing rubble mats over a 1.0km length of channel of the type altered at Scarriff (site 1). Look at the fishery benefits in terms of the cost of stocking the standing crop of salmon and trout in this zone on an annual basis. Assume the same specification in terms of the percentage of shallow water created by the rubble mats at the Scarriff site (22%).

The projections in Table 4 indicate a complete return on investment in less than four years without making any allowance for the additional income which might be generated locally by an increased level of tourist angling.

The fish values in monetary terms presented in Table 4 were calculated as follows. The cost of a stocked smolt was assumed to be £1(IR). The survival of the S2 wild smolts produced, to adult salmon status, was assumed to be three times higher than what one would expect in returns from stocked smolts - values calculated for an Irish fishery by Mills & Piggins (1983). This figure underestimates annual smolt output because no allowance is made for S1 smolt production per annum. The cost of stocking the standing crop of trout is based on current production costs in Ireland. A multiplier of two is used here on the basis that wild fish would probably have a significantly higher survival rate than stocked fish (O'Grady, 1981). It is assumed that an adequate recruitment rate of young fish into the enhanced channel would be available annually to maintain the projected standing crop figures.

Two other factors suggest that the benefits, as calculated here, may be an underestimate. Firstly, the assumed standing crop values used to calculate these figures are those achieved at the Scarriff site only three years after their construction. Hunt (1976) has shown that the maximum benefit of physical instream enhancement works in trout streams may not be evident for up to 6 years. Secondly, the contrast in results achieved at the Scarriff and Inchamore rubble mat sites (1 and 2 respectively)

Table 4. The costs and benefits of a rubble mat type enhancement programme.

Costs - for the construction of rubble mats as per Scarriff specification for 1km of channel	Benefits - measured in terms of fish stocking costs per annum	
£14,571 (Machine hire & stone purchase costs)	640 S^2 Smolts	£1920
	640 2 y.o. trout	£ 960
	320 3 y.o. & older trout	£1,280
Total £14,571	Total	£4,160

172

suggest that the quantity of invertebrate drift passing through an enhanced area may influence standing crop values. Rubble mats constructed in series over a 1.0km length of channel would, when colonised, generate a very significant invertebrate drift which might lead to the maintenance of higher salmonid standing crop figures than those measured at the Scarriff site by 1990.

7. DISCUSSION

Numerous studies in North America have identified stream depth, flow and gradient as key factors in determining the trout carrying capacity of fluvial systems (Duff and Cooper 1978, Collotzi and Dunham 1978, Pennak 1978, Binns and Eiserman 1979, Wesche *et al*, 1987 and others). The initial survey of the R. Boyne catchment confirmed that the aforementioned factors all appeared to be of critical and primary importance in determining both juvenile salmon and adult trout numbers found in specific areas of this river.

The relative success of the authors' approach in using rubble mats to create productive salmonid habitat is not surprising. Hey (in press) has highlighted the potential for salmonid stock enhancement in lowland rivers. White and Brynildston (1967) and Barton and Winger (1973) have shown that given proper planning and adequate resources, the salmonid carrying capacity of some rivers can be fully restored following physical disturbance.

It must be stressed that the success achieved using rubble mats was due in part to the availability of salmon parr and trout in this particular river to recruit into the enhanced areas.

The selection of rubble, as opposed to gravel or boulders, as "mat material", may have also played a role in the success of this exercise. Needham (1969) has shown that this type of material can harbour a greater biomass of invertebrates than the aforementioned materials.

The rubble material (in rubble mats and V-shaped structures) creates a new habitat for plant colonisation. Filamentous algae have been found to be among the first colonists of such new habitats (Crawford 1979). The dominance of these plants on the rubble mats suggests that floral colonisation of these structures is still at an early stage.

The rubble mats create a channel constriction (by reducing depth) and hence increase flow rates. Water velocity has been shown to be of major importance in determining river plant community composition (Caffrey 1990). Sites with moderate to high water velocities frequently carry a substantial moss flora, as at the Scarriff 'natural' shallow site. Aquatic plants of the genus *Ranunculus* are also characteristic of fast water (Haslam 1978). The abundance of *Chara* in the Scarriff natural shallow site may appear unusual. This genus is characteristic of hard-water benthic systems. However, both *Chara* and the closely-related *Nitella* have been recorded at a number of Irish riverine sites with high velocities, including locations on tributaries of the R. Boyne (Caffrey and King 1989).

In addition to influencing species composition, velocity can affect the phenotype or physical form of the plant present. The predominance of submerged, rather than emergent, leaves of *Scirpus lacustris* in the faster flowing waters of the V-rubble site has already been referred to. The same effect has been noted by Caffrey (1990) in fast flowing sections of other Irish rivers.

The relative difference in the standing crops of salmonids in the two "rubble mat areas" illustrates the importance of ecological conditions in zones upstream of enhanced areas in determining both aquatic floral, invertebrate diversity (Murray and Lynch, pers comm.) and fish colonisation rates post-works.

The necessity for a bio-engineering approach in relation to the design of rubble mats in specific channel areas is regarded by the authors as critical. A failure to do so could result in the creation of impoundment and/or bank erosion problems. It could also lead to poor returns in fishery terms. For instance an excessive water depth regime at summer levels, over mat areas, could limit the primary and secondary productivity of such areas. Critical water depth in this context will vary in individual catchments depending as it does on water clarity and colour. In future the authors would hope to use a "back water analyses" software programme designed by Office of Public Works drainage engineers for use in lowland catchments (Mangan, 1988). It is hoped that this package will enable one to cost in-stream physical works exercises for specific channel sections at design stage and also guard against the implementation of programmes which might impact on a channel's designed drainage functions.

The compliance of rubble mat design with the drainage requirements of the channel were assured in this instance by an examination of the effects of reducing the conveyance (water carrying capacity) of the channel at individual reaches using the step by step method based on Mannings equation (Massey, 1970). The rubble mats and V-shaped structures reduced the cross-sectional area by up to 60%. The effect of these proposals when complete was to increase the mean velocities in the affected reaches with no detrimental drainage alteration to the existing water surface profile. The increase in mean velocities compensated for the reduced conveyance of the channel.

The rubble mats could be described as "drowned" broad crested rivers. Since the rubble mats were designed to be drowned out for the Q bar flow condition they do not interfere with the channel's ability to deal with flood condition.

The poor results achieved by the second enhancement exercise (V-rubble structures) would appear to be due to the widely fluctuating summer water levels during the study period which had two consequences. Water depth over some rubbled areas in the experimental zone became inadequate to support juvenile salmonids. The reduced depth regime also appears to have been responsible for major floristic changes in the control zone which in essence meant that it no longer functioned as such.

A review of the estimated minimum annual Q values for an adjacent gauging station on the R. Boyne at Trim (Station No.0705) over 16 years (1975-1990) illustrates this point (Fig.7). These data provide one with an estimated annual minimum Q bar value of 3.1981 (m³/s) for this period. Using a least squares estimate procedure these data predict the following (return time) values (Table 5).

A review of estimated annual minimum flow Q values over the experimental period (1987 to 1990) in conjunction with the derived Q(T) expectancies indicated that when

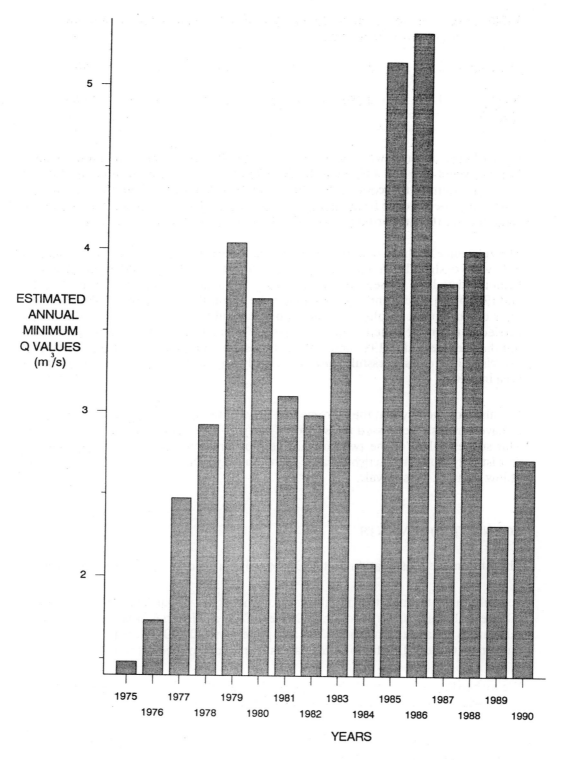

Figure 7. Lowest estimated annual Q values for the Boyne at Trim (1975 - 1990).

Table 5. Least squares estimates for Q(T) derived from annual minimum flow values from 1975 to 1990.

T (Years)	2	3	5	10	25	50
Q (T) (m^3/s)	3.006	2.589	2.242	1.918	1.614	1.437

the works programmes were carried out (1987 to 1990) the annual minimum Q values in those years (3.8 and 4.0) might be expected to re-occur with a frequency of <2 years. In contrast the comparable 1989 and 1990 values (2.31 and 2.71) have an expected re-occurrence frequency of between 2.2. and 5 years. In addition the Q bar value for the 16 year period (3.1981m^3/s) is close to the 2 year Q (T) value.

The relevance of these data to the overall experiment is the fact that the structures built were designed to function at or close to the Q bar value (3.1981/m^3s) calculated from the data base presented. Unfortunately, estimated minimum Q values in 1989 and 1990 being significantly lower appear to be primarily responsible for the relatively poor enhancement results achieved with the V-rubble exercise. As the alterations carried out were designed to function best at "normal" (Q bar) low water levels and not those expressed in 1989 and 1990 it is possible that, in the longterm, this type of exercise will prove successful. They were clearly very successful relative to the control area in 1988.

It is also noteworthy that the extreme low flows of the latter two years do not appear to have seriously depressed the salmonid carrying capacity of the rubble mat areas. This suggests that, of the two enhancement programmes, the rubble mats may be consistently more productive because of their ability to function over a broader range of low summer water levels.

ACKNOWLEDGEMENTS

The authors are most grateful to the Office of Public Works who funded this project.

Special thanks are due to a number of our colleagues in particular Mr. Tim Joyce (Office of Public Works) and Dr. J.Caffrey (Central Fisheries Board) for advice in relation to data interpretation. We are grateful to Dr. D. Murray and J.Lynch, University College Dublin for information on the macro-invertebrate fauna.

We wish to thank Inspector J. Stapleton and his staff of the Eastern Regional Fisheries Board who carried out the electrical fishing programme.

We are most grateful to Dr. P. Fitzmaurice (Central Fisheries Board) for his constructive editorial comments.

REFERENCES

Barton, J.R. & Winger, P.V. (1973) Rehabilitation of a channelised river in Utah. Proceedings of the 21st Annual Hydraulic Diversion Speciality Conference, Montana State University. 1-10.

Binns, N.A. and Eiserman, F.M. (1979) Quantification of fluvial trout habitat in Wyoming. Transactions of the American Fisheries Society, 108 (3): 215-228.

Caffrey, J. (1985) Macrophyte studies in Irish lakes. Abstract only. Annual Conference of the Freshwater Research Group, 1985. R.I.A.

Caffrey, J. and King, J.J. (1989) Aspects of charophyte ecology in three drained tributaries of the River Boyne. Bulletin of the Irish Biogeographical Society 12: 6-15.

Caffrey, J. (1990) The classification, ecology and dynamics of aquatic plant communities in some Irish Rivers. Ph.D.Thesis, National University of Ireland 254pp.

Collotzi, A.W. & Dunham, D.K. (1978) Inventory and display of aquatic habitat. Pages 533-545 in Anonymous. Classification inventory and analysis of fish and wildlife habitat. From Proceedings of a national symposium at Phoenix, Arizona, January 1977. United States Fish & Wildlife Service, FEW/OBS-78/76, Washington, District of Columbia, U.S.A.

Crawford, S.M. (1979) Farm pond restoration using *Chara vulgaris* vegetation. Hydrobiologia, 62 (1): 17-31.

Duff, D.A. & Cooper, J.L. (1978) Techniques for conducting stream habitat surveys on national resources land. United States Bureau of Land Management, Technical Note 283, Denver, Colorado, U.S.A.

Haslam, S.M. (1978) River Plants. Cambridge University Press, Cambridge. 396pp.

Hey, R.D. (in press) River mechanics and habitat creation.

Hunt, R.L. (1976) A long-term evaluation of trout habitat development and its relation to improving management-related research. Transactions of the American Fisheries Society, 105 (3): 361-364.

Kennedy, M. and Fitzmaurice, P. (1972) Some aspects of the biology of gudgeon *Gobio gobio* L. in Irish waters. Journal of Fish Biology, 4: 425-440.

Leopold, L.B., Wolman, M.G. & Miller, J.P. (1964) Fluvial processes in geomorphology. Freeman & Co., San Francisco.

Lund, J.A. (1976) Evaluation of stream channelisation and mitigation on the St. Regis River, Montana. United States Department of the Interior, Fish & Wildlife Service Biological Services Programme FWS/OBS-76/06.

Mangan, B.J. (1988) Water surface profile modelling, a complete package. M.Sc. Eng. Thesis, National University of Ireland.

Massey, B.S. (1970) Mechanics of fluids. Van Nostrand Reinhold Co. Ltd., London.

Mills, C. & Piggins, D. 1983 The release of reared salmon smolts (*S. salar* L.) into the Burrishoole River system and their contribution to the rod and line fishery. Fisheries Management, 14 (4): 165-175.

Modde, T. & Platz, B. (1990) Influence of operator position on the precision of measurements taken with hand-held velocity meters in rivers. North American Journal of Fisheries Management, 10: 247-248.

Needham, P.R. (1969) Trout Streams. Revised by C.F. Bond. Winchestor Press, New York.

O'Grady, M.F. (1981) A study of brown trout (*Salmo trutta* L.) populations in selected Irish lakes. Ph.D. Thesis, National University of Ireland.

O'Grady, M.F. (in press) Rehabilitation of salmonid habitats in a drained Irish river system. Proceedings of the Royal Irish Academy

Pennak, R.W. (1978) The dilemma of stream classification. pp. 59-66 *In* Anon. Classification inventory and analysis of fish and wildlife habitat. From Proceedings of a national symposium at Phoenix, Arizona, January 1977. United States Fish and Wildlife Service FWS/OBS 78/76,Washington, District of Columbia, U.S.A.

Wesche, T.A., Goertler, C.M. & Hubert, W.A. (1987) Modified habitat suitability index model for brown trout in southeastern Wyoming. North American Journal of Fisheries Management, 7: 232-237.

White, R.J. & Brynildson, O.M. (1967) Guidelines for management of trout stream habitat in Wisconsin. Wisconsin Department of National Resources Technical Bulletin, 39, 65pp.

Zippin, C. (1958) The removal method of population estimation. Journal of Wildlife Management 22 (1): 82-90.

RE-INTRODUCTION OF SALMON TO THE YORKSHIRE OUSE

S.N.AXFORD

National Rivers Authority: Yorkshire Region

Attempts at rehabilitation logically require as a first step that the cause of extinction of the salmon run be removed or mitigated, or else the new population is doomed from the start. In the Yorkshire Ouse, the reasons for the effective extinction of the salmon run have never been fully established and thus the scheme to re-introduce salmon to the River Ouse, started by the Yorkshire Ouse and Hull River Authority in 1965 was a speculative venture. It was relatively costly in relation to the River Authority Fisheries Budget and was not popular with many anglers who feared that the presence of increased numbers of salmon would put up the costs of fishery rentals and rates.

Examination of catch records for the R.Ouse and Humber (Figure 1) show that a prolific salmon fishery existed until the end of the nineteenth century. Between 1867 and 1882, the average catch was reported as 13.25tons per year, with 91 nets employing 270 men. After about 1890, there was a decline in catches in which the effects of pollution on migration were implicated. A substantial increase in salmon runs appears to have occurred in the 1930's leading to a peak in catches coincident with a period

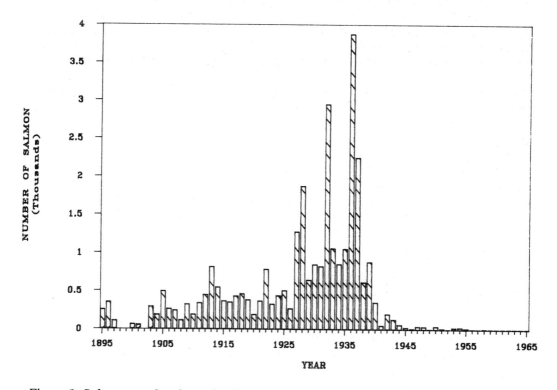

Figure 1. Salmon catches from the Ouse.

of dry springs and summers. From the start of World War II there was a very marked decline in salmon catches which seems to have reflected a substantial fall in stocks since the few remaining fishermen caught little thereafter and there has been little evidence from any source of significant runs of salmon since that time. Netting for salmon has been banned by bye-law in the Humber and lower Ouse since 1977, although even prior to this no licences had been taken up for several years.

Salmon in the lower Ouse were largely taken with draft (= seine) nets or click nets. The latter exploited the tendency of the migrating fish to move to the surface in response to reduced dissolved oxygen levels, from where they were removed by bank or boat fishermen equipped with click nets, which were like large landing nets.

Low dissolved oxygen levels in the lower Ouse related to pollution are a problem of long standing. Reports about the salmon fishery in the 1880's include a number of comments about the pollution from the rivers of the West Riding of Yorkshire and the effects of dams. Annual reports of the Yorkshire Fishery District include references to many dead salmon being observed in the tidal reaches during the summers of 1896, 1914, 1915, 1918 and 1929, for example. There were cycles of abundance in catches that were probably greatly influenced by conditions for fish passage in the estuary. For example, the wet spring of 1928 appears to have allowed a very large number of fish to ascend, thereby producing prolific rod catches. One licensee records that he took 183 fish weighing 3152 lbs, including 39 fish of over 20 lbs. Many salmon died in the upper reaches in the summer of that year.

Few direct measurements of dissolved oxygen in the tidal waters were made in the early part of this century from which to judge the changes that have taken place. Those that are available do not indicate that there was any significant improvement by the time that the scheme started (Figure 2), and clearly show the zone of low dissolved oxygen in the Goole area about 20 to 30 kilometres upstream of Trent Falls.

Although dams may have proved major obstacles to adult salmon in the nineteenth century, the number of dams acting as barriers to fish migration was steadily reduced over the years, with a pass at Naburn, the major barrier at the tidal limit being opened in 1936.

Net catches in the mid 1930's were so great that the Fishery District Board considered limiting the number of licences issued in order to ensure adequate escapement of spawning stock but it appears that no action was taken until 1947 and 1948, when they bought up some netting rights. This action did not increase catches for the rods or remaining netsmen since it appeared that the stocks had already declined to a very low level.

A number of possible explanations have been advanced for the demise of the salmon runs of the Yorkshire Ouse including:

a)   Increased impoundment, abstraction and drainage in the catchment affecting the ability of salmon to ascend obstacles and giving them a shorter period to pass through the netting or de-oxygenated zone in flood conditions.

b)   An unknown factor relating to war-time defensive measures.

180

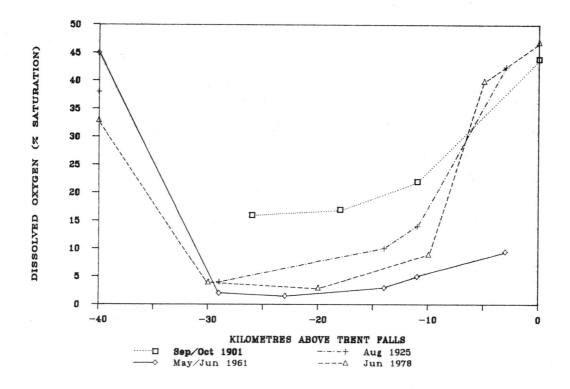

Figure 2. Dissolved oxygen levels: spot samples from surveys in the Ouse.

c)   Increased pollution load from the rivers Aire, Don and Trent and factories alongside the estuary.

d)   A succession of warm, dry springs resulting in extensive mortalities of smolts in a de-oxygenated upper estuary.

e)   Excessive netting reducing the spawning escapement to a very low level.

In retrospect, a combination of these rather than any one factor seems likely to have been involved. Certainly, there was and still is a de-oxygenated zone in the tidal Ouse in dry summers that may be impassable to migrating salmon. There is a suggestion of an improving trend in dissolved oxygen levels but progress to date has been slow (Figure 3).

The basic premise of the rehabilitation scheme was that smolt losses during migration through the de-oxygenated zone were the critical stage preventing re-establishment of salmon runs. The adults could avoid this zone by migrating before or after its formation. Thus measures were devised to trap the descending smolts upstream of the problem zone, transport them downstream around the de-oxygenated zone, and release them in the lower estuary where dissolved oxygen conditions were satisfactory but salinities were still low.

Salmon ova purchased, initially, from the River Tweed Commissioners were reared in the Costa Hatchery at Pickering then stocked during 1965 and 1966 as feeding fry

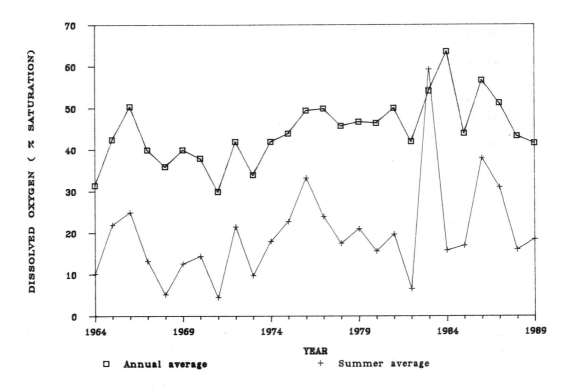

Figure 3. Dissolved oxygen at Blacktoft: yearly and summer averages at low water.

into tributaries of the River Ure that had been cleared of trout by electric fishing. In subsequent years, ova were purchased from the Kyle of Sutherland Fishery Board and similarly reared and stocked.

A smolt trap was constructed in a mill goit at Mickley, upstream of Ripon, which led off from the downstream end of a large diagonal weir and enabled the entire flow of the River Ure to be taken under low to moderate flows. A Wolfe trap of inclined timber slats was installed in spring 1967. The trap was generally operated each year thereafter throughout April and May and for 24 hours per day during at least part of this period. During high flows the weir over-topped and an unknown proportion of the smolt run was able to by-pass the trap. By marking pre-smolts in the nursery streams in one year it was estimated that at least 14% of the run was intercepted by the trap, and, in dry springs, probably a very high proportion was captured. Each year, the majority of the smolts trapped were tagged. Between 1967 and 1981, the smolts were transported in tanks by road and released at Brough on the Humber estuary, where the salinity was about half that of sea water. Details of the number of fry stocked, and numbers of smolts trapped, tagged and transported are given in Table 1.

Although smolt production would appear to be fairly poor, the numbers of fry stocked were probably much lower than indicated by the official figures in some years since they appear to have been based on the theoretical production from the number of ova bought rather than a careful estimate of numbers dispatched. Unfortunately, the smolt trap was not operated before the progeny of the stocked fry would have been likely to be trapped, so the numbers of wild smolts present before the scheme started could

Table 1. Details of stocking, trapping and recaptures.

Year	Number of stock fry	Trapping conditions	Number of smolts			Recaptures	
			Trapped	Tagged & released			
				Brough	R.Ure	Number	%
1965	57,000						
1966	150,000						
1967	201,000		500	500			
1968	289,000		819	689		1	0.15
1969	200,000		1890	1248		9	0.72
1970	190,000		4200	3980		35	0.88
1971	200,000		969	969		9	0.93
1972	140,000		1600	1320		17	1.29
1973	150,000		2190	2139		14	0.65
1974	170,000	good	4922	3000		88	2.93
1975	30,000	poor	1649	1352		14	1.04
1976		good	1340	1257		8	0.64
1977		fair	302	198	48	1	0.41
1978		good	243	120	19	1	0.72
1979		fair	280	120	100		0.00
1980		v.good	832	289	489	1	0.13
1981		fair	369		369	2	0.54
1982		good	101		89		0.00
1983		poor	184		184		0.00
1984							
1985							
1986							
1987		v.good	579				
1988							
1989							
1990		v.good	1250				

not be assessed. The last fry stocking took place in 1975, but trapping continued annually until 1983. Since very few of the smolts were more than 2 + years old, catches from 1978 onwards were of fish bred naturally in the River Ure. Some of these smolts were tagged and released in the Ure in an attempt to compare their survival with those transported to Brough. The number of returns was too small to make a meaningful comparison, but two tagged smolts released at Mickley in 1981 were later recaptured as adults, showing that they had successfully passed through the de-oxygenated zone of the tidal Ouse that year.

The tag recaptures from the Humber and its tributaries (Figure 4) illustrate that poor water quality remained a barrier to adult upstream migrants as well as smolts. Most of these fish were found dead in the lower Ouse in the region of Goole.

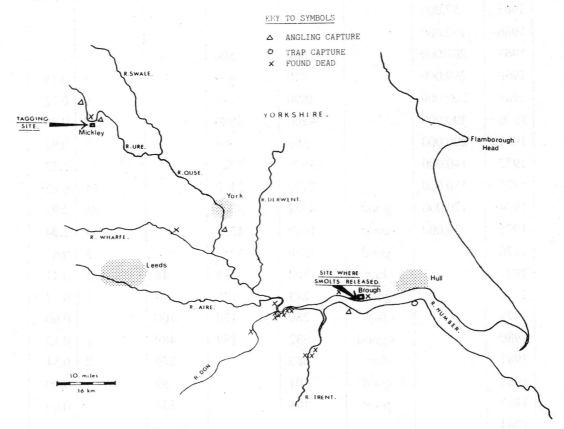

Figure 4. The River Ure and associated river systems.

The recapture rate of tagged fish has been relatively low by comparison with other studies, except from the 1974 tagging when many were recaptured off west Greenland. However, no adult migrant trap was installed in relation to the scheme, there was no commercial salmon fishery, and little rod angling for salmon took place in the Ouse or Ure that could have produced returns. The Carlin smolt tags affixed to the smolts have subsequently been found in other studies to markedly increase mortality rates and therefore the tagging operations will have greatly reduced the number of returning salmon that could restore a natural run and endangered the objectives of the scheme.

A notable feature of the recaptures of tagged salmon has been the high degree of straying displayed (Figure 5). The lack of a significant net or rod fishery in the Ouse and Ure has probably accentuated this but no other salmon tagging scheme has shown such a wide scatter of 'lost' fish. It is very unlikely that the fish taken off the Canadian coast, the Shannon estuary, from the fresh water of five rivers on the west coast of Britain and the Great Ouse in Cambridgeshire would have returned to the Yorkshire Ouse if they had been returned alive to the water after capture. However, considering that the ova came from Scotland, the fry were originally reared on a tributary of the Yorkshire Derwent, were transferred to the Ure catchment, then the smolt migration interrupted by a transfer between the Ure and the Humber, it is perhaps no wonder that they had trouble finding their 'home' river on the return migration.

The scheme was reviewed in 1981 and again in 1984 when further trapping was reduced in frequency, tagging was stopped until smolt numbers improved and an assessment made of dissolved oxygen conditions in the lower Ouse in relation to the passage of smolts and adult salmonids.

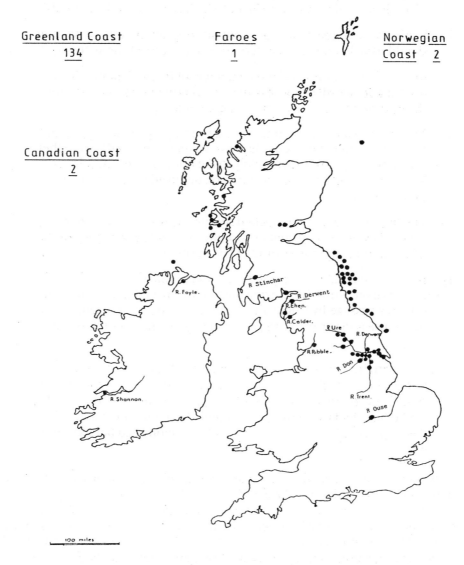

Figure 5. Positions of recaptures as adults of smolts tagged in the River Ure.

185

The smolt trap was operated in 1987 and again in 1990 for a limited part of the normal run period and at night only. Catches of naturally-bred smolts were greater than in some years when fry stocking was taking place and show an encouraging trend towards natural re-establishment of a significant salmon run.

What lessons can we learn from our experiences on the Ouse and Ure?

a) The size of the natural smolt run should have been established prior to stocking, so that stocking success could be established. Some of the smolts trapped during the period of fry planting were undoubtedly of natural origin. (It is interesting to speculate whether the reports of about 40 rod-caught salmon from the upper Ure in 1972 reflected a good escapement that produced a peak in numbers of hardy natural smolts in 1974 and a high recapture rate as adults).

b) Similarly, a suitable means of monitoring adult runs of salmon should have been implemented prior to the rest of the scheme.

c) More accurate estimates of the numbers of fry stocked should have been made in order to assess the best rearing areas and the effectiveness of trout removals from these streams.

d) The increased mortality rate caused by trapping, handling, tagging and transporting the smolts may have seriously reduced the number of adults likely to return, possibly to the point where natural breeding success would be insufficient to maintain adequate recruitment to sustain a run.

e) The distant origin of the stocked fry and the transfer procedures to which they were subjected as juveniles, upset the tendency of the adults to return to the river they left as smolts.

f) Insufficient numbers of tagged smolts were released in the river, by comparison with those transported to Brough, to determine whether passage by smolts through the de-oxygenated zone in the tidal Ouse is the critical stage determining the success of the salmon run.

g) Little progress was made in reducing the de-oxygenation thought to have been much of the reason for near extinction of the salmon run. The expensive operation of trapping and transporting smolts would have had to continue indefinitely if a good run of adults had developed because the adverse effects on smolts had been circumvented.

Major improvements are planned for trade and sewage effluents in order to increase dissolved oxygen levels in this critical zone of the tidal Ouse in the next few years, and it may, therefore, be worth considering a further attempt at rehabilitation of Ouse salmon runs. The lessons learned from this and other studies relating especially to the importance of the origin of stocks, choice of fry stocking sites, adverse effects of handling and tagging smolts and the dissolved oxygen requirements of smolts and adults should give a much greater chance of a success.

186

DECLINE AND RECOVERY OF SALMON IN THE CENTRAL BELT OF SCOTLAND

ROSS GARDINER AND IAIN McLAREN

The Scottish Office, Agriculture and Fisheries Department, Freshwater Fisheries Laboratory, Pitlochry

Over the past thirty years salmon (and sea trout) have returned to several rivers in the Central Belt of Scotland in which they had been extinct for the greater part of this century, or even longer (see Maps 1, 2, 3).

The principal cause of the extinctions was the loss of access to (and from) satisfactory spawning and nursery areas mainly caused by pollution of the lower rivers and upper estuaries. The demise of the rivers was often aggravated by the degradation of spawning and nursery areas by urban, domestic and colliery and other industrial wastes. Agricultural practices such as the clearing of extensive raised bogs or "mosses" to provide agricultural land by flushing the peat down watercourses were also destructive. In addition, the river systems were obstructed by weirs with inadequate provision for upstream passage of spawning adults. By the late 18th century the runs of salmon in much of Central Scotland were in decline. The situation in the 19th century became increasingly bad and salmon completely disappeared from many of the rivers.

Fortunately, over the last 30 years, improved treatment of domestic and industrial wastes and reductions in industrial discharges have resulted in sufficient improvements in water quality (well documented in the Annual Reports of the Clyde and Forth River Purification Boards) in the lower rivers and upper estuaries to allow re-establishment of stocks to a varied extent. As an example, a chronology, based on one previously prepared (Anon, 1987), is given for the River Clyde (Table 1).

On most of the rivers (other than the River Carron) there have been no significant efforts to reintroduce or supplement the stocks of salmon and, as water quality improved, stocks appear to have re-established themselves naturally through the entry of strays, perhaps from salmon populations from nearby rivers. There have also been small-scale introductions of salmon parr into the River Clyde (see Table 1) and recently (1990) on the Firth of Forth Avon.

In recent years salmon in this industrial area of Scotland have started returning to at least eight rivers from which they had become extinct.

On the River Gryfe, improvements in water quality in the lower river, partly as a result of closure of the polluting tanneries at Bridge of Weir, and to access for adult fish at falls at Bridge of Weir have allowed well-developed runs of salmon to be established and spawning fish are now taking advantage of areas in the main river and tributaries upstream of Bridge of Weir.

Limited numbers of adults are reported each year in the River Clyde upstream of Glasgow. There is some recent evidence of successful spawning but Blantyre Weir

TABLE 1. A CHRONOLOGY OF SALMON IN THE RIVER CLYDE

About 9500 BC   Climate ameliorates sufficiently to allow salmon to recolonise the Clyde area. In time, neolithic man, a hunter and food gatherer arrives, and exploits the salmon stock.

1165 - 1452 AD   Monks of Paisley are granted various extensive charters to net and construct traps (yairs) for salmon in Loch Lomond, Rivers Leven and Clyde and the Gareloch.

1424   Representatives of Burghs of Renfrew and Dumbarton meet at Old Kirkpatrick to discuss their conflicting rights to certain salmon fishings.

Early to mid 1700s   Start of rapid rise in population but salmon still abundant in the main river and in tributaries, such as the River Kelvin.

1771   Dredging of navigable channel downstream of Glasgow is started.

Late 1700's   Escalation in rate of industrialisation, including construction of a number of weirs hindering the passage of adult salmon, notably Blantyre Weir on the River Clyde (1785) and Patrick Weir on the River Kelvin.

1798   Common sewers directly discharging into Clyde introduced in Glasgow.

1808   Town of Dumbarton's salmon fishings are reported to be rapidly declining in value. Town Council attributes this to "porpoises, vulgarly called buckers, that pursue and destroy the salmon"!

c 1850   Blantyre Weir heightened.

1859 - 60   Loch Lomond Angling Improvement Association comes into existence.

1869   Salmon numbers above Glasgow are now at a low level but poaching still a problem. One poacher takes 14 salmon by cleek on the River Nethan.

1870   Buckland inspects River Clyde and reports on the fish pass at Blantyre Weir.

1876   Parliamentary Report into the best means of dealing with pollutions of Clyde and tributaries.

1900   Occasional salmon are reported still being sighted at Blantyre Weir.

c 1905 - 65   No salmon are reported in River Clyde upstream of Glasgow, or in River Cart, but c 1930 occasional salmon are reported stranded in dry dock at mouth of River Kelvin. Throughout this period salmon continue to run the River Leven.

Mid 1960's   Occasional salmon are noted in River Cart and its tributary, the River Gryfe.

Table 1. continued

1970's	Water quality steadily improves as a result of better sewage treatment. Salmon numbers build up in the River Gryfe.
1980/1981	A total of 6000 salmon fry of Dee/Spey origin are introduced into the King's Burn at Rutherglen.
1983 on	Adult salmon are seen each autumn attempting to negotiate Blantyre Weir.
1984	Formation of River Clyde Fisheries Management Trust to supervise and coordinate the future development of River Clyde salmon fishing rights.
1988	A Clyde tributary, the River Avon, is stocked with 8000 salmon parr.
1989-90	The Freshwater Fisheries Laboratory, in collaboration with the Clyde River Purification Board, obtains evidence by electrofishing, of some successful spawning in favourable areas upstream of Blantyre Weir.

(location shown on Maps 2 and 3) is a serious constraint as no satisfactory spawning streams are presently accessible downstream of the weir. A moratorium on taking migratory fish exists at present to aid recovery of stocks and a River Clyde Fisheries Management Trust has been set up to coordinate river management.

A viable population of salmon is now established in the River Leven on the Firth of Forth and in one of its tributaries, the Kennoway Burn. However, suitable spawning and nursery areas at present accessible are restricted.

Runs of salmon, have occurred on the River Carron recently, apparently resulting from a stocking programme on the inaccessible upper river by Stirling Salmon/Howietoun Fishery in cooperation with Larbert and Stenhousemuir Angling Club. Although stockings started in 1985, the first large scale stockings took place in October and November 1987 with 122,000 parr of mixed origin, around 30% of which were expected to smolt in 1988. A run of one-sea winter salmon (nearly all males) was reported in 1989. In 1990 there was a larger run of one-sea winter salmon (again, mainly males with some females later in the run) with some two-sea winter fish (mainly females). Scale samples from 18 of the fish caught in 1990 were consistent with these fish having resulted from the 1987 stocking. Electrofishing in summer 1990 at some of the more favourable sites on the lower main stem and tributaries has not yet produced evidence of successful spawning.

Again on the Firth of Forth there have been occasional reports of adult salmon entering the River Avon in recent years, while on the River Almond a modest population has become established, following installation of fish ladders at high weirs to allow access to suitable spawning areas. Both adults and juveniles are present in two tributaries of the River Almond, the Linhouse and Murieston Waters, but poor quality is a likely constraint on production of juveniles in the main river.

The Water of Leith which runs through Edinburgh and enters the Firth of Forth at Leith is now an attractive and clean stream but access to adults is generally not possible

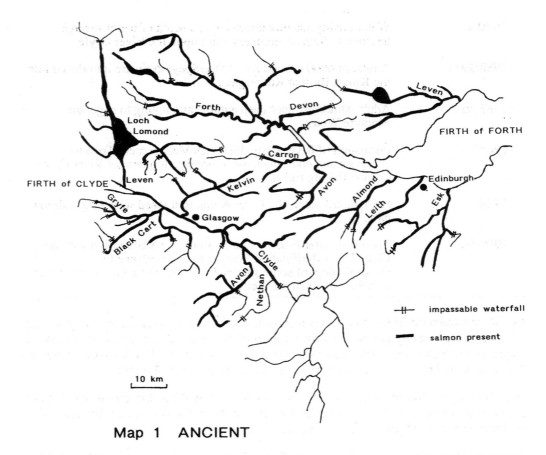

Map 1   ANCIENT

*Maps 1, 2 and 3 indicate the likely ancient distribution of salmon and in 1950 and 1990.
In general, where there are several impassable waterfalls and weirs (as on the
Rivers Leven and Esk in the Firth of Forth) only the furthest downstream of each
is shown. These maps are provisional.*

owing to tidal gates at Leith. However, there have been occasional reports of adult
salmon in the lower reaches.

A modest population of salmon has established itself in another river near Edinburgh,
the River Esk at Musselburgh, and both adults and juveniles are present. There is a
limited area of suitable spawning and nursery area at present available due to
restricted access.

On most of the rivers salmon populations have re-established themselves naturally as
water quality in the lower rivers and upper estuaries has improved. The first stage in
a "natural" recovery is for adult salmon to stray in and Solomon (1985) has pointed
out that there may have to be a minimum density of adults for any successful
colonisation to take place. If the strays successfully spawn, a build up of numbers over
several generations may take place because of the greater survival of juveniles at low
densities, provided that the factors which caused the extinction are no longer
operating and that exploitation is kept at a low level.

190

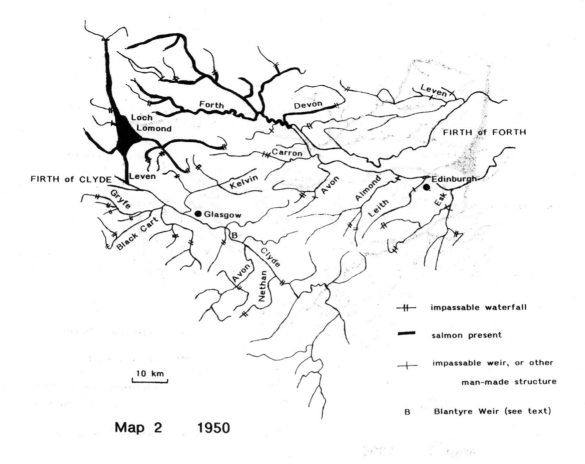

Map 2   1950

- —H— impassable waterfall
- ▬▬▬ salmon present
- —+— impassable weir, or other
          man-made structure
- B   Blantyre Weir (see text)

There are, of course, constraints on the rate of build up and on the number of salmon which can ultimately be produced and these include ease of access and the extent of losses of adult salmon during upstream migration, extent and quality of the accessible spawning and nursery areas and the extent of losses of smolts during downstream migration. Catch per unit rod effort per available salmon is higher at low stock levels (Small, 1991; Gardiner, 1991) and moderate rod effort coupled with low stock levels may result in a high proportion of the stock being taken which would also slow recovery.

Many of these constraints apply to the rivers discussed in the present paper and have been recently discussed in detail in the context of the River Clyde by Gardiner (1987) and by Curran and Henderson (1988) who looked at the ability of the Clyde estuary to meet the requirements necessary for the successful migration of both adult salmon and smolts. Access of adult salmon to the potential spawning areas upstream of Blantyre Weir is still hampered by water quality in the upper estuary, particularly in summer, and by the very difficult Blantyre Weir. Although there is now evidence of some successful spawning upstream of Blantyre Weir there is little evidence yet of any sustained build up in numbers of adult salmon.

191

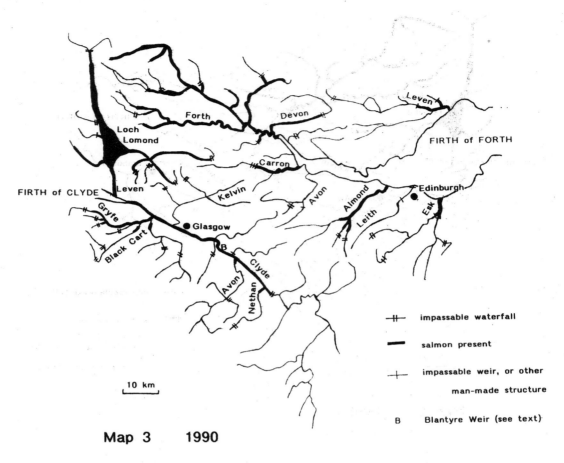

Map 3   1990

On some of the other rivers, owing to the presence of impassable weirs, access to salmon is presently restricted, and within the accessible area potential spawning and nursery areas of satisfactory quality may be localised. Nevertheless, salmon populations have successfully re-established themselves "naturally" on a number of the rivers.

ACKNOWLEDGEMENTS

We wish to acknowledge the help and advice of Ian Baird of the Forth District Salmon Fishery Board, Ross Doughty of the Clyde River Purification Board, Dave Lowson and Ian Fozzard of the Forth River Purification Board, Rob Murray of Stirling Salmon and Paul Featherstone of Howietoun Fishery and the officials and members of various angling clubs and associations and other fishery owners and managers. In addition, Drs Derek Mills, Tony Hawkins and Dick Shelton made helpful suggestions to improve the draft text. To all, our thanks.

REFERENCES

Anon. (1987). A brief history of salmon in the River Clyde. In The Return of Salmon to the Clyde. Proceedings of a one-day Conference held at the University of Strathclyde on 15 November, 1986. (Holden, A. and Struthers, G. eds), pp. 2. Pitlochry: Institute of Fisheries Management (Scottish Branch).

Curran, J.C. and Henderson, A.R. (1988). The oxygen requirements of a polluted estuary for the establishment of a migratory salmon, *Salmo salar* L., population. Journal of Fish Biology, 33 (Supplement A), 63-69.

Gardiner, R. (1987). The potential of the Clyde as a salmon producing river. In The Return of Salmon to the Clyde. Proceedings of a one-day Conference held at the University of Strathclyde on 15 November, 1986. (Holden, A. and Struthers, G. eds) pp. 21-25. Pitlochry: Institute of Fisheries Management (Scottish Branch).

Gardiner, R. (1991). Modelling rod effort trends from catch and abundance data. In Catch Effort Sampling Strategies and their Application in Freshwater Fisheries Management. (Cowx, I.G. ed.) Oxford: Blackwell Scientific Publications, in press.

Small, I. (1991). Exploring data provided by angling for salmonids in the British Isles. In Catch Effort Sampling Strategies and their Application in Freshwater Fisheries Management. (Cowx, I.G. ed.) Oxford: Blackwell Scientific Publications, in press.

Solomon, D.J. (1985). Salmon stock and recruitment, and stock enhancement. Journal of Fish Biology, 27 (Supplement A), 45-47

SUMMARY

DEREK MILLS

Institute of Ecology and Resource Management,
University of Edinburgh.

The purpose of this summary is to draw together the main points mentioned in the preceding papers and to include other facts raised in discussion or in the relevant literature. Before rehabilitation commences four questions have to be answered, namely is everyone agreed that salmon should be restored to the river, who is going to do the work, what resources are available and who is going to pay? If a number of organisations are going to be involved it is essential that they liaise closely with one another from the start through a liaison committee and a liaison officer who is responsible for co-ordination. It is also important to emphasise to those funding the project that it will take time. One must not expect to have a first class salmon river the year after the project starts and, as Dulude and Pustelnik point out, a restoration plan can only be undertaken on a long term basis, and they give 10 years as a minimum period. It is also necessary to produce a management plan on which a programme can be based so that involved staff can co-ordinate their work. Publicity for the project is also essential so that local communities feel involved and can give it their support. The summary has been written in a form which will enable those considering rehabilitation to feel their way into the scheme of things.

1. SURVEY

1.1. Water flow

In certain instances, as a result of water abstraction or diversion, attempts at rehabilitation of a river would be unrewarding unless its previous normal flow was restored. An example of this situation is to be seen on the upper Perthshire Garry where, as a result of diversion of its headwaters to Loch Ericht in the 1930s and tapping of all its upper left bank tributaries to Loch Errochty in the 1950s, the upper Garry is virtually dry during the summer months except during periods of heavy rain.Similarly, many Spanish salmon rivers have lost their salmon runs partly as a result of excessive water abstraction.

1.2 Water temperature

There should be some reservation regarding water temperature as, while some northern Canadian (Matamek) and Norwegian (Saltdaselva and Strygnselva) rivers rarely exceed $10^{\circ}C$ and the lower limit for salmon growth in them is not fixed, there is some evidence from Iceland and Greenland that water temperature affects the survival of egg, alevin and fry. For example, Jonas carried out an extensive stream survey along the west coast of Greenland with emphasis on an evaluation of the potentials for significant natural production of Atlantic and Pacific salmon. He came to the conclusion that water temperature was the limiting factor and was the reason for the failure of earlier attempts to introduce Atlantic salmon to some of these streams, although methods of planting these stages and interspecific competition with the native Arctic charr should not be ruled out. In, Iceland some of the glacial rivers in the south-east and those draining from permanent snowfields, such as the Horga and Bruara, are too cold for salmon. On the other hand, there are some Icelandic rivers fed by geothermal springs with very high temperatures which deter salmon from entering except during flood conditions. However, one, the Reykjdalsa, has had much of its hot water piped to a neighbouring community and consequently promises to become a good salmon river.

High water temperatures can affect upstream movement of adult fish, with migration being reduced to zero at mean minimum weekly temperatures of between 22.1^{o}C and 24.9^{o}C, depending on water flows. Some Spanish rivers with reduced water flows as a result of water abstraction probably have water temperatures in excess of 25°C for much of the summer and for this reason may no longer be able to support salmon, particularly in the warm isolated pools in a river with a severely reduced flow because of water abstraction.

1.3 Water quality

Suspended solids may be naturally high in some rivers, particularly glacial rivers, and may not deter fish from ascending, but high suspended solids in the spawning and nursery areas as a result of peat excavation, arterial drainage, coal mining or erosion from afforestation would be limiting. A high BOD from any organic effluent, or severely reduced oxygen levels as a result of stream eutrophication, as described by Martin O'Grady, would also be limiting. High BOD values were regularly recorded in the lower reaches of some salmon rivers resulting in a marked decline (e.g. Aberdeenshire Don, Tyne, Yorkshire Ouse and Loire.) or extinction (e.g. Clyde, Gryfe, Carron in Scotland, Tees, Trent and Thames in England, Taff in Wales, Akerselv in Norway, the Rhine in The Netherlands and Germany, the Meuse in Belgium, Netherlands and France, the Seine, Dordogne, Garonne and Bresle in France, Naton in Spain, Douro in Portugal and Jacques Cartier in Canada). In some instances high BOD values in the estuary may be the one restricting factor deterring entry to adults or killing descending smolts. On the Tees, and probably the Tyne and Yorkshire Ouse, as mentioned by both Tony Champion and Steve Axford, high BOD values in the spring of some years, when the weather is dry and smolt run delayed, may result in a significant proportion of the run being killed, as well as a proportion of the adult run. The fact that Tees salmon enter early and late in the season may well be an adaptation to the adverse conditions prevailing in the estuary of this river at other times of the year. A reduction in pollution levels has already resulted in salmon returning spasmodically to the Clyde, the Gryfe and Trent and regularly to the Thames.

High levels of heavy metals, such as lead and zinc may deter attempts at rehabilitation, as on the Ystwyth in Mid-Wales, but with water treatment to remove these metals, as was done on the neighbouring River Rheidol, restoration can proceed.

Guy Mawle refers to an appropriate water quality standard for safe passage of fish to be the National Water Council water quality class 2, namely (i) dissolved oxygen concentration 40% saturation; (ii) a biochemical oxygen demand (BOD) 9mg/1 with a mean of 5mg/1 and (iii) non toxic to fish as defined by Alabaster and Lloyd (1986).

The effects low pH values have on salmon stocks have been well documented and many rivers in southern and western Norway have lost their salmon. Low pH values are affecting some Canadian salmon rivers and also some rivers in south-west Scotland (Cree) and Wales (Towy). Liming is a temporary solution to a problem which can only be solved by strict control on gaseous emissions from power stations and oil refineries.

1.4 Spawning and nursery areas

Spawning gravel can become compacted through sedimentation as a result of land drainage, afforestation, gravel washing, peat excavation or the chemical effects of mine water and might require major treatment by raking or the use of spawning gravel cleaning machines. These areas may, however, be lost as a result of erosion and flash floods, channel excavation, gravel extraction and arterial drainage. On a tributary of the South Esk gravel is prevented from being scoured out by sinking horizontal wooden beams into the stream bed to prevent downstream gravel movement. Spawning beds and nursery areas may be irretrievably lost, as on parts of the Rhine system, or temporarily lost due to river bed excavation, as on the Torridge, or due to shortening of the river's length as a result of arterial drainage as on the Norwegian River Soya. However, the use of controlled-flow spawning channels, as on Noel Paul's Brook in Newfoundland, and the importation of gravel, as was done when an entirely new river was created in the Doohulla River system in Co. Galway, could be a successful solution to the absence of both spawning and nursery areas in relatively small rivers. The habitat requirements for spawning and rearing have been fully summarised in a *Report of a Workshop on Salmon Stock Enhancement* by David Le Cren and published by the Atlantic Salmon Trust. More recently, computer modelling is being used to predict the carrying capacity of short stretches of river.

1.5 Access

Difficulty or impossibility of access can be due to either natural obstructions or artificial barriers. A number of natural obstructions in the shape of high falls or impassable rapids have restricted, or still restrict, access to rivers or sections of river which otherwise provide ideal conditions for salmon production. Although the easing of natural obstacles preventing access to a river with no previous history of a salmon population cannot strictly be considered as rehabilitation, such an operation may be less costly than the latter and, indeed may increase the geographical distribution of salmon. For example, salmon, which were never known to occur in the Faroes, became established in two rivers, the Leynara and Saksun, after fish passes were built at steep falls at the mouths and the rivers stocked. There are many rivers where practically their whole length is unavailable to salmon because of natural falls. In some instances these would be far too expensive to open up due to their being either too high and/or too numerous. Scotland's major river system, the Tay, has two tributaries coming into this category, namely the Isla and Braan, while the Clyde has many miles of potential spawning and nursery area above the Falls of Clyde. In England, High Force on the Tees and Aysgarth Falls on the Ure also prevent salmon access to many miles of good spawning and nursery area. However, trapping and transport or transfer of adult fish upstream of such obstacles is one solution and has been successfully achieved in Newfoundland on Great Rattling Brook and the Exploits and Biscay Bay rivers as well as on the Jacques Cartier, and the Thames. If the downstream passage of smolts over such obstacles seems too hazardous then trapping and transport could be considered.

There must be some hundreds of miles of potential spawning and nursery area upstream of both natural and artificial barriers on many salmon rivers. For example, on the Tweed, 25% of the river system is presently inaccessible to salmon, while on the Clyde the projected production of salmon below the Falls of Clyde, given the necessary access and habitat improvement, has been estimated to be approximately 30,000 adult salmon. On the Trent system, assuming nearly 100 obstructions can be eased, it is estimated that the system could support a minimum of 1000 adults. In France there are some 1000km of river available to salmon that are still not populated. In many cases it is only money which prevents such areas being available to salmon. Proof that salmon production is increased by such operations has been well demonstrated on the River Erriff in Ireland and the North Esk in Scotland after installing fish passes and stocking the virgin headwaters. In some instances it may be preferable to use areas above inaccessible falls for rearing but make no attempt to open them up to adults. Lars Hansen refers to this decision being made on the Drammenselv in Norway so as to prevent adult fish introducing the skin parasite *Gyrodactylus*.

Artificial barriers in the form of dams built for hydro-electric power or water abstraction and weirs associated with navigation locks have been a major cause of decline in salmon stocks in most countries, particularly in France, Spain, the United Kingdom and in the U.S.A. on the Connecticut River. Fish passes have or are being installed at many of these sites, probably nowhere more so than France, and opportunity for subsequent rehabilitation by introducing fish is promising. Where there are problems of delay at such barriers adult, kelt and smolt transport can be considered. Adult transport has been practised successfully in North America and Sweden. Kelt transport was tried one season on the Inverness-shire Garry with no promising results, but smolt transport, carried out for a number of years on the River Bran on the Conon River system, was most successful both in terms of numbers of returning adult fish and the small degree of their straying within the river system. Although Steve Axford found it less successful on the Yorkshire Ouse where his smolts had to negotiate low dissolved oxygen levels in the estuary. Under this heading one should also consider the problems of potential diversions of migrants into fish farms, through power stations or by water abstraction.

2. INTRODUCTION OF FISH

2.1 Allow colonization by stray fish

There are many recorded instances of fish both entering rivers where no salmon have previously existed and rivers where salmon existed before conditions became unfavourable. In addition, there are records of fish tagged in one river being recaptured in another. It would be surprising if no exploratory mechanism existed in salmon to test or explore other waters and estimates of straying rates vary between 2 - 7% and up to 18% in some Norwegian rivers. On salmon rivers where insurmountable falls prohibit further movement upstream, fish are frequently seen immediately below the falls, and when these are eased it is not long before fish are recorded upstream even if there has been no history of stocking with juveniles. Although 6000 salmon fry were released into one of the Clyde tributaries in 1981, it is considered that the many salmon sighted well up the river from 1983 onwards were stray fish from the Leven system situated further down the Firth of Clyde. Similarly, the small number of salmon which returned to the Trent in 1982 were almost certainly strays, as were the fish which first repopulated the Taff. It has been suggested that the presence of juvenile salmon in a river may increase the rate of straying, particularly if the river discharges into the sea in the coastal pathway of fish returning to neighbouring rivers. There may be some merit in allowing stray fish to colonize new waters, as those of their progeny that returned and subsequently reproduced would probably be those that had adapted to the local environment and be the ones from which one could build up a broodstock.

2.2 Trap and transfer of adult fish

The capture of adult fish by trapping or electrofishing and their subsequent transport upstream to spawning areas has been practised for some time on Newfoundland rivers and more recently on the Jacques Cartier and the Thames and Taff. In addition to transporting adults to spawning areas, it may be necessary to initially "top up" these areas with the hatchery-reared progeny of local broodstock.

2.3 Stock juvenile stages

A valuable report on the *Principles and Practice of Stocking Stream with Salmon Eggs and Fry* by Egglishaw *et al.* and published by the Department of Agriculture and Fisheries for Scotland provides the necessary guidelines to those planning to restock waters either devoid of salmon or below the water's carrying capacity. The results of stock enhancement using any of the juvenile stages has been well reviewed by Kennedy in the proceedings of the Third International Atlantic Salmon Symposium - *Atlantic Salmon - Planning for the Future*. Most estimates of potential smolt production from plantings of eggs and fry have been based on areas of stream available for stocking, however, one should not overlook the fry rearing potential of lakes and in parts of eastern Canada and Iceland lacustrine production of smolts can be quite significant. Attempts have been made to rear smolts in lakes by releasing fry. Even acid lakes should not be overlooked for this purpose, and in Norway a lake with a pH of 4.4 was used after liming to raise the pH. This practice has been successful up to a point, but the main problem has been the unseasonal time for smolt migration from these lakes. A solution would seem to be catching and transporting the smolts at the normal time of migration. However, the semi-natural rearing of smolts in ponds in Prince Edward Island has been more successful and one sited on the Morell rive system is capable of rearing 80,000 smolts annually.

Verspoor recommends the stocking of material at the earliest possible stage of the life cycle and at the egg or unfed fry stage he considers the most preferable. This will give natural selection the best opportunity to remove poorly adapted genetic types, as some maladaption of the genetic types will manifest early in development.

2.4 Source of fish

There is increasing emphasis being placed on the genetic makeup of the fish to be stocked and geneticists are warning of potential damage to existing stocks if fish of the wrong "sort" are introduced. This is wise and valuable advice but not always encouraging for managers wishing to make a start on rehabilitating rivers for which this information is lacking and the availability of appropriate stock limited or non-existent. The genetic adaptation of salmon populations to local environmental conditions mean that in general salmon will have a lower survival rate and reproductive success in the new environment than in their native water. Ritter found in eastern North America that the adult return rates of stocked salmon were lower the further the native environment of the stocked salmon was from the stocked stream. Problems in time of smolt migration can arise when juvenile stock derived from a tributary low down the river system are stocked into much higher tributaries in the catchment. There have been recorded instances on the rivers Tummel and Spey where the introduced stock, from lower tributaries, migrated from the system as smolts up to a month later than the "natural" smolts. This could have serious implications where the timing of the passage of smolts through the estuary was crucial. In the case of rivers with no previous history of being salmon rivers, such as those in the Faroes, or rivers where the salmon stocks were extinct, such as the Carron in Central Scotland, the Taff in Wales, Thames and Trent in England and the Jacques Cartier and Morell in Canada, stocking may be by trial and error. For example, it was some time between the first plantings of fry in the Faroes and the subsequent return of adult fish, and probably it was only the continued stocking of Icelandic salmon fry which resulted in an eventual colonization of these rivers as an appropriate genome became established. The Faroese now use some of these established salmon as broodstock for their rivers. Similarly, stocking the Thames and Taff has had to be done using eggs, fry and parr from various sources.

For rivers having no native stock, Noel Wilkins has suggested that it is possible to create a run from hatchery stock, as happened on the River Lee in Ireland. He describes a strategy which involves stocking artificially produced S1 pre-smolts in the lower reaches of the river but above an upstream trap and artificially produced S2 parr in suitable nursery areas in the upper reaches of the river. The S1 pre-smolts will be "imprinted" to the river in the year of planting and may form the basis of an adult run to the river within one or two years. The S2 parr will provide smolts which will have survived river conditions for one year before migration and which have therefore commenced the process of environmental adaptation. The mixture of S1 and S2 fish, and their diverse hatchery origins, will help to provide genotypic and phenotypic diversity. These steps should be repeated each year until a run of adults develops at which time some should be allowed upstream and others used as broodstock and their progeny used for subsequent stocking. Wilkins suggests a similar, but modified, scheme for augmenting the salmon stock of a catchment containing a small inadequate indigenous population by using hatchery produced parr and smolts derived from local parents. However, both these schemes involve a reliable trap and the use of a hatchery, both expensive items.

On the Morell River, Prince Edward Island, in order to develop an early-run salmon stock (between June and August) eggs were imported from early-run parentage of Miramichi River origin, as no native stock existed. A selective breeding programme was then implemented using multi-sea winter and one-sea winter fish, some of which were subsequently reconditioned from the kelt stage and spawned as many as six times.

The problem still remains for many managers as to where to obtain suitable eggs or fish, particularly when it is to augment existing stocks. Sometimes eggs are obtained from a wide range of sources. On the Merrimack and Connecticut eggs were obtained from 15 and 18 sources respectively since restoration has been carried out on these two river systems. So often in recent years desperate requests for ova have come to Scotland from Spain and France and one wonders how successful establishment has been of material from northern latitudes in near tropical conditions. Considerable pressure can be put on managers by those funding any rehabilitation programme, as "stocking" can be a great P.R. exercise and it is often very difficult to convince Trust fund managers, anglers and administrators that stocking with eggs and fish from any source is inadvisable. It has been well-documented that such exercises can be a waste of time and money.

However, David Solomon provides helpful recommendations:

- Options for rivers devoid of salmon: (a) choose stock from a part of a river with a similar environment (e.g. size of stream, gradient, water temperature, flow regime and type of estuary). (b) obtain stocks from anywhere they are readily and cheaply available, ideally from a multitude of sources, in the hope that either genetic differences are of little adaptive significance, or that presenting the river with a wide range of genetic material will provide the basis for a new well adapted genetic stock by natural selection.

- Options for depleted stocks: work entirely from local material, and build up a stock by hatchery production or redistribution of adults. However, there are some reservations to this strategy in that a relict population from one part of the catchment may be unsuited for introduction to other parts with different prevailing conditions; there may be some resistance to taking scarce broodstock from the deplete natural population for hatchery production, and there may been dramatic changes in the environment so that the stock which it is planned to release are no longer adapted to the new environment.

In addition one could add:

- The setting up of gene banks, which has been done in Norway and is recommended by NASCO, may alleviate some of the problems of stock selection.

3. MONITORING

The monitoring of both the fate of the introduced juveniles and returning adults should be essential. The former can be traced by electrofishing, traps, microtags and the use of genetic markers, the latter can be checked using traps, electronic counters, redd counts, microtags and genetic markers. The use of traps on their own usually involves a large expenditure, so where possible, it may be cheaper to incorporate them into fish pass design as is being done on the Tawe in Swansea, or install them in fish passes when appropriate, as on the Dordogne. Fish counters with video systems are ideal but expensive and suitable sites for their installation are surprisingly difficult to locate, as is presently being experienced by the Tweed Foundation on the 96 mile-long River Tweed.

The semi-quantitative electrofishing for the monitoring of juvenile salmon distribution is probably the cheapest and most effective form of monitoring the success of a rehabilitation scheme and this is practised most efficiently on the River Bush in Northern Ireland. However, an adequate check using electrofishing is not always easy, as has been experienced on such large rivers as the Dordogne and Jacques Cartier.

The appraisal of restoration schemes is much clearer on rivers which have been devoid of salmon, in that the return of adults after pollution control, improved access or following stocking can be correlated directly to the rehabilitation measures. However, David Solomon warns of the dangers of a wrong interpretation being put on the results from monitoring returning adults. Demonstrating a level of return of tagged fish to the estuary or to the angling catch does not in itself prove that a good spawning stock will result.

4. MANAGEMENT

In any rehabilitation scheme river management in the form of stream improvements is most important, and indeed, such improvements may be all that is required and no stocking is needed. Fish transport may be necessary in certain instances.

4.1 Stream improvements

These will include the removal of temporary obstructions, such as fallen timber and, as Martin O'Grady has shown is necessary, the clearance of deciduous trees growing close to the river banks causing "tunnelling" which reduces the productivity of the river. Other improvements include the removal and prevention of the deposition of silt by concentrating flows to cause scouring; increasing spawning and nursery areas by either raking or breaking up the compacted gravel or by introducing rubble, gravel or providing spawning channels; increasing food production, which may occur naturally as a result of tree clearance and removal of silt; the creation of holding pools and the stabilization of eroding river banks; the creation of river corridors, as is recommended by the Forestry Commission in its *Forests and Water Guidelines,* and is also being practised on rivers in Devon and elsewhere; the maintenance of drainage channels, and flow control and adjustment on arterial drainage schemes.

Bird predator control may be necessary, but serious consideration should be given to the implications which might arise from other conservation interests. Even the removal of some fish predators, such as brown trout, has been known to cause ill feelings, and consequently lack of co-operation, from trout anglers. However, the removal of pike has been widely practised in Scottish waters. This has been done with some justification as, over a nine year period, over 12,000 pike were removed from the River Bran in northern Scotland in an endeavour to reduce predation on smolts derived from large annual plantings of between 84,000 and 1,500,00 unfed fry in an attempt to establish a run of adult salmon into this river made accessible with the installation of a number of fish passes. It was estimated that over three smolt seasons the proportion of pike eating smolts was between 14 and 25%. The costs of such an exercise can be offset by selling the catch.

All such stream improvement work costs money. In some countries it may be possible to enrol the help of the army, providing its enthusiasm for explosive can be curbed. An assessment of the cost and design of improvement schemes where there have been arterial drainage works can be made using a "back-water analysis programme", referred to by Martin O'Grady, to achieve maximum enhancement value and ensure minimal interference with the drainage design.

4.2 Fish transport and kelt reconditioning

The subject of fish transport has already been discussed. It can be a useful management procedure, although in certain instances, as on the Yorkshire Ouse, the transport of smolts can be a failure if environmental conditions are unfavourable at the release site. However, on the River Guddena in Denmark pre-smolts are driven slowly in a large floating pen some 100km to the outer estuary and released beyond any forms of pollution and inshore predation.

Kelt reconditioning is being practised fairly widely now and is a regular management feature on rivers such as the Merrimack, Morell, Jacques Cartier and Thames, with the eggs taken from these fish being used for restocking. The fish are simply held in freshwater and fed until they mature again the next season.

5. RESEARCH

River rehabilitation provides a number of valuable research opportunities, particularly when the salmon population has been extinct for some time. The scope of research will depend on what monitoring facilities are available. Where there is adequate funding, a trap, with staff to man the structure at all times, is essential and will yield the sort of valuable information provided by the River Bush studies. Where a trap can either not be provided or where it is physically impossible to instal, then trapping facilities at fish passes would be needed. Where there are no fish passes or dams or weirs at which to site them then fish counters are the next alternative. Without these facilities population studies would need to be based on catch statistics, electrofishing surveys and redd counts and anglers' observations.

Genetic studies would also be most valuable and, in rivers where the salmon population has been extinct, a study of the extant reared strains stocked could be compared with their wild founder populations using enzyme electrophoresis or mtDNA analysis, to detect any loss of genetic variability or alteration of genetic composition giving indications of inbreeding. Studies using genetic markers could provide a useful assessment of the performance of the stocked and native populations.

A measurement of the success of various stocking policies employed (i.e. stage and time at which introduced) would be valuable in rivers previously devoid of salmon, as there would be no confusion between returning adults of native and introduced stock. Where there are native fish present the problems of identification could possibly be overcome using genetic markers as has been achieved on some Spanish rivers. The value of such studies can be seen from the results obtained by Lars Hansen on the Drammenselv, where 400kg of adult salmon were produced for every 1000 smolts released (60-65% of this production was harvested by marine fisheries) and, interestingly, 450kg of adult salmon were produced for every 1000 underyearlings released.

Radio tracking studies of fish approaching and within the river system, and also at dams and fish passes, would be most valuable. Fish behaviour studies, particularly at dams and fish passes, need to be increased, as recent results at Pitlochry Dam on the River Tummel have raised a number of questions regarding movements at the power station tailrace and fish pass entrance. An interesting investigation, for example, could be the deterring effect on fish of power station generator sound profiles and the subsequent movement and survival of adults transported upstream.

With adequate trapping facilities, as on the River North Esk, the River Bush, the Girnock Burn, a tributary of the Aberdeenshire Dee, and the Ims in Norway, various population parameters could be obtained enabling estimates of exploitation rates and stock recruitment relationships. Such data would provide a basis for controlling subsequent exploitation.

6. EXPLOITATION

6.1 At what stage is a fishery started ?

The stage in rehabilitation at which a fishery is started must depend on whether the river already supports a salmon population or one is in the process of developing. This question does not seem to have been addressed very widely. On the River Clyde the River Clyde Fisheries Management Trust has produced detailed project proposals but no mention is made of when and how a fishery should start. Probably the success of the scheme and local pressure will be the greatest influence to when a sport fishery develops. On the River Gryfe, for example, there was no attempt to prevent anglers fishing for salmon from the time the first salmon were seen returning after closure of a polluting tannery, although the local anglers improved the fish pass arrangements at a local weir and endeavoured to introduce some protective measures. Elsewhere, a sport fishery now occurs both on the Akerselv and in the neighbouring Oslofjord as a result of stocking since 1981 of the once polluted Akerselv, and in the Faroes there has been heavy angling pressure since at least 1980 on five rivers to which the first salmon returned in 1957. So the decision on when to open a river to angling would appear to depend on local conditions.

The ownership position varies between countries and naturally the question as to who owns any resulting salmon fishing should be resolved before salmon are either introduced to a new river or reintroduced to a river from which they have become extinct. The question of ownership can be a problem and it may be difficult to trace where salmon fishings have not been exercised as a result of the salmon becoming extinct, and this situation has been experienced on the Clyde.

6.2 Initial restrictions

Initial restrictions might wisely start with a ban on all fishing until the river has been monitored for some time and it is seen that a population has become established. This could be followed for a period when the fish are caught and released and then a daily or seasonal (or both) bag limit introduced and fishing method and effort restricted. There might be some merit in considering carcass tagging.

6.3 Usual controls

The usual controls on exploitation will need to include annual, weekly, and even daily (as in Iceland) close times, issue of licences, restrictions on fishing method and effort and notification of catch.

6.4 When should net fishing be introduced?

The stage at which net fishing should be introduced, if at all, will depend on the success of the rehabilitation scheme and whether there are any inherited net fishing rights. These may include aboriginal rights, as in Canada and Lapland. At present there is considerable conflict in Canada over Indian treaty fishing rights. Even though these may be legal there appears to be difficulty in imposing fishing effort and catch restrictions.

Other factors which may influence decisions to start commercial river fishing could be the extent of exploitation in neighbouring coastal waters and the policy of those responsible for the rehabilitation.

7. CONSTRAINTS

7.1 Costs

The costs of rehabilitation can be very high, for example, in France, over 150M francs was devoted to salmon over a 14 year period. Costs need to be carefully estimated and a cost-benefit analysis is probably necessary if financial support is being sought. The costs of the Thames salmon rehabilitation scheme were running at £65,000 a year in 1988, giving a production cost of £163 - £235 for each returning adult. However, it is sometimes questionable whether or not the value of salmon conservation should always be considered in monetary terms. One might argue what monetary benefit is there to the community of re-introducing the osprey and the red kite to their previous haunts or introducing the white-tailed eagle to the west coast of Scotland? The answer seems to be that people want to have them around and are prepared to subscribe to trusts and protection societies. However, in the case of salmon one has difficulty in adopting this philosophy because of its economic value. If one was to remove the monetary benefit from the equation would people still be prepared to pay to have salmon in their rivers? This seems to have been answered positively in the case of the Connecticut Restoration Scheme where conservative estimates of the benefits of the scheme set benefit levels for the New England public at just over $100M. These estimates are derived from the public's willingness to pay increased taxes or other fees and also purchase a licence to fish.

Funding may come from government and local government sources, charitable trusts, fishing associations and sponsors. The Committee of the Jacques Cartier River benefited from a number of grant programmes which provided almost $2M. The Quebec government itself contributed some $700,000 and the Federal government just over $1M. The local communities along the river felt the scheme sufficiently worthwhile and donated almost $150,000.

There are additional and more novel ways of raising money to fund operating costs. The possibility of selling fresh or smoked fish has been discussed on the Morell River and also the use of surplus salmon in ways which would provide additional fishing opportunities. For example, reconditioned kelts could be released in newly-created or restored pools open to anglers on a daily fee basis. The sale of surplus eggs is another possibility.

The value of salmon restoration is admirably summarised by Kay, Allee and Brown in an article entitled *Is salmon restoration worth it?* published in the Proceedings of the Symposium on Present and Future Atlantic Salmon Management in 1988.

7.2 Political resistance

7.2.1 Alternative traditional fishery
There may be some people who do not want to have salmon in their rivers and plans for opening up of additional river areas to salmon may result in resistance from trout or coarse fish anglers on the grounds that they may lose their fishing rights as salmon become established and salmon angling takes priority, and also because of the effects that juvenile salmon might have on trout stocks. Plans for easing the Falls of Clyde to give salmon access to the upper Clyde met with fierce resistance from trout anglers who were concerned at what might happen to their fishing. Likewise, some Yorkshire anglers were concerned that an increase in numbers of salmon in the Ouse and Ure would put up the costs of fishery rentals and rates. On the Nepisiguit a Trout Protective Association has been formed which opposes any further introduction of salmon above the Grand Falls. Already, on the lower beats of the Tyne, coarse fish anglers have been excluded in order to give salmon fishermen the exclusive right of the fishery.

There is evidence that when salmon have access to some trout waters stocks of the latter decline. This has been recorded on some northern Norwegian rivers and on the upper Moisie in Quebec. On the other hand the juvenile salmon can be at risk from capture and retention by trout and coarse fish anglers, as they are on the Dordogne from fishermen using maggots. As a result, the minimum size at which trout can be obtained has had to be increased to insure anglers release salmon parr.

One way of overcoming these objections is to bring trout and other anglers into the discussions from the beginning, as was done on the Morell River, and on the Nepisiguit a Nepisiguit River Fisheries Management Committee has now been set up with representatives of both trout and salmon interests.

7.2.2 Alternative conservation interests
Conservation bodies concerned with other animal species may resist the introduction of salmon on the grounds that it will upset the existing ecosystem. For example, plans to extend, with the aid of a fish pass, the upstream distribution of salmon on the Laxa i Adaldalur in northern Iceland is being resisted by the Icelandic Nature Conservation Council. This is on the grounds that the resulting juvenile salmon might both overgraze the bottom fauna to the detriment of the unique river ducks, the Harlequin and Barrow's Goldeneye, and upset the unique animal community structure for which the Myvatn area has a worldwide reputation. There is also objection from trout anglers who are concerned that the salmon might affect the numbers of large brown trout for

which this area is renowned and that access to their fishing might be restricted as salmon angling developed.

7.2.3 Conflicts with other land and water users

There can be major conflicts with various land and water uses such as afforestation, agriculture, land reclamation, hydro-electric development and water abstraction schemes. Any one of these can also arise after a salmon rehabilitation programme has commenced and negate any benefits. Information on the likelihood of such developments should be obtained before rehabilitation begins.

7.2.4 Conflicts over ownership

Even when it is known who owns the various fishings on the river, problems can arise from an owner, who has leased his fishing to, say, a local angling or improvement association, terminating his lease as the value of the fishing improves, and reletting it at a higher price to a more wealthy concern and thus excluding local people who probably participated in the restoration scheme. Such a situation can lead to reprisals where the salmon comes off worst. Such a situation has arisen on the River Doon in west Scotland where, after 10 years of rehabilitation work by the local community who formed themselves into the River Doon Angling Improvement Association, many sections of the river previously fished by local clubs have been sold to 'outsiders' at inflated prices, much to the annoyance of local people. On the Tyne also it seems inevitable that local angling clubs will be dispossessed of their rented water as the owners appreciate the profits available from letting to syndicates or wealthy visitors.

7.3 Illegal fishing

The prevalence of illegal fishing may be a deterrent to rehabilitation until it can be eliminated or reduced to an acceptable level. The introduction of carcass tagging may be a solution to the problem in some situations.

7.4 Poaching

If poaching is likely to be a threat some consideration has to be given as to whether to proceed fully with any restoration scheme. The threat of poaching, which was beyond the limited bailiff resources to control due to the isolated area through which the river ran, caused the local district salmon fishery board to close the River Bran in Scotland to returning adults a few years after the river was just becoming established as a salmon river. Many other projected schemes are open to the same threat and adequate policing is essential if these are to be a success. Ken Whelan refers to salmon protection barriers at each end of a salmon sanctuary area (a barrier protection scheme) proving successful on the Northwest Upsalquitch.

7.5 Aboriginal fishing rights

If there are historically established aboriginal fishing rights then some form of agreement has to be reached before rehabilitation starts so that exploitation can be controlled from the moment adult fish start returning in increasing numbers. In addition, it is sensible to invite aboriginal fishing representatives on to any association so as to help with the proposed rehabilitation. This has happened on the Nepisiguit River, where the Pabineau Indian Band participate in the rehabilitation programme.

7.6 High seas fisheries

Although there may be no evidence that the high sea fisheries off Greenland and the Faroes have a significant effect on any particular fishery, there is a general feeling that any attempt at rehabilitation which involves large costs should not be undertaken until these fisheries are closed. This was evident from remarks made by an engineer responsible for installing fish passes on the Allier, who felt that further work should not proceed until the Greenland fishery was closed. It is feared by some that the Greenlanders and Faroese could demand a higher quota as salmon production from rehabilitated rivers increases.

7.7 Coastal marine environment

The coastal marine environment in some localities could be a constraint in respect of the prevailing sea water temperatures at the time of smolt migration and the presence of fish predators. At each end of the salmon's geographic range there are only short periods when the sea and river temperatures are favourable for upstream and downstream migration and if the smolt migration, for example, is delayed by dams, by the time they enter the sea the unfavourable sea temperatures may influence survival, this could be one of the reasons for the relatively poor return rates on the Connecticut River at the southern end of the salmon's range in North America.

Predation on smolts as they enter the sea may be high at times, particularly if their time of sea entry coincides with the local coastal shoaling of gadoid fish as occurs in some Norwegian fjords and has been observed in Ireland and by Tony Champion in the Tyne estuary. Adult fish my have to run the gauntlet of predation from seals in neighbouring colonies.

7.8 Availability of appropriate stocking material

The availability of appropriate stocking material may affect rehabilitation success until eggs or fish of an appropriate genetic strain are available. Guy Pustelnik attributes the low adult return rate on the Dordogne partly to this lack of material.

8. BENEFITS

8.1 Community involvement

The success of any rehabilitation scheme is enhanced immensely if it has the support of the local community. It should therefore be the aim of those planning river restoration to ensure that the community is involved in any way possible. It is important that members from all fishing interests, as well as other sectors of the community who will benefit from the scheme, are represented. Furthermore, there should be adequate publicity given to the scheme in the form of literature, talks, school projects, angling courses, visitor centres and possibly a hatchery, so that one can achieve what has been referred to, with respect to restoration of the Jacques Cartier and other rivers such as the Dordogne and the Norwegian river Laerdal, as a "collective pride".

8.2 Conservation image

Environmental conservation is now of major public concern and salmon river restoration is one way of demonstrating that people have the future of the river environment at heart. The public at large who see salmon in the river, even though they are not salmon fishermen, know that the river must be healthy. The responses to a questionnaire in New England indicated that there was a symbolic and environmental value to the return of the salmon that extends beyond personal experience. Three-fifths of the respondents expressing some interest in salmon agreed with the suggestion that salmon should be returned to New England rivers to restore the balance of nature. Three-quarters of the respondents agreed that the return of salmon is an important sign that river pollution has been cleaned up. So salmon have the ability to create a public awareness of the environment. This fact is probably more significant than one might imagine as salmon have been depicted as a conservation image on the postage of at least three countries, Greenland, the United Kingdom and France, in the last few years.

8.3 Provision of fishing for local people

Although it was stated earlier that once salmon fishing has been restored access to it gradually falls into the hands of the more wealthy, this situation does not occur throughout the whole of the salmon's range. In many parts of eastern Canada, in parts of Norway, the Faroes and Ireland it is available to all at modest prices. Provision of fishing for local people will ensure community involvement and also voluntary policing of the resource. Time share arrangements, which are developing rapidly in Scotland at present, must not be allowed to exclude local people from fishing.

8.4 Increased revenue and local employment

The creation of a sport, and probably a commercial, fishery can provide a wide range of employment opportunities including those for guides, ghillies, boatmen, bailiffs, river wardens and netsmen and hotel, hatchery and tourist information staff. Others receiving local benefits would be shopkeepers, tackle dealers, net manufacturers, boat builders and smokehouse operators. So salmon river rehabilitation can help to restore or introduce wealth along a whole river system and also prevent a gradual population decline from previously prosperous and remote areas.

Finally, it should be remembered that it is not only fishery managers and scientists who are involved in salmon rehabilitation decisions but also politicians, administrators, fishermen's unions, economists and other water users. Any one of such groups may have quite different preferences to those of the others. Because of this, numerous negotiations are required to acquire detailed and balanced information to allow each group to understand each other better and to focus discussion on the most essential parts of the programme and resolve any problems objectively.

POSTER DISPLAYS

NATIONAL RIVERS AUTHORITY (Sponsor of publication of the Proceedings)

The display showed aspects of salmon rehabilitation work carried out by the NRA. A video illustrated the work of the various NRA functions including flood defence, water quality, water resources, fisheries conservation, navigation and recreation and how fisheries interrelates with these other functions. Leaflets, entitled "Fisheries, Facts and Figures", were available and described the aims and objectives of the fisheries function and tabulated key statistics.

NATIONAL POWER (Part Sponsors of the conference and publication of the Proceedings)

National Power is the largest of the British electricity-generating companies. As the largest user of surface water, mostly for cooling purposes, the Company has a considerable commitment to maintaining water quality. The Company also employs fish biologists carrying out research and monitoring around power station intakes and outfalls. The database for some sites reaches back some 20 years.
Terry Langford, Environmental Information Services Manager.

WATER RESEARCH CENTRE

Illustrated an NRA/MAFF funded study (based at NRA, Exeter) of the effect of changes of land use and environmental factors in the Torridge catchment to determine the reason for the deterioration in river quality and in salmonid populations.
Iain Naismith, Water Research Centre.

ATLANTIC SALMON TRUST

Described the various radio-tracking techniques with reference to work on the rivers Dee and Tay and the results of the River Polla investigation into the effects of interbreeding of escaped farmed salmon and wild fish.
Michael Martin, AST Council of Management and Julia Thorold, Public Relations Manager, J & B Rare, sponsors of Polla Project and projects in France and Spain.

INSTITUTE OF FISHERIES MANAGEMENT

Portrayed the aims and objectives of the Institute - listing the categories of membership and the correspondence certificate and diploma training courses. Space was devoted to the annual study courses, the activities of the various branches throughout the UK and attendance at exhibitions and game fairs where Institute publications were on sale together with books from other publishers at discount prices.
Robin Templeton, Treasurer and Vice Chairman of the Institute.

THAMES SALMON TRUST

Depicted the work in progress to reinstate a stock of salmon to the River Thames. The work is undertaken by the National Rivers Authority - Thames Region, with funding for major capital projects being provided by charitable donations to the Trust. Following the dramatic clean-up of the Thames tideway and the commencement of the salmon rehabilitation scheme in 1979, salmon now return to the river regularly. The annual run is currently of the order of 150 to 400 fish and is showing an increasing trend in spite of two major drought years. A fish pass construction programme to open up the catchment for returning fish is now well under way. A fish propagation programme using Thames returnees together with selected wild genetic strains has been initiated and should supply all stock requirements within three years.
Peter Gough, Fisheries Officer, NRA: Thames Region.

MAFF FISHERIES LABORATORY, LOWESTOFT

Display on the use of micro-tagging in the evaluation of rehabilitation projects.
Ted Potter, Head of Salmon and Freshwater Fisheries Research Group.

SCOTTISH OFFICE, AGRICULTURE AND FISHERIES DEPARTMENT, FRESHWATER FISHERIES LABORATORY, PITLOCHRY

An outline of the situation in rivers in the industrial Central Belt of Scotland, highlighting those rivers which had either lost their salmon stocks entirely or where stocks had declined almost to the point of extinction and where, as a result of improved water quality, salmon are once more returning.
Ross Gardiner, Freshwater Fisheries Laboratory, Pitlochry.

ELECTRICITY SUPPLY BOARD OF IRELAND

The River Shannon Management Programme - The Shannon hydro-electric scheme, which was commissioned in 1929, is described and details of a salmon restocking programme carried out from 1961 to date are presented. A plan for a three-year electrofishing survey of the entire catchment is also given. Results from the 1990 survey showed that juvenile salmon are absent from the upper catchment (330 km^2). The main elements of the management programme were also shown. These consist of genetic appraisal of salmon populations in main subcatchments; multi-sea-water and grilse breeding programmes at Parteen Hatchery; a coded wire tagging programme for ranched smolts, and investigation of procedures at Ardnacrusha power station in relation to the hydrological requirements of descending smolts and ascending adults.
Martin O'Farrell, Consultant to the Fisheries Conservation Section of ESB and
J.C. O'Dowd, Generation Manager, Hydro Group, Ardnacrusha.

FISH EAGLE CO. (Sponsor of publication of the Proceedings)

Working display of the identification systems for fishery management and research, with particular reference to river enhancement.
John Taylor, Director, Fish Eagle Co.